THE JOY OF
HEALTHY
GRILLING

THE JOY OF
HEALTHY
GRILLING

JOE FAMULARO

PHOTOGRAPHER: Thom DeSanto
FOOD STYLIST: Andrea B. Swenson

All inquiries should be addressed to:
Barron's Educational Series, Inc.
250 Wireless Boulevard
Hauppauge, New York 11788
http://www.barronseduc.com

International Standard Book No. 0-8120-9875-7

Library of Congress Catalog Card No. 97-35092

Library of Congress Cataloging-in-Publication Data
Famularo, Joseph J.
    The joy of healthy grilling / Joe Famularo.
        p.   cm.
    Companion volume to: The joy of grilling.
    Includes bibliographical references and index.
    ISBN 0-8120-9875-7
    1. Barbecue cookery.   2. Low-fat diet—Recipes.   I. Title.
TX840.B3F285   1998
641.5'784—dc21   97–35092
                                                            CIP...

PRINTED IN HONG KONG
9 8 7 6 5 4 3 2

CONTENTS

This book is dedicated to my brothers
Jerry and Charlie

Acknowledgments

A lot of people added fuel to my fire—not in alphabetical order, but this is how I'm listing them. But first let me thank so many friends who graciously shared their grill know-how, and their own recipes. I especially want to thank Eileen Canzoneri who developed the nutritional analyses without a word of complaint as recipes were sent back with reduced fat and requests for new analyses; Helen and Tony Crimmins who laboriously tested and helped me revise many recipes; and to Sue and Joe Garufi who patiently keyboarded the manuscript again and again, with smiles on their faces and to their son David who monitored the telephone requests for work and more work.

To others, my sincere thanks: Sandy Daniels for her inspiration; my nephew Charles Famularo for his enthusiasm; Louise and John Imperiale, my sister and brother-in-law; Bernie Kinzer, whose critique of the food makes it so much better; Christopher Laus, who assists me in the home kitchens; Tina Radecka, a great cook and friend; Candace Thieme, who keeps me healthy with her healthy living counsel; Amy Van Allen, my editor at Barron's; and to Jerry Ann and Gene Woodfin, great cooks who like to add a little fat to the fire. Out of alpha order, and last but not least, my deep gratitude to Grace Freedson who keeps the fire burning.

CHAPTER 1
AN INTRODUCTION TO HEALTHY GRILLING

Americans love to grill. Americans want to eat more healthfully. These two facts are the reasons for this book. Food trends may come and go, but the art of grilling is a method of preparing food still practiced in most homes—some even call it the American national cuisine. Once limited to summer, grilling is now a year-round activity, even when the weather is bad. Grilling can be done indoors today, as manufacturers have designed grills that can be installed in old as well as new kitchens. Outdoor grills have improved significantly, too, especially in design and operation, and are priced so just about anyone can have one.

Grilling (or oven broiling, a similar technique) creates flavor by caramelizing the natural sugars in food through direct heat. Added flavor, in addition to easy clean up, may explain America's passion for grilling. Although grilling is an ancient cooking technique, it is an art and not an exact science. Americans like this because it is rustic and leaves room for creativity.

Charcoal grilling can be hazardous to your health if done improperly. Fat dripping from the food onto burning coals will promote clouds of carcinogenic hydrocarbons, which then permeate the food. In addition to concerns about carcinogens, a very hot fire will char the outside of the food before cooking the inside to its proper doneness. The best way to avoid this problem is to use low-fat foods, avoid heavily oil-based sauces and basting liquids, and cook over moderate heat.

I have grilled for many years, and have learned that anyone who wants to eat healthier grilled food, without sacrificing flavor, has to modify not only how he or she grills, but also the kind of food that is cooked on the grill. I wrote this book to show how modifications, such as using low-fat marinades and lean meats, will maximize health benefits without sacrificing flavor.

I also have included some recipes that are prepared in foil on the grill, which will deliver flavorful packets of food. Foil packets are sometimes pierced or left slightly open to allow the grill flavor to penetrate the food. If the packet is sealed and put over direct fire, the juices will caramelize, as in sautéing on top of the stove, but the flavor is smokier

THE LINK BETWEEN DIET AND HEALTH

The most noticeable food trend today is the link between diet and health. New government food guidelines, new nutritional analyses printed on food packages, manufacturers' commitments to creating low- or no-fat products, and new studies on diet, obesity and health all document the shift to healthier eating.

From a health standpoint, most fresh meat and produce do not carry the kind of nutritional labeling that is required on processed food.

The recipes in this book have been developed with U.S.D.A. guidelines in mind, and provide nutritional analyses. Foods such as lean meats and spray oils have been suggested to help reduce saturated fats.

THE CHOLESTEROL QUESTION

The American Heart Association recommends that cholesterol intake be limited to 300 milligrams a day and that fats represent no more than 30 percent of total calories, with only one third of those calories coming from saturated fat.

Saturated fats (butter, lard, and coconut and palm oils, for example) are hard at room temperature. Unsaturated fats have either no effect on the blood cholesterol level or may actually lower it. Monounsaturated fats (olive and peanut oils) are neutral. Polyunsaturated fats such as canola, corn, safflower, and sesame, help lower the amount of cholesterol in the blood.

and more intense than food cooked on the stove top. This healthy, new grilling technique suits me to a T, and I think you will find that it will suit you, too.

Look at the Four Basic Rules for Grilling Tasty, Healthy Low-Fat Foods. They summarize the main techniques that I've used in the book. Most of the recipes contain only ten grams of total fat, with saturated fat levels well below five grams. Where traditional recipes use three or four tablespoons of olive or vegetable oil, mine use one tablespoon or less, or call for spray oils. Almost every recipe is flavored with herbs, spices, and/or vegetables and fruits to perk up the flavor. These are ingredients such as garlic, onions, scallions, and all types of peppers, with food values that won't compromise fat and calorie counts, and with flavors that make a big impact. Portion sizes also have been trimmed.

FOUR BASIC RULES FOR GRILLING TASTY, HEALTHY LOW-FAT FOODS

❶ Use leaner cuts of meat and poultry. Remove all visible fat from beef, pork, and lamb before grilling, and remove all skin and fat from poultry.

❷ Grill and cook with less added fat. Decrease the amount of oil, and when using oil, select canola or olive oils for their healthful monounsaturated fat content. Or better still, use spray oils, some of which are available in cans with metered spouts. Use reduced or nonfat mayonnaise, sour cream, and yogurt.

❸ Reduce the use of salt and sugar by using more herbs, spices, and fruit juices to gain flavor. Replace thick, rich, fatty gravies with salsas and/or vegetable purées. Liberal use of freshly ground black pepper usually will obviate the need for salt.

❹ Plan meals with less meat, more fish, and even more vegetables. Grilled vegetables make a great lunch or supper when three or four of them are served together on a plate. When meat is part of the meal, decrease the amount of meat by decreasing the serving size. As a rule, I've suggested a serving size of four ounces per person.

Here's healthy, delicious grilled food. Fire up your grill and let's get started.

CHAPTER 2
THE ART OF GRILLING

Cooking over an open fire has become an everyday event all over the country, and its popularity continues to grow. The actual technique of grilling foods has not changed that much from the ancient art. For example, the pit, for the most part, has been replaced by the firebox, although die-hard barbecue addicts will insist on the pit method. The *barbacoa,* the native American green-wood grill, has become a metal grid. Grilling techniques are easier these days and afford us more time to concentrate on other details and refinements, such as preparing marinades and rubs as well as the accompaniments to complement the grilled foods.

The two basic grilling methods are open grilling and closed grilling. When using the open-grilling method, or grilling without a hood, the fire will be hotter because it is more ventilated. Food will cook quickly, so it is better to use thinner slices of food (i.e., sliced onions instead of whole). When you grill with the hood down— that is, covered grilling—you will have considerably more control of the fire, as you can regulate the draft with vents.

It is a good idea to have both hot and cold spots on the grill so you can move food around as it reaches the desired doneness. This is done by building a fire on one side of the grill, or, if using a gas grill, lighting just one of the two jets.

FUEL OPTIONS

CHARCOAL BRIQUETS

These have been the main fuel for grilling because briquets burn longer than most other materials. They are reasonably priced, readily available, and do a good job overall, although they may take a little longer to create the proper fire for grilling than gas. Be sure to keep the charcoal dry; it is difficult to start a fire properly with damp charcoal. (Tip: When you open a new package, store the remaining charcoal in an airtight container.) Do not use briquets that contain additives, such as the ones containing chemicals that promise quick lighting. Such additives and chemicals are harmful, taste awful, and simply are not necessary.

Try to buy briquets bound with vegetable starches—sometimes called "natural" briquets. They are not easy to find, but they burn longer than any other type of charcoal on the market.

LUMP CHARCOAL

Now available in hickory and other natural wood flavors, this ideal fuel is easy to light and creates a heat more intense than briquets. This is pure charcoal and will spit when lighted, so be alert while you're at the grill to avoid flying sparks.

Both briquets and lump charcoal must be burned to achieve a gray-ash state, while still glowing red inside, in order to cook properly and safely. Many professional cooks prefer mesquite lump charcoal because its intense heat reaches a

◣◢◣◢◣◢◣◢◣◢◣◢◣
**PAIRING FOOD
AND WOOD**
For vegetables:
mesquite, pecan,
maple

For seafood: alder,
fruitwood (especially
apple and cherry),
mesquite, oak, sas-
safras, grapevines

For pork: fruitwood,
hickory, maple, oak,
sassafras

For beef: hickory,
mesquite, oak,
grapevines

For poultry: alder,
fruitwood (apple
and cherry), hickory,
maple, mesquite,
sassafras

Warning: Do not use
cedar, pine, spruce,
or other resinous
woods, leftover
scraps of lumber,
or any wood you
cannot identify.

temperature of about 1,000°F (538°C), and thereby quickly seals in the flavors and juices of whatever is cooked over it. Mesquite charcoal is made from mesquite wood that has been slowly burned until it carbonizes. Hardwood charcoal also is made from wood chunks, but it is a bit more difficult to find. Hardwood charcoal burns very hot and adds a lot of smoky flavor; sometimes it is too strong for delicate foods.

I use less hardwood charcoal and spread it in a thinner layer on the floor of the grill box than I would when I use briquets.

GRILLING WITH WOOD CHIPS

Wood chips actually are a flavoring agent, not a fuel, but it seems appropriate to discuss them here with the various coals. Chips, wood chunks, or vines must be soaked in water for at least 30 minutes before adding them to the fire; this allows them to smoke rather than flame. For fires using charcoal briquets or lump charcoal, drained wood chips or chunks should be sprinkled evenly over the fire shortly before adding the food, perhaps two to five minutes. For gas or electric grills, a "log," or open-ended foil package containing drained chips or chunks, should be placed over the lava rock. A good handful of chips is usually required for one hour's grilling time. If you want a stronger flavor, add more chips, and replenish them when the smoke dies down.

Dried herbs and branches also should be presoaked, then added to charcoal fires just before adding food to the grill. Using dried herbs is a simple way to add flavor, and don't hesitate to add large sprigs of herbs, even fresh ones, soaked in water first, of course. If used on a gas grill, make an open-ended foil package, and puncture holes in the foil to allow the aromas to escape and flavor the food. Cover the grill to prevent the smoke from blowing away.

MAPLE WOOD CHIPS

Consider using maple chips and chunks for added flavor, especially when grilling vegetables. Maple produces a softer smoky flavor than other wood chips, and is slightly sweet. If you can't find maple wood chips, then look for cherry or apple for a similar effect.

ALDER WOOD CHIPS

Alder is the variety of wood traditionally used to smoke Pacific Northwest salmon. It has a soft smoky flavor that is gentle enough to season salmon and other fish without an overpowering taste. Alder chips can be bought in small bags where grilling equipment and supplies are sold.

HICKORY AND OAK WOOD CHIPS

In the South, hickory is king. It is as basic to Southern cooking as collard greens. The smoky flavor from hickory wood is intense, and it is perfect for pork, ribs, poultry, and most red meats. In many places, hickory is preferred to oak, but oak is great-tasting also. Oak is very versatile and provides a full range of flavors.

TYPES OF GRILLS

Basically, a grill has a metal box for fuel and a grid for cooking over the heat source. The grill may have a cover, and may operate on charcoal, gas, or electricity. As simple as a grill may be, many varieties are marketed today, each with specific advantages. Briefly, they fall into the following categories.

HIBACHI

This small, low-priced, portable unit can go anywhere (your backyard, porch, or to the beach). It uses lump charcoal or briquets.

BRAZIER

Also known as the open grill, it can be stationary or portable (usually on wheels). It has a fire bowl, usually made of heavy steel, with a mechanism that raises and lowers the grid to control the heat. The brazier is inexpensive and of varying quality. It uses lump charcoal or briquets.

COVERED KETTLE

This is similar to the brazier, but it has a cover, vents, and a stationary rack. It may come with a rotisserie—electric or battery operated. This is probably the most popular charcoal barbecue unit used today because grilling food under a cover reduces the cooking time and increases the

---

CLEANING THE GAS GRILL

To clean lava rock and ceramic briquets, cut a piece of heavy-duty foil and place it on top of them. The foil should not touch any side of the grill, in order to provide proper ventilation. Light the grill and keep it at high temperature for about ten minutes, or the amount of time specified in the manufacturer's manual; any buildup of food or grease will burn off the rocks.

Brush the burners with a stiff wire brush every six months or so to unclog portholes. For persistent clogs, use a wire or thin metal skewer. Clean the Venturi tubes with an old coffee percolator brush or toothbrush.

CLEANING THE CHARCOAL GRILL

Keeping the grill clean is important to good grilling. It is best to clean the grill with a wire brush after removing the food from the grill, but before the grill has completely cooled. All food residue should be removed, and the grill should be clean and sparkling. If blackened bits of food cling to the grid, it will be difficult to remove newly grilled food.

If the grill is not cleaned after you finish grilling, be sure to clean it before you start a new fire, then again after you use the grill again; this applies to both charcoal and gas grills. Also, add a light spray of oil to the grid after it is cleaned, then again before you add food to the fire.

smoky flavor. Because the heat is more controlled than in an open grill, the food also cooks more evenly. The kettle (any covered grill, whether round or rectangular) is an oven, smoker, and a grill all in one.

HOODED GRILL

This is the same as the kettle, but its shape is square or rectangular. With the hood open, it cooks as an open grill. As a rule, fuel grates and cooking racks or grids are adjustable. Some units have temperature gauges built into the hood, but they are questionable as accurate thermometers. Other appointments may include a rotisserie, side shelves, and rib racks. The cost may be from less than $100 to several thousand dollars. This type of grill is also called a "wagon grill."

INDOOR GAS GRILLS

Also called a flat-top grill, highly polished sheets of metal are set over gas jets on racks or grids; proper ventilation is a necessity. An indoor grill usually is built into the counter top, or is a feature of a stove or range. This grill is gaining popularity for home use, but has been basic equipment in restaurants for years.

ELECTRIC GRILL

This may be an indoor or outdoor grill, portable or stationary. When grilling on an electric unit, it is especially important to marinate, mop, or rub the food since this grill is smokeless. Electric grills don't work as well as other grills. They seem to work well with a small piece of chicken or fish, but they lack the smoky grill flavor we get from grilling directly over charcoal.

The most popular grills today fall into the kettle or hooded categories—either fueled by charcoal or gas. They are more efficient, use less fuel, and provide more control of the heat. The larger types of these grills have an added advantage in offering enough grilling space to allow direct and indirect heat. Indirect grilling, as mentioned on page 19, is done by setting the heat source to one side of the unit; in a gas grill, light just one of the two gas units. Many grill recipes call for setting food in cooler parts of the grill, or over indirect heat.

Although grill aficionados prefer grilling over lump charcoal or briquets, many grilling experts will agree that a gas grill can give good results. One reason is that wood chips can be used in a gas grill to add smoky flavor. The recipes in this book will work on charcoal or gas grills. If using an electric grill, the grilling times may vary.

GRILL TOOLS

One of the most important considerations when choosing grill tools is QUALITY. A few good tools are better than many inexpensive, poor-quality ones. Tools should have long handles with protection from the heat. Following is an alphabetical listing of tools, NOT by order of importance.

BASTING BRUSHES

I prefer angled brushes with long handles and good bristles (usually made from boar hair).

CHARCOAL STARTER

A good starter is one of the most important tools; I couldn't grill without one. Most starters look like an oversized coffee can with a protective handle and a perforated shelf inside to hold the coals, under which newspaper is placed to start the ignition process. Once you use this type of fire starter, you will use no other. I use two, if I think I'm going to need a larger coal bed. I start one, and then the second a little later. The coals ignite at the same time in the starter, and do so rather quickly (in about 20 minutes). Using a starter is safe, provided you place it on the grill once the newspaper is lit, or on a concrete or stone surface away from any flammable material. It is an inexpensive tool worth its weight in gold.

FOIL

Always use heavy-duty foil for the grill; it will have many uses, such as lining the grill and making foil packages. Use heavy-duty foil to cover food off the grill, before cutting or serving it.

HINGED WIRE BASKETS

These are available in various sizes for a variety of foods, such as one in the shape of a fish used for grilling whole fish without the risk of it falling into the fire. Most of these baskets are made of cross-hatched wire, and are ideal for sliced vegetables, to keep them from falling into the fire.

KEBAB RESTS

These are not as popular as they should be, only because they don't seem to be in the stores as often as the other tools, but I like them and use them frequently. Kebab rests are metal racks with notches on each end on which to rest the skewers. These keep the food from touching the grill.

MITTS

Good mitts should be insulated and long, to protect your hands and arms from extreme heat.

SKEWERS

I recommend using both wooden and metal skewers. Use metal skewers with potatoes, turnips, and other root vegetables because the metal heats while on the grill and helps to cook the inside of the vegetables. (If the root vegetables are cut into one-inch chunks, grilling time will be between 15 and 20 minutes.)

When using wooden skewers on the grill, be sure to presoak them for at least 30 minutes to keep them from burning. Wooden skewers have many uses, especially for cooking tidbits on the grill. Suggestions are given throughout the book on when to use wooden skewers. They are indispensable in testing most grilled foods for doneness.

SPATULAS AND TONGS
Both are important. Spatulas should be offset, which means the blade should be set lower than the handle. You will need a spatula to turn individual servings of fish and other delicate foods, especially if you are not using the hinged wire basket. Tongs should be stainless steel and spring-hinged.

WIRE BRUSH
A wire brush is used to clean the grill. Get one with brass bristles and a steel-wool pad. When the fire has cooled, clean the grid with a wire brush by running the brush up and down the lengths of the grid. This is a must and, as far as I know, the only way to properly clean the grill.

LET'S GET GRILLING

STARTING THE FIRE
The easiest way to start a fire is to use a chimney starter instead of charcoal lighter fluid, kindling, presoaked charcoal briquets (not a good addition to grill cookery), or an electric starter. This great invention also is known as a metal flue, and I like it because it is a no-fail, easy-to-use way to get a fire started. Crumple two sheets of newspaper into the bottom section of the cone so they rest against the grid. Fill the flue 3/4 full with charcoal. Set the cone on the bottom of the grill or on the grate, then light the newspaper. The flames from the newspaper will spread upward to the charcoal and ignite it. In about 20 minutes, the coals will become light gray; then, and only then, carefully turn over the cone to empty the hot coals onto the grill bottom. Whether you choose briquets or lump charcoal, you will need a bed two inches deep and a little wider than the food you plan to grill. If you have a large grill, start one chimney and then another.

KNOWING WHEN THE FIRE IS READY
Successful grilling depends on a good fire. It should be hot enough to maintain a steady heat, but not so hot that it blackens the food. The most common error in grilling is adding the food to the heat source before the coals are ready. Think "patience" before adding the food. There are two ways to tell if the fire is ready for the food: (1) white ash MUST cover the coals, and (2) the coals must be at the proper grilling temperature. When the coals are light gray or gray-white, shake the grill gently to rearrange the coals, allowing one half inch or so space between the coals. This will moderate the heat, and will allow the drippings to fall in between the coals. This is important to prevent flare-ups that could blacken the food.

To test for the right temperature, place your hand, palm down, about six inches over the fire. If you have to pull away in two or three seconds, you may add the food to the grill, as this is the right temperature for searing. Once the food is seared, you can adjust the grid to a higher setting to cook the food more slowly, if you have an adjustable grill. If you do not have an adjustable grill, put the food on the grill when you can keep your hand directly over the fire for four or five seconds; this will mean that the fire is medium-hot, ideal for most grilling in this book.

ADDING MORE COAL TO THE FIRE

Most charcoal fires last for about one hour, but if you need more time, light another batch of charcoal in the starter. Add the newspaper to the bottom, fill the cone 2/3 full with charcoal (more or less, according to need), light the paper, then set the starter on a concrete or stone base. When the charcoal is ready, add it to the edges of your ongoing fire, moving some of the new coal to the center, if needed.

ADJUSTABLE VENTS

Many grills have vents on the bottom or sides. Some grills have vents built into the hoods. The vents definitely influence the temperature of the coals; cooler if closed, hotter if open. Eventually you will learn to control flare-ups without the use of water by speeding up (opening the vent) or slowing down (closing the vent) the burning rate of the coal.

DIRECT AND INDIRECT HEAT FOR GRILLING

For direct grilling, the food is placed on the grill directly over the heat source. This technique is used mostly with foods that will cook in 30 minutes or less. If kept over direct heat for a longer period of time, the food will dry out, char, and blacken.

For indirect grilling, the food is placed on the grill over a "cold spot." This usually means that the food is placed to the side of the heat source. With indirect grilling, the cover must always be down. The food is cooked by circulating heat, with a lower temperature—and longer grilling time— than if put over direct heat. Recipe directions will clearly advise if indirect grilling is required. Otherwise, put food on the grill directly over the heat source.

BASTING LOW-FAT FOODS

Many of the recipes in this book call for basting food while it is on the grill.

Basting is important because the recipes call for food with little or no fat, and minimum amounts of oil to keep the food moist. Basting, therefore, is necessary to keep food moist on the grill. I find it easiest just to brush on the mixture. Of course, that means opening and closing the grill, but since grill times for low-fat foods are shorter than they are for fattier foods, basting will be done only two or three times, at most, during the grilling time.

BASTING WITH THE MARINADE

Many of the recipes in this book call for basting with the marinade used to season the food. Generally, it is a good idea to boil the marinade after the food has been removed and before it is to be used for basting. This is a safety measure to destroy any bacteria that may be hiding in raw food. If you follow the recipe steps carefully (refrigerating food in marinades, not leaving food at room temperature past the time specified in the recipe, and boiling marinades that have come in contact with raw food), you should not have to worry about food-borne illnesses.

USING FOIL ON THE GRILL

Heavy-duty foil is very useful when grilling foods. If you do not have an extra small-hole grid, the kind to prevent smaller foods from falling into the fire (such as a Griffo Grid), put a large sheet of heavy-duty foil on top of the grid and punch small holes into the foil with a metal or wooden skewer. This will allow the smoky flavor to develop as the food cooks. Do this with the cover down, in order to trap the smoke.

THE DRUGSTORE WRAP

There are two basic methods of wrapping food in foil for use on the grill. One is a tighter package that allows you to turn food without spilling it. This wrap is called the "Drugstore Wrap." This wrap is more difficult to open and close and should not be punctured. Following are steps to form the Drugstore Wrap.

❶ Use a piece of heavy-duty foil, large enough to enclose the food, leaving enough excess foil to make several folds on the top and sides of the package.

❷ Place the food in the center of the foil, bringing the edges up over the food, and folding two or three times to secure the wrap.

❸ Fold in the sides of the foil two or three times to secure the package tight against the food.

THE BUNDLE WRAP

The second type of wrap is called the "Bundle Wrap," and is used for foods that don't need to be turned on the grill, for example, when grilling whole apples or a head of cauliflower. It is a good wrap for chopped vegetables of all kinds; it opens and closes easily. The top of the package usually isn't secured, and you should puncture holes in the sides to let some of the smoke into the package; alternatively, leave the top of the package open. Here's how to form the package:

❶ Use foil about three times the size of the food to be wrapped, and center the food on the foil.

❷ Bring the four corners together and fold to seal. Leave some space between the foil and the food for the steam inside the packet, and leave some gaps in the foil to let smoke in. If you make a tight seal, use a small skewer to punch several holes near the top of the packet to let smoke in, preventing the juices from oozing out.

When using foil on the grill, the foil will get hot, so be careful when handling the packets. Also, liquid will accumulate in the packet as the food cooks. To get as much flavor as possible, spoon these juices over the food as it cooks. The food will be basting in its own juices.

People always ask me how do grilled flavors penetrate the foil. In many cases, I suggest leaving the top of the foil packets slightly open to increase the absorption of the smoky flavors. Puncturing the foil in several places with a skewer or small sharp knife will offer the same effect. As for tightly sealed packets (used when turning is required), the intense heat cooks and flavors the food in a way not possible in a hot oven or on the stove top. The intense heat will prompt the natural sugars in the food to caramelize more quickly.

GRILLING SAFETY RULES

❶ Never use charcoal for indoor cooking or heating; toxic carbon monoxide fumes may collect, with lethal consequences.

❷ Alcohol, gasoline, and kerosene are not to be used for lighting charcoal or other fuels. They will explode or flash when lit, and can cause serious burns.

❸ Open the hood slowly and carefully to prevent burns, since hot air and steam may build up in a covered grill.

❹ The grill area should have proper circulation. Smoke should drift away, and not gather around the cook, family, or guests.

CHAPTER 3
THE MAGIC OF MARINADES, SAUCES, AND SALSAS

INTRODUCTION

There is no limit to the flavors that can be developed with marinades, and the seemingly limitless variety of ingredients will bring forth the cook's creativity. It is satisfying and exciting to create a marinade, a sauce, or a salsa that is uniquely one's own. It seems as if each chef or home cook has his or her special concoction, wet or dry, for fish, poultry, meat, and vegetables. Everyone that I've talked to agrees that marinades, sauces, and salsas really are important to grilling and will often make the difference between success and failure on the grill.

Most meat and poultry in this country is good, in the sense that it is tender and rarely needs to be tenderized; years ago the primary reason to marinate food was to tenderize it. Even after two nights of marinating, some meats still were as tough as shoe leather. Fortunately, that is not the case these days. Today, most cooks marinate food to add flavor, and that is why most food prepared for the grill is "rubbed" with a spice mixture, "mopped" with a sauce, or immersed in one of the many marinades made with wine, vinegar, lemon, or other fruit juices, oil, and seasonings.

ADDING FLAVOR WITH MARINADES AND RUBS

Some marinades may be sauces, too. The basic barbecue sauce that follows marinates food, but can be used as a sauce when reheated and spread on food as it comes off the grill. The Hot and Tangy Marinade is another example of a marinade that is reheated as sauce. Not all marinades, however, can be used as sauces. When reheating a marinade to be used as a sauce, bring it to a boil, then lower the heat and simmer four minutes.

There are flavorful rubs and mops, such as Spicy Fennel Fish Mop and Mustard Spice Rub, that are used specifically for seasoning before and during grilling. Unlike marinades, in which food is steeped in cupfuls of flavored juices, the rubs and mops are drier and literally are rubbed into the surfaces of the food to be grilled. Rubbed and mopped foods need to marinate as well, often overnight.

THE MAGIC OF DRY RUBS

Dry rubs are blends of spices and herbs. The rubs often do not include liquid, but sometimes a little oil, wine, lemon juice, or other liquid is mixed in with the dry ingredients. If liquid is added, the dry rub becomes a paste. These rubs add considerable flavor to what you grill. Don't hesitate to develop some of your own rubs and pastes.

When using a dry rub, add a spray of oil, rub the oil into the food, then rub the dry mixture into the food. Dry-rubbed food may be left at room temperature for 30 minutes to one hour; if marinating longer, refrigerate the food.

Dry rubbing food is an old technique and was done mainly to preserve food; these days it is used to add flavor. Don't add too much salt or sugar to dry rubs. Salt will extract juices from the food and sugar will burn easily on the grill. Use them, but use them sparingly.

THE CONDIMENT CRAZE

The kitchen rage today is to serve food with condiments, especially relishes and salsas. There seems to be an infinite variety of them; I've included some of my favorites in this book: Peach Honey Relish, Cranberry Apple Conserve, as well as Spicy Melon, and Pepper and Pineapple salsas, to mention a few. There are many more relishes and salsas elsewhere in the book, and it is worth a minute's time to review the index to find something appealing.

These marinades, sauces, and salsas contain negligible amounts of fat, particularly saturated fats, and are exceedingly low in calories, especially considering the flavor impact they deliver. They are ideal accompaniments for grilling, for they can jazz up an otherwise ordinary grilled chicken breast or turnip slice.

MARINATING AND COOKING FOOD PROPERLY

When marinating or storing relishes or salsas, use nonreactive containers such as glass or ceramic dishes or strong plastic bags to hold the mixture. If using a dish, choose one in which the food can be placed in a single layer, not necessarily covered by the marinade, as the food will be turned several times during the marinating time. In most recipes, I've omitted salt or made it optional. If you want to add salt, add it after the food is grilled. Salt draws out juices, and there's no point in grilling "dehydrated" food.

I almost always suggest grilling food that is at room temperature. So, if you plan to refrigerate food while it marinates, remove it 20 to 30 minutes before grilling it. Fish does not require a long marinating time, so refrigeration for 15 or 20 minutes usually is unnecessary—in other words, it is all right to marinate your fish at room temperature for a short period of time. If marinating for more than 15 or 20 minutes, the food must be refrigerated.

To keep food on the grill moist (especially boneless, skinless chicken breasts), baste frequently with the marinade. If the marinade contains tomato, sugar, jam, or other sugary substances, baste toward the end of the grilling time to avoid blackening the food—sugar tends to burn when cooked over high heat.

Caution: Although I recommend using spray oils most of the time, don't spray the oil on food that is already on the grill, as the fire surely will flare. Butter has been eliminated in most of these recipes, but if you use butter, don't add it to food that is already on the grill, as that will cause flaring, too.

Vegetables and fruit also marinate well, so don't overlook the possibilities of added flavor with these grilled foods, which can be simply delicious.

Lastly, try to create your own marinades, sauces, and salsas; they're healthy, tasty, and fun.

BASIC BARBECUE MARINADE AND SAUCE

MAKES 1 CUP (240 ML) FOR 2 LBS (900 G) OF POULTRY, BEEF, OR PORK

This is a good marinade that also can be used as a sauce. After heating the mixture, cool before using it as a marinade. Reheat the marinade to serve it as a sauce. Before putting the marinated food on the grill, drain well, as the marinade contains both ketchup and sugar, and will blacken more quickly. Use this marinade as a basting sauce after the food has been on the grill midway through cooking time.

1/2 cup (120 ml) ketchup

1/3 cup (80 ml) cider vinegar

3 tablespoons packed dark-brown sugar

2 tablespoons each: vegetable oil, prepared mustard, and Worcestershire sauce

2 garlic cloves, minced

juice of 1 whole lemon (3 tablespoons)

2 tablespoons bourbon (optional)

❶ Combine all ingredients in a nonaluminum saucepan. Stirring, bring to a boil.

❷ Reduce the heat and simmer 4 minutes to allow the flavors to blend, and to cook off the bourbon, if using.

KETCHUP

Ketchup is a popular ingredient in marinades and sauces. Of a pureed consistency, ketchup is made with tomatoes, walnuts, mushrooms, and the extract of salted anchovies. Some say the word comes from the old Chinese term, *ketsiap,* meaning "fish brine." (Catsup is another form of the word.)

Each tablespoon			
Calories	40	Total Fat	1.8 g
Protein	0.2 g	Saturated Fat	0.2 g
Carbohydrates	6 g	Cholesterol	0 mg
Dietary Fiber	0.2 g	Sodium	116 mg

MY BROTHER JERRY'S KENTUCKY RUB

MAKES ABOUT 1/2 CUP (120 ML) FOR 2 LBS (900 G) OF PORK

My brother Jerry, a judge in Kentucky, is a fine cook and boasts about his special rub-paste that he uses on pork. He makes it ahead and keeps it in the refrigerator for more than a week. Here's the way he makes it.

1 small to medium-size onion, peeled and coarsely chopped

2 garlic cloves, peeled

1/4 cup (60 ml) good Kentucky bourbon

2 tablespoons dark brown sugar

1 tablespoon coarsely ground black pepper

1 tablespoon corn oil

1/4 teaspoon red pepper flakes

1 Combine all ingredients in the bowl of a food processor, then blend until a paste is formed.

2 Use immediately, or store in a tightly covered jar in the refrigerator.

Each tablespoon			
Calories	52	Total Fat	1.8 g
Protein	0.2 g	Saturated Fat	0.2 g
Carbohydrates	5 g	Cholesterol	0 mg
Dietary Fiber	4 g	Sodium	2 mg

FRESH HERB SAUCE

MAKES ABOUT 1/2 CUP (120 ML) FOR 8 SERVINGS

This herb sauce can be used to season grilled vegetables, chicken, pork, beef, soups, and bread. It also is very good on a grilled potato with a teaspoonful of nonfat sour cream. Or smear the herb sauce over corn before or after grilling. Serve the sauce as a condiment with sliced turkey breast. Spread it on bread, then place it on the grill for a few minutes with the cover down. Add a teaspoonful of the sauce to a bowl of soup, just before serving.

3 garlic cloves, peeled and cut into halves

1/3 cup (80 ml) each, fresh: basil, mint, and parsley

juice of 1 whole lemon (3 tablespoons)

1 tablespoon olive or canola oil

freshly ground black pepper to taste

❶ Place the garlic in the bowl of a food processor and mince it by pulsing 2 or 3 times.

❷ Add the herbs, and pulse 2 or 3 more times.

❸ Add lemon juice, oil, and pepper and continue pulsing until the sauce is blended. Serve at room temperature.

HERBS AND THEIR FRAGRANCE

One of the most effective ways to enhance the flavor of food, especially when cutting back on fat, is to use herbs creatively. Recognizing this fact, supermarkets have shelves and bins full of fresh herbs.

Fresh herbs stay fresh longer if you wrap them in damp paper towels, then put them in plastic wrap or bags, and store them in the refrigerator.

Each tablespoon			
Calories	20	Total Fat	2 g
Protein	0.2 g	Saturated Fat	0.2 g
Carbohydrates	1 g	Cholesterol	0 mg
Dietary Fiber	0.3 g	Sodium	2 mg

HOT AND TANGY MARINADE

MAKES ABOUT 3/4 CUP (180 ML) FOR 3 LBS (1 1/2 KG) OF CHICKEN

This is a sauce as well as a marinade, and it is delicious. Chicken and pork can marinate in it overnight. Drain food well before adding it to the grill. Baste with the marinade after the food is half-cooked, and reheat more of the mixture to serve as a sauce.

1/4 cup (60 ml) each: cider vinegar, ketchup, and fresh lemon juice

2 tablespoons margarine, melted

2 tablespoons prepared horseradish

1 teaspoon Worcestershire sauce

2 or 3 drops hot red pepper sauce

salt to taste (optional)

❶ Combine all the ingredients in a small nonaluminum saucepan with a tight-fitting lid, then bring to a boil.

❷ Lower the heat, then simmer 10 minutes.

Each tablespoon			
Calories	25	Total Fat	1.9 g
Protein	0.2 g	Saturated Fat	0.3 g
Carbohydrates	2.4 g	Cholesterol	0 mg
Dietary Fiber	0.1 g	Sodium	89 mg

ASIAN SHERRY-GINGER MARINADE

MAKES 3/4 CUP (180 ML) FOR 2 LBS (900 G) OF FISH

This marinade and basting sauce adds an exciting Oriental flavor to fish. I can't think of any kind of fish that would not benefit from this marinade.

1/2 cup (120 ml) low-sodium soy sauce

2 tablespoons dry sherry

juice of 1 whole lemon (3 tablespoons)

3 tablespoons freshly grated ginger

3 tablespoons finely sliced scallions

2 garlic cloves, minced

3 drops hot red pepper sauce

1 teaspoon freshly ground black pepper

❶ Combine all ingredients in a glass or nonaluminum bowl, and mix well.

❷ Pour over the fish 30 minutes before grilling, and use to baste while fish is on the grill.

SOY SAUCE, AN AMERICAN STAPLE

Soy sauce is a common ingredient in marinades and other grilling sauces.

Soy sauce is made from a mixture of cooked soybeans, and wheat or barley flour, which is salted and fermented. The liquid is dark brown and salty, and tastes somewhat like bouillon. There are low-sodium versions of soy sauce, and almost all recipes in this book call for the low-sodium variety.

Each tablespoon			
Calories	20	Total Fat	0.1 g
Protein	0.9 g	Saturated Fat	0 g
Carbohydrates	3 g	Cholesterol	0 mg
Dietary Fiber	0.2 g	Sodium	334 mg

ITALIAN HERB MARINADE

MAKES ABOUT 3/4 CUPS (180 ML) FOR 2 LBS (900 G) OF FISH OR VEGETABLES

This is a wonderful marinade for fish, meat, and vegetables. Vegetables need only 15 to 30 minutes in this marinade, but be sure to baste the vegetables frequently while on the grill.

1/2 cup (120 ml) plus 2 tablespoons fresh lemon juice

2 tablespoons olive oil

2 large garlic cloves, minced

2 tablespoons chopped onion

1 tablespoon each, finely chopped fresh: basil, oregano, and flat-leaf parsley or 1 teaspoon dried

freshly ground black pepper to taste

salt to taste (optional)

1 In a large bowl, combine lemon juice and oil; whisk until blended. Add other ingredients, then mix well.

2 Place fish, meat, or vegetables in a large dish, and add marinade. Marinate up to 30 minutes for fish and vegetables, several hours for meat. Use marinade for basting while food is on the grill.

THE WONDERS OF GARLIC

When I was growing up, I was told that my grandfather's heavy consumption of garlic spared him from the Spanish flu epidemic of the early 1900s. Today, studies document the health benefits of garlic: Garlic reduces blood pressure, clears bronchitis, and tones the digestive system because of its antiseptic properties.

Garlic comes in several varieties: white, pink, and mauve. Purchase bulbs with firm cloves. Cut off any discoloration on a clove, or it will spoil the taste of your dish.

Each tablespoon			
Calories	23	Total Fat	2.3 g
Protein	0.1 g	Saturated Fat	0.3 g
Carbohydrates	1 g	Cholesterol	0 mg
Dietary Fiber	0.1 g	Sodium	0.4 mg

THAI PEANUT SAUCE

MAKES ABOUT 1 CUP (240 ML) FOR 16 SERVINGS

This is a hot, spicy sauce, and a teaspoonful goes well with many grilled foods, even a simple baked potato or vegetable kebab.

2/3 cup (160 ml) water

1 1/2 teaspoons cornstarch

  4 garlic cloves, minced

1/3 cup (85 g) chunky peanut butter

1/3 cup (80 ml) seasoned rice vinegar

  2 tablespoons low-sodium soy sauce

  2 teaspoons sugar

1/2 to 1 teaspoon red pepper flakes

❶ Combine water and cornstarch in a small saucepan. Whisk until the cornstarch is totally dissolved. Bring to a boil, reduce the heat and whisk constantly until the mixture thickens. Set aside to cool.

❷ In the bowl of a food processor or blender, combine the remaining ingredients, using only 1/2 teaspoon red pepper flakes. Pulse several times to blend. Transfer peanut butter mixture to the cooled cornstarch mixture, and whisk until blended. Taste and adjust spiciness with remaining red pepper flakes.

RICH, COMPLEX, AROMATIC SOY SAUCE

Soy sauce has become so popular in this country that it can be found in most supermarkets and small groceries. It adds flavor and color to marinades, and can be used with vegetables, meat, poultry, and seafood.

I look for soy sauce that is naturally brewed and aged, to ensure full flavor. Use low-sodium soy sauce as it will have about 50 percent less sodium than the others.

Each tablespoon			
Calories	38	Total Fat	2.7 g
Protein	2 g	Saturated Fat	0.5 g
Carbohydrates	3 g	Cholesterol	0 mg
Dietary Fiber	0.5 g	Sodium	88 mg

MUSTARD SPICE RUB

MAKES ABOUT 1/2 CUP (120 ML) FOR 1 LB (455 G) OF MEAT

This is one of my favorite rubs for meat, especially beef and pork. Don't fret over the optional addition of cognac; the alcohol will cook off once the meat is on the grill, leaving only the flavor.

1 large garlic clove, minced

1 tablespoon each: dry mustard, ground coriander, paprika, ground black pepper, and canola oil

2 tablespoons cognac (optional)

❶ Combine the garlic with the spices in a mortar with a pestle; mash to grind and blend well. Work in the oil and cognac.

❷ Rub the meat on all sides, and let marinate, covered, overnight in the refrigerator.

❸ Bring the meat to room temperature 1 hour before grilling. If there is no time to marinate overnight, rub the marinade on the meat, and leave it at room temperature for 1 hour before grilling.

Each tablespoon			
Calories	28	Total Fat	1.9 g
Protein	0.3 g	Saturated Fat	0.2 g
Carbohydrates	1 g	Cholesterol	0 mg
Dietary Fiber	0.4 g	Sodium	1.2 mg

SAKE, SOY, AND GINGER SAUCE

MAKES 1/2 CUP (120 ML) FOR 1 TO 2 LBS (455–900 G) OF FISH

These Oriental flavors are ideal when grilling small fish, fish steaks, fillets, and kebabs. This sauce is great on a kebab of tuna, monkfish, or swordfish, or any combination of these.

1/4 cup (60 ml) low-sodium soy sauce

1/4 cup (60 ml) sake

  2 garlic cloves, minced

  2 tablespoons finely chopped scallions

  2 tablespoons peeled and minced fresh ginger.

1 Combine all ingredients in a glass bowl; mix well.

2 Coat the fish liberally 30 minutes before grilling.

THE SAVORY SCALLION

Scallions are in the market year-round and play an important role in grilling. They look like skinny leeks, but are really young onions; they are picked before a full bulb is developed. Green onions are more mature scallions; they are picked later and have bulbs. Purchase them with crisp, green tops and clean white bottoms. They don't last as long as fully mature onions, so use them within several days.

To store, wrap them in plastic wrap or in a plastic bag, and refrigerate. One cup of chopped scallions has only 32 calories and less than one gram of total fat, with no cholesterol.

Each tablespoon			
Calories	29	Total Fat	0.1 g
Protein	1 g	Saturated Fat	0 g
Carbohydrates	2 g	Cholesterol	0 mg
Dietary Fiber	0.1 g	Sodium	251 mg

SPICY FENNEL FISH MOP

MAKES ABOUT 1/2 CUP (120 ML) FOR 3 LBS (1 1/2 KG) OF FISH

The fennel seed in this marinade provides an exciting Mediterranean flavor, ideal for fish.

1 tablespoon ground fennel seeds

1 dry red chile seeded and crumbled, or 1/2 teaspoon red pepper flakes

1 tablespoon kosher salt

1 teaspoon black peppercorns, cracked

2 large garlic cloves, minced

2 tablespoons olive oil

juice of 2 whole lemons (about 3/8 cup/89 ml)

❶ Grind fennel, chile, salt, peppercorns, and garlic in a mortar with a pestle, or in a spice grinder. Slowly add oil and lemon juice, and blend.

❷ Brush marinade on fish 30 minutes before grilling; let sit at room temperature. When grilling a whole fish, marinate inside and outside of fish, and baste often while on the grill. Marinate kebabs or fish fillets 30 minutes before grilling, and also baste while on the grill.

Each tablespoon			
Calories	38	Total Fat	3.5 g
Protein	0.4 g	Saturated Fat	0.5 g
Carbohydrates	1.8 g	Cholesterol	0 mg
Dietary Fiber	0.2 g	Sodium	801 mg

SHERRY AND ORANGE MARINADE

MAKES 3/4 CUP (180 ML) FOR 1 TO 2 LBS (455–900 G) OF POULTRY OR PORK

The flavors of orange and sherry combine well here, and are excellent for grilling chicken. Use it also to marinate pork cutlets or tenderloin, and as a basting sauce for many vegetables.

1/4 cup (60 ml) sherry

1/4 cup (43 g) firmly packed brown sugar

2 tablespoons fresh orange juice

1 teaspoon finely chopped orange zest

freshly ground black pepper to taste

❶ Combine all ingredients in a nonaluminum saucepan. Stirring constantly, cook over medium heat until the sugar dissolves; cool.

❷ Place chicken or pork in a shallow dish and add marinade; marinate overnight.

❸ Bring to room temperature before grilling. Grill meat to desired doneness, brushing leftover marinade over meat during last few minutes of grilling.

ORANGE AND LEMON ZEST, A FRESH TOUCH OF FLAVOR

Zest is the thin colored part of the peel from any citrus fruit. The zest can be cut easily with a vegetable peeler or paring knife, but avoid cutting away any pith, or bitter white part of the peel, with the zest. Another approach is to rub the whole lemon, or orange, against a cheese grater. To avoid the pits, turn the fruit to a new spot after rubbing back and forth a few times.

Zest gets its flavor from essential oils in the outer part of the rind.

Each tablespoon			
Calories	24	Total Fat	0 g
Protein	0 g	Saturated Fat	0 g
Carbohydrates	4.8 g	Cholesterol	0 mg
Dietary Fiber	0 g	Sodium	1.9 mg

SPICY PEPPERCORN MARINADE

MAKES 3/4 CUP (180 ML)

This marinade can be used with most kinds of fish to be grilled whole. Be sure to get some on the inside of the fish.

2 tablespoons whole peppercorns, any color or mixed, cracked

2 teaspoons kosher salt

1/4 teaspoon red pepper flakes

1 teaspoon ground coriander

2 tablespoons finely sliced scallions

1/2 cup (120 ml) bottled clam juice or fish broth

2 tablespoons olive oil

1 Grind peppercorns, salt, pepper flakes, and coriander in a mortar with a pestle or in a spice grinder.

2 Transfer to a small bowl and blend in clam juice and oil.

3 Pour over the whole fish, and marinate 1 hour, including 20 minutes marinating at room temperature. Baste fish frequently with marinade while fish is on the grill.

Each tablespoon			
Calories	23	Total Fat	2.3 g
Protein	0.2 g	Saturated Fat	0.3 g
Carbohydrates	0.8 g	Cholesterol	0.3 mg
Dietary Fiber	0.3 g	Sodium	378 mg

WHITE WINE AND SCALLION MARINADE

MAKES ABOUT 2 CUPS (480 ML) FOR 2 LBS (900 G) OF FISH

This excellent marinade and basting sauce may be used with most kinds of fish. Baste the fish continually while it is on the grill.

1 cup (240 ml) white wine

2 tablespoons olive oil

1/4 cup (43 g) finely chopped scallions

1/4 cup (32 g) finely cubed (1/4 inch/5/8 cm) carrots

1/4 cup (28 g) finely chopped fresh flat-leaf parsley

1/2 teaspoon freshly ground black pepper

❶ Combine all ingredients in a small, nonaluminum saucepan, and bring to a boil, stirring frequently.

❷ As soon as the mixture boils, remove from the heat and let cool.

❸ Marinate fish 30 minutes before grilling. Baste often while fish is on the grill.

FLAT-LEAF PARSLEY IS TASTIER THAN CURLY

Flat-leaf parsley is considered by food connoisseurs to have more flavor than curly. So go ahead and use the prettier curly parsley for garnishing your dishes, but use the flat-leaf variety when the recipe calls for parsley as a seasoning. For example, parsley is an important ingredient in the White Wine and Scallion Marinade recipe shown here.

Each tablespoon			
Calories	26	Total Fat	2 g
Protein	0.1 g	Saturated Fat	0.2 g
Carbohydrates	0.5 g	Cholesterol	0 mg
Dietary Fiber	0 g	Sodium	1.8 mg

CRANBERRY APPLE CONSERVE

MAKES ABOUT 3 CUPS (3/4 L)

This conserve is a great companion for grilled turkey, chicken, and pork. The sweet-tart taste complements white meat. However, it also works well with vegetables. Try putting a tablespoonful in the center of a grilled half summer squash, or as an accompaniment with slices of grilled butternut squash.

1 (12-oz/340-g) package cranberries, picked over and rinsed; fresh or frozen

1 apple, peeled, seeded, and finely chopped

1/2 cup (120 ml) fresh orange juice

1/2 cup (120 ml) low-sodium chicken or vegetable broth

1 teaspoon grated orange zest

1 teaspoon finely chopped rosemary, or 1/2 teaspoon dried

1 or 2 pinches ground cinnamon

1/4 cup (57 g) chopped pecans or walnuts

1 Thaw cranberries, if frozen. Place all ingredients, except the pecans, in a saucepan. Bring to a boil, then lower heat to a simmer; cook, partially covered, until mixture thickens, about 10 minutes.

2 Remove from the heat. Add the pecans and toss well. Serve warm or at room temperature.

Each tablespoon			
Calories	10	Total Fat	0.4 g
Protein	0 g	Saturated Fat	0 g
Carbohydrates	2 g	Cholesterol	0 mg
Dietary Fiber	0 g	Sodium	16 mg

MANGO AND JICAMA SALSA

MAKES ABOUT 1 QUART (1 L)

The wonderful flavors in this recipe combine to make an unusually good salsa that has many uses. I use it frequently with a plate of grilled vegetables.

1 1/2 cups (248 g) diced fresh mango

1 cup each diced: jicama, seeded cucumber, red onion, and fresh grapefruit

1 teaspoon sugar

1 or 2 minced, seeded jalapeños

1/2 cup (120 ml) fresh lime juice

❶ Combine all ingredients in a glass container with a tight-fitting lid.

❷ Chill overnight.

TROPICAL MANGO

Mangoes are best when they are fully ripe.

Mango is rich in beta carotene and vitamin C. One half of an average-size mango has about 65 calories. When purchasing, bear in mind that size is no indication of quality or ripeness. As the fruit ripens, it develops orange, yellow, and sometimes red hues.

Each tablespoon			
Calories	7	Total Fat	0 g
Protein	0.1 g	Saturated Fat	0 g
Carbohydrates	1.7 g	Cholesterol	0 mg
Dietary Fiber	0.3 g	Sodium	0 mg

PEACH HONEY RELISH

MAKES ABOUT 2 CUPS (480 ML)

This relish has many uses. I especially like it with a slice of grilled corn bread, and a very thin slice of low-fat ham. It also is delicious with sliced, grilled chicken breast or sliced, grilled pork tenderloin.

1 lb (455 g) peaches

1 tablespoon honey

1 tablespoon finely chopped fresh mint, or
   1 teaspoon dried

1 tablespoon fresh lemon juice

1 teaspoon fresh minced ginger

pinch of red pepper flakes

❶ Peel and pit the peaches, then chop them coarsely. Place peaches in a large glass or stainless steel bowl; add the remaining ingredients.

❷ Cover with plastic wrap, and leave at room temperature for 30 minutes.

A WORLD OF HONEY

Have you tried all the wonderful flavors of honey? There's lavender honey, wild rose honey, orange-blossom honey, and linden honey.

Honey is a natural liquid sugar. I find it infinitely more interesting to use a table-spoon of honey in a marinade, sauce, or salsa, than an ordinary spoonful of sugar as I've done in the recipe for Peach Honey Relish.

Each tablespoon			
Calories	8	Total Fat	0 g
Protein	0 g	Saturated Fat	0 g
Carbohydrates	2.2 g	Cholesterol	0 mg
Dietary Fiber	0.2 g	Sodium	0 mg

PEPPER AND PINEAPPLE SALSA

MAKES ABOUT 1 1/2 CUPS (360 ML)

This is an all-around condiment as it is delicious with many grilled foods. This salsa is chunky and flavorful, and has lots of color. Use it with vegetables, fish, poultry, and pork.

1 red bell pepper, cored, seeded, and finely chopped

1 cup (300 g) finely chopped fresh ripe
 pineapple, or canned crushed pineapple, drained

1/2 cup (152 g) finely chopped red onions

1/4 cup (28 g) finely chopped cilantro or flat-leaf parsley

1 finely chopped jalapeño, or a pinch of red pepper flakes
 juice of 1 whole lemon (3 tablespoons)

1 teaspoon honey or sugar
 salt to taste (optional)

❶ Combine all ingredients in a glass bowl, and leave at room temperature for 30 minutes to 1 hour.

❷ Refrigerate up to 24 hours, but bring to room temperature before serving.

Each tablespoon			
Calories	6	Total Fat	0 g
Protein	0 g	Saturated Fat	0 g
Carbohydrates	1.6 g	Cholesterol	0 mg
Dietary Fiber	0.2 g	Sodium	0 mg

SPICY MELON SALSA

MAKES ABOUT 1 QUART (1 L)

This is a healthy, versatile condiment that can be used with appetizers, fish, meats, and a variety of vegetables.

- 1 cup (175 g) each, finely diced ripe: honey-dew, cantaloupe, and watermelon
- 1 tomato, peeled, seeded and diced
- 1/2 cup (152 g) finely diced red onion
- 1/4 cup (28 g) finely chopped fresh mint
- 1/4 cup (60 ml) fresh lemon juice
- 1 teaspoon finely minced jalapeño pepper, or more to taste
- 1 teaspoon sugar
- pinch of salt

❶ Combine all ingredients in a large bowl.

❷ Cover with plastic wrap, and let sit at room temperature for 30 to 40 minutes to allow flavors to blend. If made ahead of time, refrigerate; bring to room temperature before serving.

THE ANCIENT HERB MINT

The Latin *mentha,* or mint, has hundreds of varieties, wild as well as cultivated. The Romans used mint in their cooking, and spread it throughout their empire.

Mint adds considerable zest to salsas and other foods.

Mint can also be used to make a delicious jelly. Mint jelly is the classic accompaniment to roast leg of lamb.

Each tablespoon			
Calories	4	Total Fat	0 g
Protein	0.1 g	Saturated Fat	0 g
Carbohydrates	1 g	Cholesterol	0 mg
Dietary Fiber	0 g	Sodium	1.6 mg

CHAPTER 4
APPETIZERS AND SOUPS WITH SMOKY FLAVORS

INTRODUCTION

If you are grilling lunch or supper, why not let the fire do double duty and prepare some appetizers, or even soup. Most appetizers coming off the grill are simply wonderful in that they go directly into the mouth. And they can be simple, small bites, such as Spicy Gingered Shrimp or Oriental Tuna Kebabs. Such snacks, speared for the grill, can be served hot off the grill, without additional fuss. People seem to love food like this as they wait for another cocktail or a main course.

Not all appetizers need to be eaten directly off the grill. Many recipes offered in this chapter also make excellent first courses at sit-down meals: Antipasto of Grilled Onions and Tomatoes, wonderful Bruschetta of Grilled Eggplant, Tomatoes, and Basil make easy, tempting first courses.

You won't miss the deep-fried shrimp or other foods that are smothered in fattening batters and left to crisp in hot oil that are usual appetizer fare. Family and guests in the vicinity of the grill will smell the wonderful barbecue aromas and flavors—a simple way to work up an appetite. Charred peppers, tomatoes, and grape leaves filled with goat cheese are just a few of the attractive, mouthwatering appetizers that can be prepared on the grill.

ANTIPASTO OF GRILLED ONIONS AND TOMATOES

MAKES 4 SERVINGS

The flavors of grilled onions and tomatoes, combined with olives in a balsamic dressing, atop crusty bread is as delicious as food can be. The smoky flavors add an exotic note, and I honestly can make a meal of this by adding some cooked greens, or a Boston lettuce or curly endive salad.

1 large sweet onion, such as Vidalia, peeled and thinly sliced into rings

2 large tomatoes, cut into 1/2-inch (1 1/4-cm) slices

1 large turnip, peeled, sliced 1/4 inch (5/8 cm) thick, then sliced into 1/4-inch (5/8-cm) matchsticks

4 cured black olives, pitted and finely chopped

2 teaspoons each: balsamic vinegar and olive oil

1 tablespoon finely chopped fresh basil, or 1 teaspoon dried

freshly ground black pepper to taste

4 thin slices of Italian or French bread

❶ When the fire is ready, lightly spray the grid with oil. Add the onions, tomatoes, and turnip, then grill 7 to 10 minutes, turning as needed. When done, transfer them to a bowl.

❷ In a small bowl, combine olives, vinegar, oil, basil, and a liberal amount of pepper. Mix well and pour over vegetable mixture. Toss to mix.

❸ Quickly toast the bread on the grill and put 1 slice on each of 4 plates. Spoon the onion mixture over the bread, using all the sauce. Serve right away, and pass the pepper mill.

Serving suggestion: Add a slice of grilled polenta to the plate to make a good lunch.

THE BALSAMIC WAVE

Balsamic vinegar, a trendy item these days in the United States, has been on the scene in Italy for generations. There, it is considered a staple. Good balsamic vinegar is aged at least three years. In Modena, Italy, it has been made and packaged for hundreds of years, the ancient casks handed down from one generation to the next. The vinegar's distinct flavor not only enhances salad dressings, but also creates a fine base for a marinade.

Each serving (not including polenta)			
Calories	162	Total Fat	4 g
Protein	4 g	Saturated Fat	0 g
Carbohydrates	28 g	Cholesterol	1 mg
Dietary Fiber	3 g	Sodium	271 mg

BRUSCHETTA WITH GRILLED EGGPLANT, TOMATOES, AND BASIL

MAKES 24 APPETIZER SERVINGS OR 4 MAIN-COURSE SERVINGS

For appetizers, cut a French or Italian baguette into 1/4-inch (5/8-cm) slices, and dry the slices in an oven or atop a grill. Or, for a main course, grill four larger slices of Italian or French bread, then brush them with oil and rub them with garlic.

1 (1-lb/455-g) eggplant, rinsed, dried, ends removed, and sliced 1/2 inch (1 1/4 cm) thick

1 tablespoon olive oil

2 large ripe tomatoes, cored, skinned, seeded, and chopped into 1/2-inch (1 1/4-cm) pieces

10 large fresh basil leaves, thinly sliced, or 1 teaspoon dried

juice of 1 whole lemon (3 tablespoons)

freshly ground black pepper to taste

salt to taste (optional)

❶ Prepare the grill. Lightly brush the eggplant slices with oil. When the fire is ready, place eggplant slices on a lightly oiled grid, and grill 4 to 5 minutes on each side, until the slices are tender. To test for doneness, insert a wooden skewer; if it meets no resistance, the slices are cooked. Remove to a cutting board. Cut eggplant into 1/2-inch (1 1/4-cm) cubes, and put in a bowl.

❷ Add tomatoes, basil, lemon juice, and a liberal grinding of pepper; stir to blend. Season with salt.

❸ If serving as an appetizer, put the eggplant mixture in an attractive bowl in the center of a serving platter. Place bread around the bowl, asking your guests to help themselves. If using as a first course for 4, put the grilled bread slices on a plate, and spoon some of the eggplant mixture over each slice. Serve immediately.

Each appetizer serving			
Calories	114	Total Fat	2 g
Protein	4 g	Saturated Fat	0.3 g
Carbohydrates	21 g	Cholesterol	1 mg
Dietary Fiber	1 g	Sodium	205 mg

BASIL, QUEEN OF THE HERBS

In the *Great Herbal*, published in 1526, it was written that "Basil taketh away melancholy and maketh merry and glad."

If you haven't grown basil, you should.

Basil grows easily and profusely. It looks good, smells beautiful, and freezes superbly. A spoonful of pesto alongside most grilled vegetables is truly wonderful. Try the pesto recipe on page 275 for a low-fat alternative.

ROASTED GARLIC HUMMUS ON BREAD SLICES

MAKES 30 SERVINGS

This is an easy-to-prepare and inexpensive appetizer that you and your guests will enjoy. The roasted garlic bulb can be prepared ahead of time.

Roasted Garlic (recipe follows)

1 (19-oz/539-g) can chickpeas, drained and rinsed twice

2 tablespoons sesame paste (tahini)

juice of 1 whole lemon (3 tablespoons)

1/2 teaspoon ground cumin

1/4 teaspoon red pepper flakes

1 loaf sourdough baguette, cut into 1/4-inch (5/8-cm) slices

1 Prepare Roasted Garlic and set aside.

2 Combine the chickpeas, sesame paste, lemon juice, cumin, and red pepper flakes with 1 tablespoon water in the bowl of a food processor; purée until smooth. If the mixture is too thick, add another tablespoon water and process again to reach desired consistency.

3 Add the garlic pulp, and pulse to incorporate.

4 Grill the bread slices, being careful not to char, or dry them out in a low oven, 250°F (121°C), until they crisp, 30 to 40 minutes.

5 To serve, put the garlic hummus in a bowl in the center of a large serving dish, and arrange the bread slices around the bowl. Let people spread their own portion of hummus on each bread slice.

ROASTED GARLIC

1 whole garlic bulb

1/2 teaspoon each: canola oil and fresh
lemon juice

1 small rosemary sprig

freshly ground black pepper to taste

salt to taste (optional)

❶ Cut 1/2 inch (1 1/4 cm) off the top of the garlic bulb, so individual cloves are exposed; cut an 8-inch-square sheet of heavy-duty foil. Place the garlic bulb on the foil: add oil and lemon juice to the cut end of the garlic bulb. Place the herb sprig across the bulb, and season with pepper and salt. Wrap the foil around the bulb by making a Bundle Wrap (page 10).

❷ When the fire is ready, place the packet on the grid over the hot coals and cook for about 40 minutes, turning carefully several times. Remove the packet from the grill, and let sit until cool enough to handle. Squeeze the cooked garlic bulb by hand, and the delicious, soft pulp will come forth. Set aside.

HAIL ROSEMARY

Rosemary has many uses in grilling, especially with meats and sauces. It is a unique flavoring agent. Use this herb sparingly, as it has a strong flavor and may overtake other flavors. If you use it dried, be sure to crush the leaves to help release the flavor, but remember that a little goes a long way.

The herb is best fresh, and it is abundant in some states, notably Virginia, North Carolina, and California.

Each tablespoon of hummus (without bread)			
Calories	31	Total Fat	1 g
Protein	1.4 g	Saturated Fat	0.1 g
Carbohydrates	4.3 g	Cholesterol	0 mg
Dietary Fiber	1 g	Sodium	1 mg

GRILLED GOAT CHEESE IN GRAPE LEAVES

MAKES 16 APPETIZERS

These are tasty morsels that should be eaten as soon as they come off the grill. Some grape leaves are too large for this preparation; either cut them into halves, or snip off and discard what you don't need, in order to make smaller containers.

16 bottled grape leaves, rinsed and dried

2 teaspoons olive oil

2 oz (57 g) goat cheese, softened

2 oz (57 g) nonfat cream cheese, softened

4 teaspoons hot pepper jelly

❶ Prepare the grape leaves, and lay them on a flat work surface. Lightly brush with oil, reserving some oil for later.

❷ In a small bowl, combine the cheeses, mixing until well blended. Using teaspoonfuls of the mixture, form small marble-size balls. Place one ball on each leaf. Add 1/4 teaspoon jelly to each. Fold each leaf like an envelope to completely cover the cheese and jelly. Lightly oil the outside of each grape-leaf packet.

❸ When the fire is ready, place the packets on a lightly oiled grid. Grill on each side about 1 minute, just enough to melt the cheese and lightly brown the grape leaves. Serve hot with toothpicks.

Each appetizer			
Calories	25	Total Fat	1.4 g
Protein	2 g	Saturated Fat	0.6 g
Carbohydrates	2 g	Cholesterol	2 mg
Dietary Fiber	0 g	Sodium	33 mg

SPICY GINGERED SHRIMP

MAKES 12 APPETIZERS

Considering the taste that just one of these shrimp delivers, this is probably one of the easiest and best dishes in the book. You may add finely minced garlic to the marinade, if you want, and use finely chopped candied ginger instead of fresh.

1/4 cup (60 ml) seasoned rice vinegar

1/4 cup (60 ml) frozen orange juice or lemonade concentrate, thawed

1/4 cup (76 g) finely chopped onion

1 tablespoon freshly grated ginger

1/2 teaspoon red pepper flakes

12 large fresh shrimp (about 3/4 lb/340 g), shelled, deveined, rinsed, and dried well

❶ In the bowl of a food processor or blender, combine all ingredients except the shrimp. Pulse until well mixed.

❷ Place the shrimp in a shallow dish, and pour the citrus-ginger mixture over top. Cover tightly with a lid or plastic wrap, and refrigerate 30 minutes. Soak 12 (12-inch/30-cm) wooden skewers in water for 30 minutes; skewers must be completely submerged in the water. Meanwhile, prepare the grill.

❸ When the fire is ready, thread 1 shrimp onto each skewer. Place skewers on a lightly oiled grid and grill, basting frequently with the marinade, 2 minutes on each side. Remove skewers from the grill and serve immediately.

Each appetizer (1 shrimp)			
Calories	21	Total Fat	0.2 g
Protein	2 g	Saturated Fat	0 g
Carbohydrates	3.3 g	Cholesterol	11 mg
Dietary Fiber	0.2 g	Sodium	11 mg

RICOTTA AND GRILLED TOMATOES ON TOAST

MAKES 16 APPETIZERS

This is an easy appetizer that can be pulled together right at the grill. The combination of ingredients is very flavorful.

 1 cup (8 oz/227 g) part-skim ricotta cheese
 2 tablespoons plain, nonfat yogurt
 2 tablespoons finely chopped scallions
16 very thin slices baguette bread
16 cherry tomatoes
   spray oil
   freshly ground black pepper to taste

❶ Combine ricotta, yogurt, and scallions in a bowl; cover and refrigerate.

❷ Place bread slices in a single layer on a cookie pan, and bake at 250°F (121°C) 30 to 40 minutes, or until they become crisp; bread slices should not be too brown.

❸ Thread the tomatoes onto 2 long metal skewers; spray both sides with oil, and grill about 3 minutes on each side.

❹ To serve, put a teaspoon of the cheese mixture onto each toasted baguette slice, and top with a grilled tomato. Season with pepper and serve.

RICOTTA

Some people think ricotta is not cheese because it is made from the whey left over from other cheeses, such as mozzarella, pecorino, and provolone. Ricotta is like cottage cheese, but perhaps more bland. Like cottage cheese, it is white and creamy. In Italy, it is an important ingredient in fillings for ravioli, lasagne, and cannelloni. Ricotta also is used in desserts, such as cannoli. Here, I combine ricotta with two other ingredients, before spreading it on toast, and topping each with a grilled tomato. It makes a great appetizer.

Each appetizer			
Calories	128	Total Fat	2.4 g
Protein	5 g	Saturated Fat	1 g
Carbohydrates	22 g	Cholesterol	6 mg
Dietary Fiber	1 g	Sodium	226 mg

GRILLED SWEET POTATOES WITH LOW-FAT SOUR CREAM SAUCE

MAKES ABOUT 16 APPETIZERS

2 large sweet potatoes
   spray oil
   freshly ground black pepper to taste
   salt to taste (optional)
   Low-Fat Sour Cream Sauce (recipe follows)

❶ Peel the sweet potatoes, then slice crosswise into 1/4-inch (5/8-cm) slices; lightly spray with oil and sprinkle with pepper and salt. Prepare the grill.

❷ When the fire is ready, lightly spray the grid with oil, then place the potato slices on top. Grill until lightly browned, about 3 to 4 minutes on each side.

❸ Remove the potatoes to a large plate. Arrange them in one layer, keeping warm in a 275°F (135°C) oven while preparing sauce.

❹ When ready to serve, place a dollop of sour cream sauce on each slice.

LOW-FAT SOUR CREAM SAUCE

MAKES ABOUT 1/2 CUP (120 ML)

1 tablespoon canola oil
2 tablespoons seasoned rice vinegar
1 tablespoon Dijon-style mustard
   juice of 1 whole lemon (3 tablespoons)
1 garlic clove, minced
   freshly ground black pepper to taste
1/3 cup (80 ml) nonfat sour cream

❶ In a small bowl, combine oil, vinegar, mustard, lemon juice, garlic, and pepper; blend well.

❷ Fold in the sour cream and place a dollop of it on each grilled potato slice.

Each appetizer			
Calories	27	Total Fat	1 g
Protein	1 g	Saturated Fat	0 g
Carbohydrates	4 g	Cholesterol	0 mg
Dietary Fiber	1 g	Sodium	17 mg

GRILLED SALMON ON RYE TOAST WITH DILLED NONFAT SOUR CREAM

MAKES ABOUT 24 APPETIZERS

The nice thing about this appetizer is that almost everything, except the final assembly, can be done ahead. In fact, it is important to grill the salmon in advance and let it cool, in order to slice it more neatly. The sour cream sauce can be made ahead also, and refrigerated until ready for use.

6 slices from a small, thin square rye bread loaf

1 (1-lb/455-g) boneless, skinless salmon fillet

1 teaspoon canola oil

   freshly ground black pepper to taste

1 teaspoon sugar

1/3 cup (80 ml) nonfat sour cream

   juice of 1/2 lemon (1 1/2 tablespoons), or more to taste

1 teaspoon capers, drained, rinsed, and dried

1/4 cup (14 g) finely chopped fresh dill, or 4 teaspoons dried

2 or 3 lemon wedges, seeds removed

❶ Preheat the oven to 250°F (121°C). Cut the crusts off the bread slices, then cut each slice into 3 strips. Arrange in a single layer on a cookie sheet, and bake until the bread dries out, about 40 minutes. Set aside to cool. Prepare the grill.

❷ Pat the salmon dry with a paper towel, then lightly brush with oil. Liberally coat both sides with pepper and sugar. Lightly oil the grid. When the fire is ready, place the salmon on the grill, and, with the cover down, grill about 8 minutes. Pierce with a small wooden skewer to test for doneness. Remove carefully from the grill, and place in refrigerator to cool several hours before slicing.

❸ In a small bowl, combine sour cream, lemon juice, capers, and dill; mix well. Set aside or refrigerate. If refrigerated, bring to room temperature before serving.

❹ Cut each slice of bread into 4 pieces. Then thinly slice the salmon and place a salmon slice on each piece of bread. Top each salmon slice with a dollop of the sour cream mixture. Season with more lemon juice and pepper, or serve with lemon wedges on the side.

Each appetizer			
Calories	62	Total Fat	2 g
Protein	6 g	Saturated Fat	0.3 g
Carbohydrates	6 g	Cholesterol	13 mg
Dietary Fiber	1 g	Sodium	68 mg

GRILLED SALMON AND CUCUMBER ON TOAST TRIANGLES

MAKES 4 APPETIZERS

This is an easy appetizer or first course to make, if you are planning to grill a main dish. If you're not using a charcoal fire for other food and don't want to go to the trouble of creating a fire, simply broil the salmon. If you have a gas or an electric grill, grill the salmon.

1/2 lb (230 g) boneless, skinless, fresh salmon fillet, cut crosswise into 2 pieces

1 cup (115 g) finely chopped peeled and seeded cucumber

2 tablespoons chopped fresh dill

3 tablespoons nonfat mayonnaise

2 tablespoons fresh lemon juice

hot red pepper sauce to taste

freshly ground black pepper to taste

4 slices whole-wheat bread

❶ When the fire is ready, oil the grid, place the salmon on the grid, and grill 3 to 4 minutes on each side. Remove from the grill and cool. Break salmon into flakes, and put in a bowl.

❷ Add cucumbers and dill. In a separate bowl, combine mayonnaise, lemon juice, hot sauce, and pepper; mix well. Stir mayonnaise mixture into the salmon mixture, then fold with a rubber spatula.

❸ Grill or toast the bread. Remove the crusts and spoon some of the salmon mixture on each slice. With a sharp knife, cut each slice diagonally in half. Serve 2 triangles on each of 4 plates. Season with additional black pepper.

THE FLAVOR OF DILL

I always think of caraway when I smell dill. Although its main function is to flavor pickles, dill also is used to flavor sauerkraut and vinegar. Dill is used a good deal in Russian and Scandinavian cooking. The feathery green leaves of the plant have a softer flavor than the seeds, but the seeds also can be used with the same foods. Dill seed is good in sauces, salad dressings, and marinades. Fresh chopped dill is paired with salmon in Grilled Salmon and Cucumber, all perfect companions.

Each appetizer			
Calories	200	Total Fat	5 g
Protein	16 g	Saturated Fat	0.8 g
Carbohydrates	24 g	Cholesterol	32 mg
Dietary Fiber	4 g	Sodium	319 mg

GRILLED ORIENTAL TUNA KEBABS

MAKES 16 APPETIZERS

This is a most pleasant alternative to the cheese-and-crackers appetizer syndrome. These tuna cubes are fresh, hot, tasty, and healthy, and from my experience, people love things on skewers, especially at cocktail parties.

1 (1-lb/455-g) tuna fillet, 1 inch (2 1/2 cm) thick, cut into 1-inch (2 1/2-cm) cubes

2 tablespoons low-sodium soy sauce

1 tablespoon dry sherry

1 tablespoon pickled ginger, minced

1 tablespoon pickled-ginger juice (from a jar)

1 teaspoon sesame oil

2 garlic cloves, minced

  pinch of red pepper flakes

5 or 6 scallions, cut into 16 (1-inch/2 1/2-cm) pieces, white part only

1 In a large shallow glass dish, place tuna cubes in a single layer. In another shallow dish, soak wooden skewers in water for 30 minutes.

2 In a small food processor bowl, combine remaining ingredients, except the scallion pieces. Pulse to process until mixture is well blended. Pour the mixture over tuna cubes, turning to coat all sides. Add the scallion pieces, and toss to coat. Marinate 20 to 30 minutes.

3 Thread 1 tuna cube and 1 scallion piece onto each skewer. When the fire is ready, lightly oil the grid. Place the skewers on the grid, and grill 3 minutes on each side, turning once; if you like rare tuna, reduce grilling time. Baste frequently while skewers are on the grill. Serve immediately.

Each appetizer			
Calories	47	Total Fat	1 g
Protein	7 g	Saturated Fat	0.4 g
Carbohydrates	1 g	Cholesterol	11 mg
Dietary Fiber	0.2 g	Sodium	74 mg

GRILLED TURKEY CHILI SOUP

MAKES 6 SERVINGS

The chili flavor is apparent without the fat from ground beef. This is a good soup and easy to make. If you want a more pronounced chili taste, add more chili powder, a little at a time.

1/2 lb (230 g) fresh turkey cutlets

1 (15 1/2-oz/440-g) can red kidney beans, drained and rinsed twice

1 (14 1/2-oz/411-g) can stewed tomatoes with green chiles (see note)

1 (8-oz/230-g) can, tomato sauce

4 cups (1 L) low-sodium beef broth

1 tablespoon fajita sauce

1/2 teaspoon chili powder

1/4 teaspoon ground cumin

juice of 1/2 lemon (1 1/2 tablespoons)

4 teaspoons nonfat sour cream or plain yogurt (optional)

❶ Prepare the fire, and lightly oil the grid. Grill turkey cutlets 3 or 4 minutes on each side; cool briefly. Cut cutlets into chunks, then finely chop in a food processor, using the pulse setting; do not purée—think of ground meat. Transfer turkey to a medium-size soup pot.

❷ Add the remaining ingredients, except sour cream. Mix well and bring to boil. Reduce heat to a steady, slow simmer, then cook, partially covered, 20 minutes. Serve hot with a dollop of sour cream.

Note: If the stewed tomatoes do not include green chiles, add 1 (4-oz/113-g) can chopped green chiles.

THE PEPPER MILL AND OTHER SPICES

Everyone knows the difference between the spicy bite of freshly ground black peppercorns and the blandness of the already-ground variety. Almost every recipe in this book calls for freshly ground black pepper. It is important to use a pepper mill to get the full flavor of this spice.

The difference in taste and aroma also is true with other freshly ground spices. Whenever possible, try to ground spices fresh for maximum taste.

Each serving			
Calories	157	Total Fat	1 g
Protein	19 g	Saturated Fat	0.2 g
Carbohydrates	18 g	Cholesterol	32 mg
Dietary Fiber	2.3 g	Sodium	290 mg

GRILLED POLENTA WITH WALNUTS AND FENNEL

MAKES 12 APPETIZER SERVINGS OR 6 MAIN-COURSE SERVINGS

This polenta makes a wonderful entrée. I use either cornmeal or polenta depending on availability. You can use coarsely ground cornmeal or any of the many packaged polenta products in the supermarkets for this dish. If using the packaged polenta, follow cooking directions on the package.

1/3 cup (51 1/2 g) chopped walnuts

1/2 level teaspoon fennel seeds

4 1/3 cups (1 L) water

pinch of salt

1 cup (151 g) yellow cornmeal or polenta

2 tablespoons butter substitute

1 teaspoon olive oil

❶ Toast walnuts and fennel seeds in a hot, dry skillet over medium heat, 2 to 3 minutes, stirring constantly. Set aside.

❷ Boil the water with a pinch of salt, in a large saucepan. Slowly add cornmeal, or polenta, stirring constantly to avoid lumping. Lower the heat, and cook about 30 minutes, smoothing out any lumps if they appear. The cornmeal or polenta should pull away from the sides of the pan when done.

❸ Stir in walnuts, fennel, and butter substitute, blending well. Transfer the mixture to a 10-inch (25 3/8-cm) glass pie dish or an 8-inch (20 1/4-cm) square glass dish. Smooth the surface, and let polenta cool at room temperature, until firm, about 1 hour. Meanwhile, prepare the grill.

❹ Slice the polenta into wedges or squares, then lightly brush with oil. When the fire is ready, lightly oil the grid. Then grill the polenta 8 to 10 minutes on each side, turning once.

Serving suggestion: Serve with Fresh Tomato Sauce (page 217).

Each serving (not including sauce)			
Calories	129	Total Fat	5.4 g
Protein	3 g	Saturated Fat	0.5 g
Carbohydrates	18 g	Cholesterol	0 mg
Dietary Fiber	2 g	Sodium	116 mg

GRILLED CORN AND CHILI SOUP WITH RED BEANS

MAKES 8 SERVINGS

The smoky flavors in this healthy soup are so delicious, you will want to try other "grilled" soups. In this recipe, simply grill the corn, peppers and a packet of other vegetables. Bring them together in a soup pot, with one or two more ingredients, and you will enjoy a fantastic soup.

4 ears fresh corn with husks

3 large green chiles, (such as poblanos or Anaheims) or 1 (4-oz/113-g) can green chiles, drained and chopped

3 garlic cloves, minced

1 large red onion, cut into 1/2-inch (1 1/4-cm) dice

2 carrots, cut into 1/2-inch (1 1/4-cm) dice

1 celery rib, cut into 1/2-inch dice

1 lb (455 g) tomatoes, cored, peeled, and seeded, then cut into 1/2-inch (1 1/4-cm) pieces, or 1 (14.5-oz/411-g) can chopped tomatoes

1 tablespoon finely chopped fresh oregano, or 1 teaspoon dried

1 tablespoon sugar

3 (15-oz/425-g) cans red kidney beans, drained and rinsed

6 to 8 cups (1 1/2 to 2 L) low-sodium vegetable broth (see note)

1 tablespoon low-sodium soy sauce

1 tablespoon fajita sauce (see note)

1/4 cup (7 g) finely chopped chives

1 cup (100 g) finely sliced Chinese cabbage

❶ Pull husks away from the corn, without pulling the husks off. Remove the silk from each ear of corn, then smooth husks back into place, tying with a string if necessary. Place the corn in a pan of water for 10 minutes. Drain corn, then place over hot coals; grill 10 minutes, turning them several times. Remove from grill, and set aside until cool enough to handle; remove husks and cut off the kernels.

❷ Grill, peel, and seed the chiles (see sidebar), then cut them into 1/2-inch (1 1/4-cm) pieces.

Continued on next page

HOW TO GRILL CHILES

Grill whole fresh chiles until skin is charred and bubbly, turning occasionally to grill evenly. Remove chiles from the grill, and place in a paper bag to "sweat" until cool enough to handle. Finally, peel and seed the chiles.

❸ Cut 2 (18-inch/45 3/4-cm) squares of heavy-duty foil; stack them and set aside. Combine the garlic, onion, carrots, celery, tomatoes, oregano, and sugar in a bowl. Mix well, then place in the center of the foil. Make a Bundle Wrap (page 10), leaving a vent in the packet to let steam escape. Put the packet in a covered grill, and cook until tender, about 20 minutes.

❹ In a large soup pot, combine corn kernels, chiles, the contents of the vegetable packet, the beans, vegetable broth, soy sauce, and fajita sauce. Bring to a boil, then reduce the heat to a slow, steady simmer, and cover. Cook until the beans are heated through, about 15 minutes. Taste and adjust the seasoning with additional fajita sauce if you prefer a smokier flavor; add 1 teaspoon at a time.

❺ In a small bowl, combine chives and cabbage. Top each portion of soup with a heaping teaspoon of the chive mixture. Serve immediately.

Note: Made with 6 cups (1 1/2 L) of broth, this recipe will make a thick soup. If you want a thinner consistency, increase the amount of vegetable broth to 8 cups (2 L).

Fajita sauce or marinade is found in specialty food stores, or in supermarkets where Tex-Mex ingredients are sold. It is made with water, vinegar, refined wood smoke, vegetable protein, natural citrus flavors, caramel, garlic, spices, and herbs. Fajita sauce often is used to marinate and baste meats on the grill.

Each serving			
Calories	230	Total Fat	1 g
Protein	14 g	Saturated Fat	0.2 g
Carbohydrates	43 g	Cholesterol	0 mg
Dietary Fiber	5 g	Sodium	632 mg

GRILLED SWEET ONION SOUP WITH PORT WINE

MAKES 6 SERVINGS

The addition of port wine is a "truc" (trick, in French), an old friend of mine adds to her onion soup. The smoky flavor comes from grilling the onions, but be sure to use the large Texas or Vidalia varieties.

2 large, sweet onions (such as Texas Sweet) peeled and sliced

spray oil

6 (3/4-inch/1 7/8-cm) slices Italian or French bread, baguette-size loaf

1 1/2 slices (1 1/2 oz/43 g total) low-fat Swiss cheese, cut into 6 pieces

freshly grated Parmesan cheese

6 cups (1/2 L) defatted, low-sodium beef broth

1/2 cup (120 ml) port wine

freshly ground black pepper to taste

1 Prepare the onions, then spray oil on both sides of each slice. When the fire is ready, very lightly spray oil onto the grid. Add the onions, then grill on one side just until the onion slices take on some color, about 5 minutes; do not scorch or blacken the onions completely—move them around the grid to cooler spots to keep from blackening—but some charring is desirable. Cool just enough to handle, then chop onions coarsely; transfer to a medium-size soup pot.

2 While the fire is still hot, toast the bread on both sides; remove and set aside. Place 1 piece of Swiss cheese on top of each bread slice, then sprinkle with Parmesan. Keep warm in a low oven (250°F/121°C) until needed.

3 Meanwhile, add the broth, port wine, and a liberal amount of pepper to the soup pot. Bring to a boil, reduce the heat, and slowly simmer. Cover and cook 20 minutes, or until the onions are tender.

4 Spoon the soup into 6 warm bowls, and float a bread-and-cheese slice in each bowl.

Each serving			
Calories	192	Total Fat	3.4 g
Protein	10 g	Saturated Fat	1.7 g
Carbohydrates	24 g	Cholesterol	8.4 mg
Dietary Fiber	1 g	Sodium	244 mg

GRILLED HALIBUT SOUP WITH THAI FLAVORS

MAKES 4 SERVINGS

The base for this soup may be made one day ahead, and reheated just before adding the grilled halibut. Other seafood may be used, such as shrimp, scallops, fresh cod, bass, or other white-meat fillets. Many supermarkets carry Thai cooking items, and the fish sauce for this recipe should be among them. If you can't find it, use 1/2 of a fish bouillon cube, or check an Asian supermarket.

2 teaspoons canola oil

1 medium-size onion, finely chopped

1/2 red bell pepper, cut into thin strips

2 garlic cloves, minced

1 1/2 teaspoons curry powder

    pinch of red pepper flakes

1 cup (302 g) peeled, cored, seeded plum tomatoes (fresh or canned), cut into small dice

2 cups low-sodium fish broth or clam juice

2 tablespoons *nam pla* (Thai fish sauce)

    freshly ground black pepper to taste

3 tablespoons fresh lime or lemon juice

    spray oil

1 lb (455 g) boneless, skinless halibut fillets cut into 4 pieces, or 1 lb halibut steak(s) or other fish

2 cups (150 g) hot cooked white rice

1/3 cup (61 1/2 g) finely chopped scallions, flat-leaf parsley, or cilantro

❶ In a medium-size soup pot, heat the oil over medium heat. Add onion and bell pepper, and sauté until they turn soft, about 5 minutes. Add garlic, curry, and red pepper flakes, and cook 1 minute longer, stirring frequently.

❷ Add tomatoes, fish broth, fish sauce, if available, and black pepper. Cook, uncovered, 5 minutes, stirring frequently. Stir in lime juice.

❸ Prepare the grill, and oil the grid lightly. When the fire is ready, lightly spray both sides of the fish with oil, then place it on the grill. Grill about 4 minutes on each side, turning once. Remove from the grill. If using steaks, remove the skin and bones without breaking up the fish; try to keep the pieces as large as possible. If using fillets or shrimp, this obviously is not necessary.

Continued on next page

4 Place 1/2 cup (38 g) hot cooked rice in each of 4 warmed soup bowls with rims (this fish soup won't look right in rimless bowls). Divide the fish among the bowls, on top of the rice. Spoon the soup to the sides of the fish, then sprinkle scallions over top. Serve hot.

Each serving			
Calories	364	Total Fat	10 g
Protein	29 g	Saturated Fat	1 g
Carbohydrates	39 g	Cholesterol	40 mg
Dietary Fiber	3 g	Sodium	463 mg

HOW TO MAKE YOUR OWN CURRY POWDER

Indian curry does not include fennel, which usually is included in Southeast Asian curry.

1/4 cup plus 2 tablespoons (3 oz/85 g)
   coriander seeds
1/4 cup (2 oz/57 g) cumin seeds
  1 tablespoon (1/2 oz/14 g) fenugreek seeds
  1 tablespoon (1/2 oz/14 g) fennel seeds
  1 tablespoon (1/2 oz/14 g) mustard seeds
   spray oil
  2 tablespoons coarsely chopped fresh
   lemon grass, or 2 teaspoons dried
   (see note)

1 Sauté the seeds separately in a barely oiled skillet for 1 to 2 minutes to release their aromas. After they have cooled, combine with the lemon grass and finely grind the mixture.

2 Store the curry powder in a tightly covered jar at room temperature.

Note: The Dutch condiment manufacturer Conimex sells powdered lemon grass, called sereh *powder. If you cannot find fresh or dried lemon grass, use 1/2 teaspoon minced lemon zest.*

CHAPTER 5
GREAT TASTING SEAFOOD ON THE GRILL

INTRODUCTION

The average person needs about 55 grams of protein a day. Most Americans consume more than that because of the large quantities of red meat and poultry we eat. Health experts advise that we cut down on red meat—eating it only two or three times a week. They also suggest removing the skin from poultry, and eating more whole grains and legumes, which are low in fat. We are encouraged to eat more fish, and for good reasons: fish is low in calories, low in fat, and high in protein. A four-ounce serving of fish provides 140 calories, most of which come from protein. This four-ounce portion also gives us about half of our protein needs for the day. Fish also has important omega-3 fatty acids, which according to current literature, seem to help prevent strokes and heart disease.

Shellfish has cholesterol, but it is lower in saturated fat than red meat. The ever-increasing interest in reducing our fat intake makes seafood a perfect addition to our diet. All seafood—even salmon, a "fatty" fish—is low in fat, most of which is polyunsaturated. Grilling is an excellent way to cook fish because almost no additional fat is needed—just a quick spray of oil will do.

A SEA OF CHOICES

The demand for fish has prompted a nationwide increase in the number of super-market seafood sections and fish specialty stores. Improved transportation has made seafood from Australia or Chile almost as common in the United States as seafood from the Atlantic coast. The availability of farm-raised fish—domestic and foreign—has increased. One fishmonger recently remarked to me that most of the fish he sells comes from Chile.

BEST WHEN FRESH

Fish and shellfish obviously are best when fresh, but determining freshness takes a keen eye and a sensitive nose. Look your fish in the eye—bright clear eyes are the surest signs of freshness; if the eyes are cloudy or sunken, choose another. Whole fish, fillets, and steaks should have moist, lustrous flesh, and shouldn't give off a "fishy" odor.

Take fish home immediately after buying it and place it in the coldest part of the refrigerator until ready to use; try to use the fish within one day. To preserve nutrients, dip fish in a bowl of cold water. You may find some recipes that say to "rinse" the fish before preparing; this means to dip it in cold water, not hold it under running water.

The texture of fish will change after it has been frozen. If you must freeze it, be sure the fish is wrapped airtight, in several layers of plastic. A good method of freezing fish, if you have the time, is to dip it in water, then immediately place it in the freezer. Once a glaze forms, repeat the process several times, until the fish is

▼▲▼▲▼▲▼▲▼▲▼▲
FISH FILLETS

A fillet is the boneless strip of flesh that results when the fish is cut, lengthwise, away from the rib bones. Fillets can be grilled with or without the skin. I usually remove the skin, unless the fillet is very small and tender.

Fillets should be cut crosswise into strips, squares, or rectangular pieces before they are put on the grill; this makes them easier to handle. Fillets are cut into squares in the following skewered-fish recipes.

coated with ice, then wrap it in foil, and store it in the freezer until ready to use. If the fish are small, put them in a clean milk or juice carton, then fill the carton with water. Once the carton is frozen, the fish will be encased in ice. Do not refreeze fish that was previously frozen.

Farm-raised or wild, fresh or frozen, domestic or imported, people are cooking fish at home, and that fish often is finding its way to the grill.

SOPHISTICATED SEAFOOD

Preparing fish on the grill has taken on a new sophistication. Just take a quick look at the marinades, sauces, salsas, and condiments that accompany the fish recipes in these pages. There are several reasons why grilled fish is so popular: it's healthy, it's tasty, and it's easy to prepare. Fish fillets and steaks make grilling at home a snap. They not only are easy to handle, but fish fillets and steaks also require considerably less marinating time than meat and poultry, usually just 15 to 30 minutes.

If your fishmonger won't skin the fillet, you can do it at home. Using a sharp knife, move the blade just under the skin, while pulling the skin away from the flesh with your free hand. Because the skin is oily, it often will slip from your fingers; use a paper or kitchen towel to get a better grip on the skin.

The rule for cooking fresh fish—a ratio of ten minutes per inch of thickness—doesn't apply to the grill, especially when cooking fillets or small steaks. If the fire is the proper temperature, it rarely takes ten minutes to grill four ounces of fish.

Grill fish over high heat to seal in the natural juices. Since most fish is moist to begin with, only a little basting is needed. Be careful not to overcook fish, as it will dry out and toughen.

Of the many ways to test doneness, the simplest test for me is to insert a wooden skewer into the fish. If the skewer penetrates the flesh easily, the fish is cooked; if it meets resistance, the fish will need more time on the grill. Fish continues to cook after it has been taken off the grill; that's called "standing time." It is best to remove the fish from the grill, even if it is slightly undercooked. I almost always grill fish with the cover down; this shortens the grilling time.

The color of the flesh also will indicate when the fish is done. Fresh raw fish has a translucent, pearly quality. As soon as that pearliness disappears, and the color looks solid or opaque, the fish is sufficiently cooked. In most varieties of fish, the flesh will become solid white when fully cooked. Some varieties, such as salmon and sword-fish, turn pale pink or pale gray, respectively. Fish will begin to flake when it is done, but waiting until it flakes easily can result in overcooked dry fish.

THE LEAN FISH IN THE SEA

There are ten categories of lean saltwater fish whose fat content is between 1 percent and 5 percent. Much of the fat is in the liver, which is usually removed when the fish is dressed. Most of these fish have mild-flavored, firm, white flesh, and if basted properly, are delicious on the grill.

1. Cod: This is the key fish in New England, and the Atlantic cod is king of the catch. Close relatives of cod are Atlantic pollock, haddock, whiting, and cusk.

2. Flatfish: From the West Coast, we get petrale sole, Pacific halibut, and Dover sole. From the East Coast, we get fish from the flounder family, including lemon sole, or fluke.

3. Snapper: One of the best-tasting fish, snapper, comes from the warm waters of the Atlantic, from North Carolina to Florida, and from the Gulf of Mexico. Red snapper may be the best known, but there are hundreds of other snap-pers, such as yellowtail, hog, and silver snapper, which are equally as delicious.

4. Porgy: These fish are sweet, with a firm texture, and are found mainly on the East Coast.

5. Skate and Ray: Skate used to be thrown away because most of the fish is inedible, but the wings are sweet and taste somewhat like scallops. The names are used inter-changeably; however, skate generally refers to the variety that is eaten, and ray refers to the variety fished for sport, such as the electric ray and giant manta ray.

6. Drum: These fish are found in the east, south, and west, and include the white sea bass, red drum, spotted sea trout, California corbina, spot, and Atlantic croaker.

7. Sea Bass: Sea bass is sometimes called rockfish and is found on both coasts. Black sea bass, grouper, and white perch are Atlantic fish; grouper is subtropic. The giant sea bass is a West-Coast dweller.

8. Rockfish: This includes fish whose flesh is white to pink, such as the highly marketed ocean perch (also called red-fish), and the vermilion rockfish from the West Coast.

SHELLFISH

When buying clams, oysters, and mus-sels, make sure they are alive. The shells should be tightly closed, or they should close if you touch them. Steamer (soft-shell) clams are an exception. Their shells always gap somewhat, but, if they are alive, the neck will constrict when touched.

Crabs and lobsters should be alive and lively. If lobsters and king crabs have been frozen, they should not have any white freezer-burn spots. All shellfish should have a clean, fresh aroma. A faint iodine odor is caused by habitat, and is not a sign of spoilage. A smell of ammonia, however, is a bad sign, and that fish should be avoided.

9. Wolf Fish: This probably is the least known, but when this fish is in the markets, it is sold as ocean catfish.

10. Miscellaneous: This includes dolphin, or mahi mahi, which is readily available in many parts of the United States. Other flavorful fish include tile fish, from warm waters; sea robin, or gurnard; and angler, an Atlantic fish better known in England than in the United States.

MAKING THE CUT

With the many varieties of fish available, it can be hard to know which fish is good grilled whole, or which varieties are better trimmed to fillets and steaks. The following offers a quick glance to help you decide how to prepare your catch of the day.

WHOLE FISH TO GRILL

Bluefish	Pompano	Sea Trout
Flounder	Porgy (Scup)	Shad
Mackerel	Red Snapper	Sheepshead
Mullet	Salmon	Striped or Rock Bass

FILLETS TO GRILL

Cod, Scrod	Monkfish	Shad
Cusk	Pacific Snapper	Sole
Flounder	Perch	Tilefish
Grouper	Pollock	

FISH STEAKS TO GRILL

Cod	Salmon	Tilefish
Halibut	Shark	Tuna
Kingfish	Swordfish	

SHELLFISH TO GRILL

Cherrystone Clams	Lobster	Shrimp
King Crab Legs	Lobster Tails	Soft-Shell Crabs
Little Neck Clams	Oysters	Squid

GENERAL RULES FOR COOKING FISH ON THE GRILL

❶ Don't overmarinate. When using a marinade to baste, boil it first.

❷ Use an oiled, hinged grill basket to help keep fish intact.

❸ Fish and seafood should be placed about five inches above the heat source.

❹ Do not overcook.

❺ To test for doneness, penetrate the flesh with a wooden skewer; if it goes through easily, the fish is done.

GRILLED SALMON WITH LEMON AND LIME ZEST

MAKES 4 SERVINGS

This is a simple, wonderful way to serve salmon that can be presented in a number of ways. I like it over sliced, ripe tomatoes: first drop one large tomato in boiling water, then count to 15. Remove the tomato with a slotted spoon, and place the tomato in cold water. Core and peel the tomato, then cut it into four slices; put one slice on each of four plates. Sprinkle each with freshly ground black pepper and freshly squeezed lemon juice; top with finely chopped chives, scallions, or red onions. Place the grilled salmon on top. The salmon also can be served over freshly steamed spinach, boiled rice, or mashed potatoes.

2 garlic cloves, minced

1 tablespoon chopped fresh tarragon, or
   1 teaspoon dried

1 tablespoon chopped fresh flat-leaf parsley

1 tablespoon each: olive oil and lemon and
   lime zest

   juice of 1 whole lime (3 tablespoons)

   salt to taste (optional)

   freshly ground black pepper to taste

1 lb (455 g) boneless, skinless, salmon fillet,
   cut into 4 equal strips

1 lemon, quartered and seeded

❶ In a small bowl, combine all the ingredients, except the salmon and lemon wedges, and mix well. Spread mixture over all sides of the salmon pieces, then let stand at room temperature 15 minutes, or longer in the refrigerator. Meanwhile, prepare the grill.

❷ When the fire is ready, grill the salmon 3 to 4 minutes on each side. Serve with lemon wedges on the side, or as suggested above.

Each serving			
Calories	169	Total Fat	7.4 g
Protein	23 g	Saturated Fat	1 g
Carbohydrates	2.3 g	Cholesterol	59 mg
Dietary Fiber	0.5 g	Sodium	77 mg

TARRAGON, THE ESSENTIAL HERB

Tarragon has a delicate, fragrant taste of anise or licorice. It is excellent, if used with discretion, in many fish dishes, including shellfish. It is an important element to Salmon with Lemon and Lime Zest. Tarragon also enhances the taste of vegetables and salad dressings. Sprinkle some on tomatoes, potatoes, asparagus, mushrooms, peas, or add it to your vinaigrette dressing. French tarragon can be grown in most gardens in northern climes, or in a pot on a windowsill. Mexican marigold, prevalent in southern climes, is a good substitute when tarragon is not available, although its anise flavor is not as pronounced. The French love tarragon, and it is an essential ingredient in several of their national dishes, such as *poulet a l'estragon*, chicken with tarragon.

FISH BROTH

MAKES 2 1/2 TO 3 QUARTS (2 3/8 TO 2 3/4 L)

Here is a recipe for a good fish broth. You can freeze it in one-cup portions and use it as needed. In my experience, the heads and bones of a one- to two-pound fish make a tastier broth.

3 quarts (2 3/4 L) water

3 1/2 lb (1 1/2 kg) fish (such as red snapper, monkfish, sea bass, haddock, skate, or cod) cut into large pieces (see note)

2 cups (480 ml) dry white wine

2 onions, coarsely chopped

2 carrots, thinly sliced

2 celery ribs with leaves, thinly sliced

10 parsley stems without leaves, coarsely chopped

large zest strips from 1 whole lemon

2 bay leaves

2 sprigs fresh thyme, or 1 teaspoon dried

1 dried chile pepper, or 1/2 teaspoon
red pepper flakes

❶ Combine all the ingredients in a very large soup pot.

❷ Bring to a boil over high heat, uncovered, skimming away the froth that rises to the surface. Reduce the heat to a slow, steady simmer, and cook, covered, until the fish breaks apart when stirred, about 45 minutes.

❸ Pour through a fine-meshed strainer (or one lined with 2 layers of cheese-cloth). Using a large wooden spoon, mash the fish and vegetables against the side of the strainer to extract as much liquid as possible.

❹ Use immediately, or refrigerate up to 3 days. If you're not planning to use the broth within 3 days, freeze it in 1- and 2-cup portions for easy handling; broth will keep in freezer up to 3 months.

Note: Include heads and bones when preparing fish broth, to ensure a flavorful stock.

Each serving			
Calories	40	Total Fat	1.9 g
Protein	5 g	Saturated Fat	0.5 g
Carbohydrates	0 g	Cholesterol	2 mg
Dietary Fiber	0 g	Sodium	363 mg

GRILLED SALMON WITH SESAME AND GINGER

MAKES 6 TO 8 SERVINGS

A whole salmon is grilled here with Oriental flavors, which are maximized by wrapping the marinated fish in foil. I prefer grilling salmon with the head on. Although to make it more appetizing, I take three slices of ginger, dab them in finely chopped parsley, then place the ginger, overlapping, on top of the eye before serving. If you grill this on an open grill, add about ten minutes to the total cooking time. This is an impressive and tasty dish.

1 whole salmon (about 3 lb/1 1/2 kg), cleaned, with or without the head

1/3 cup (80 ml) low-sodium tamari

2 tablespoons finely chopped fresh ginger

1 tablespoon sesame chili oil

1 tablespoon vegetable oil

1/3 cup (61 1/2 g) finely chopped scallions

1 Rinse and dry the salmon; place it on a double thickness of heavy-duty foil, large enough to envelop the salmon in a Drugstore Wrap (see page 10). Prepare the grill.

2 In a small bowl, combine remaining ingredients, except the scallions; brush the inside and outside of the fish with the marinade, using all of it. Securely wrap the salmon, and place it carefully on the grill when the fire is ready. Cover, and grill 25 minutes, turning only once, being careful not to loosen the foil package.

3 To test for doneness, remove the package from the grill. Open a small area of the wrap, and insert a wooden skewer into the thickest part of the salmon; the skewer should meet no resistance, and the flesh should appear flaky. If the salmon is still translucent and needs more grilling time, rewrap the package, then place it back on the grill for several more minutes.

4 To serve, unwrap the package, and turn the salmon onto a large platter. Pour the juices over the fish. Sprinkle scallions over top.

Each serving			
Calories	379	Total Fat	19 g
Protein	46.6 g	Saturated Fat	3 g
Carbohydrates	3 g	Cholesterol	125 mg
Dietary Fiber	0.4 g	Sodium	814 mg

CRISPY CALAMARI WITH CURRY SLAW

▼▲▼▲▼▲▼▲▼▲▼
**HOW TO PREPARE
A SQUID**
Place the squid on a flat surface in front of you, and stretch it lengthwise, left to right, with the tentacles to your right. Cut just below the eyes; this will free the tentacles. There are ten tentacles, and in the center is the mouth; cut off the mouth, and discard it. Pull the skin off the tentacles and discard. Reserve the tentacles. Squeeze the body, and pull out and discard first the head and viscera and then the transparent center quill. Wash the remaining sac well, and peel off the outer skin. Slice across the sac to make rings, if desired.

MAKES 6 SERVINGS

Calamari, or squid, grills easily and quickly, and is wonderful with this curry slaw. Calamari has become very popular and can be found in most supermarket fish departments and all fish stores.

2 1/2 lb (1 1/8 kg) fresh or frozen medium-size squid (after cleaning there should be 1 1/2 lb (680 g) squid bodies (including chopped tentacles)

spray oil

juice of 1 whole lemon (3 tablespoons)

2 large garlic cloves, minced

1 tablespoon finely chopped fresh flat-leaf parsley

6 lemon or lime wedges

Curry Slaw (recipe follows)

❶ Clean the squid, or buy them ready to cook (see page 106). Slice squid bodies into 1/2-inch (1 1/4-cm) rings. Dry well, then put the squid in a glass or stainless steel bowl. Spray 2 or 3 times with oil, and add lemon juice and garlic; toss well. Let marinate 20 to 30 minutes at room temperature.

❷ Prepare the grill. Lightly spray the grid with oil. When the fire is ready, add the squid pieces; this may have to be done in two batches, depending on the size of your grid.

❸ The squid will change shape and color quickly. Toss while on the grid until lightly browned, 3 to 5 minutes. Transfer squid to a platter. Add parsley and toss; arrange lemon wedges to the side of the squid. Serve with Curry Slaw.

Each serving			
Calories	90	Total Fat	3.2 g
Protein	8.5 g	Saturated Fat	.6 g
Carbohydrates	14.9 g	Cholesterol	107 mg
Dietary Fiber	.9 g	Sodium	158 mg

CURRY SLAW

MAKES 6 SERVINGS

Buy tender, young cabbage for this dish—the leaves will be tightly packed and it won't smell as strong as a mature cabbage, which may have cracks and a strong odor. There also is less waste on a younger head, as fewer leaves have to be thrown away.

> 1 1/2-lb (800-g) cabbage, shredded
> 1 small red or yellow bell pepper, finely chopped
> 1 small onion, finely chopped
> 1 1/2 tablespoons sugar
> 1/3 cup (100 ml) seasoned rice vinegar
> 1/3 cup (100 ml) low-sodium vegetable or chicken broth
> 1 1/2 tablespoons canola oil
> 1 tablespoon curry powder
> 1 teaspoon dry mustard
> 1 teaspoon celery seeds
> freshly ground black pepper to taste

❶ In a large glass bowl, combine cabbage, bell pepper, onion, and sugar; toss and set aside.

❷ Bring remaining ingredients to a boil in a nonaluminum saucepan, stirring to blend. Remove from the heat, and pour over the cabbage mixture. Cover and refrigerate 2 hours before serving.

Each serving			
Calories	80	Total Fat	4.2 g
Protein	1.9 g	Saturated Fat	.4 g
Carbohydrates	10.5 g	Cholesterol	.3 mg
Dietary Fiber	3.1 g	Sodium	22 mg

SPICY CLAMS ON THE GRILL

MAKES 4 SERVINGS

Look for clams that are kept in a tank with circulating water; they will have already shed their sand. These cook best in a covered grill.

12 cherrystone or 24 littleneck clams

1/2 medium-size onion, cut into 4 pieces

2 garlic cloves, halved

2 tablespoons chopped fresh flat-leaf parsley

1 baby carrot, cut into 4 pieces

juice of 1 whole lemon (3 tablespoons)

spray oil

freshly ground black pepper to taste

1 Brush the clam shells clean, then soak the clams in cool water for 3 hours, if you have not bought them pre-cleaned. Drain and shuck them, reserving the juice. Place each clam on its lower shell, discarding the top shells.

2 Place onion, garlic, parsley, and carrot in the bowl of a food processor. Pulse to coarsely chop, but do not overprocess—the vegetables should look as if you finely chopped them by hand. Transfer the mixture to a bowl; add the lemon juice and 2 or 3 sprays of oil to the onion mixture. Season with black pepper, then toss well. Carefully distribute this mixture over the clams.

3 Prepare the grill; use a flat, hinged wire basket to hold the clams. Arrange the clams on the half shell in the basket. Just before placing the basket on the grill, sprinkle some of the reserved clam juice over each clam. Close the grill cover, and grill the clams for about 5 minutes, or until the juices are hot and bubbling. If your grill has no cover, cover the basket with foil.

Each serving			
Calories	32	Total Fat	0.3 g
Protein	4 g	Saturated Fat	0 g
Carbohydrates	4 g	Cholesterol	9 mg
Dietary Fiber	0.5 g	Sodium	18 mg

BLACK GROUPER WITH THREE-ONION MARMALADE

MAKES 4 SERVINGS

This recipe calls for grouper, but I have made it with other mild-flavored fish. Much of the flavor of the onions is absorbed by the potatoes. Any leftover marmalade will keep several days in the refrigerator.

1 lb (455 g) black grouper or similar fish fillet, cut into 4 pieces, rinsed and dried

spray oil

freshly ground black pepper to taste

1 very large white onion (such as Vidalia), peeled, halved, and thinly sliced

1 leek, white part only, washed carefully and thinly sliced

4 scallions, thinly sliced

1 large garlic clove, minced

1/2 cup (120 ml) dry white wine

1/3 cup (80 ml) white wine vinegar

1/4 cup (43 g) brown sugar

pinch of red pepper flakes (optional)

2 cups (518 g) hot mashed potatoes

1 Prepare the grill. Spray grouper pieces with oil, and liberally season with pepper. Leave at room temperature 15 minutes before grilling.

2 Combine remaining ingredients, except potatoes, in a skillet. Bring to a boil, then reduce heat to a slow, steady simmer; cover, and cook 10 minutes. Remove the cover, and cook until the liquid has almost evaporated, about 5 to 10 minutes. Remove from the heat, keeping warm.

3 When the fire is ready, grill the fish about 4 minutes on each side.

4 To serve, divide mashed potatoes among 4 warmed plates. Add a piece of grilled grouper to each plate, then place 2 tablespoons onion marmalade to the side of each piece of fish; serve immediately.

Each serving			
Calories	313	Total Fat	2.3 g
Protein	31.4 g	Saturated Fat	1 g
Carbohydrates	38 g	Cholesterol	55 mg
Dietary Fiber	4 g	Sodium	392 mg

GARLICKY KEBABS WITH CILANTRO, PARSLEY, AND PAPRIKA

MAKES 8 SERVINGS

Because of the density of swordfish flesh, this preparation requires a longer marinating time than for most fish. A small baked potato or steamed new potatoes go well with this dish.

2 lb (900 g) skinless, boneless dark-meat fish (such as swordfish, monkfish, or shark), cut into 1-inch (2 1/2-cm) cubes

2 red or yellow bell peppers, cut into 16 (1-inch/2 1/2-cm) squares

6 garlic cloves, peeled and quartered

1 bunch each, fresh: cilantro and parsley

1 tablespoon paprika

1/2 teaspoon hot red pepper sauce

1/2 teaspoon ground cumin

    salt to taste (optional)

2 tablespoons vegetable oil

    spray oil

2 lemons, each cut lengthwise into 4 pieces, then seeded

❶ Prepare the fish cubes and peppers, then place them in a single layer in a large glass dish.

❷ Combine remaining ingredients, except oil and lemon pieces, in the bowl of a processor, and pulse to finely chop. With the motor still running, slowly add the oil; when thoroughly combined, pour mixture over the fish and peppers. Toss well, cover with plastic wrap, and refrigerate for 2 hours. Remove from the refrigerator 30 minutes before grilling. Prepare the grill.

❸ Thread fish and peppers alternately onto 8 skewers. When the fire is ready, oil the grid. Grill the skewers, with the lid closed, about 8 to 10 minutes, turning the skewers several times to cook all sides. Divide skewers among 8 plates, and serve a lemon wedge with each portion.

CILANTRO AND CORIANDER

Cilantro and its seeds, coriander, have been popular in Asian and Mediterranean cooking for centuries. Its leaves are dark green, flat, and round with jagged edges. They have a pungent, refreshing taste that gives many salsas their unique flavor. Coriander seeds should be heated in a lightly oiled skillet to release their flavor before use in a recipe. Coriander is used in curries and pastries, and flavors some gins and liqueurs. You can buy the seeds whole or ground.

Each serving			
Calories	180	Total Fat	8 g
Protein	23 g	Saturated Fat	2 g
Carbohydrates	3 g	Cholesterol	44 mg
Dietary Fiber	1 g	Sodium	106 mg

GRILLED FISH HOUSE-SPECIAL SANDWICH

MAKES 4 SERVINGS

This is a great fish sandwich, and can be served in an informal atmosphere—great for the patio, back porch, or lawn for feeding the troops. The aioli or tartar sauce, whichever you prefer, can be made ahead, making this dish easier to pull together at the last minute.

1 tablespoon each: olive oil, teriyaki sauce, and prepared mustard

1 lb (455 g) boneless, skinless, swordfish steak, cut into 4 pieces
freshly ground black pepper to taste
spray oil

4 small Italian or French rolls, split and grilled
Tartar Sauce (page 276), or Lemon Aioli Sauce (page 97)

4 lettuce leaves

4 (1/4-inch/5/8-cm) slices tomato

4 (1/8-inch/15/16-cm) slices red onion

❶ In a small bowl, combine the oil, teriyaki sauce, and mustard. Mix well, and brush it on both sides of each piece of fish; season with pepper. Place the fish on a plate, cover with plastic wrap, and refrigerate for a minimum of 2 hours. Bring to room temperature before grilling.

❷ Prepare the grill; lightly spray the grid with oil. When the fire is ready, place the fish on the grid, and grill 3 minutes on each side. Meanwhile, grill the rolls, and divide them among 4 plates.

❸ Just before the fish is done, spread 1 tablespoon sauce on the bottom half of each roll, and top with a lettuce leaf. Place one piece of fish on top of each lettuce leaf. Top each portion with tomato and onion slices. Spread 1 tablespoon sauce on each of the remaining roll halves, then divide them among the plates. Season with pepper, and serve the sandwich open-faced.

Each serving			
Calories	280	Total Fat	10 g
Protein	32 g	Saturated Fat	2 g
Carbohydrates	14 g	Cholesterol	57 mg
Dietary Fiber	0.8 g	Sodium	473 mg

GRILLED SEA BASS WITH FRESH FENNEL

MAKES 4 SERVINGS

Fresh fennel is a beautiful and tasty vegetable. Fish and fennel are natural companions tastewise, and this recipe proves it.

2 tablespoons olive oil

1 large fresh fennel bulb, trimmed, rinsed, dried, and finely chopped (reserve some fern for garnish)

1/2 red bell pepper, cored, seeded, and finely sliced

1/2 teaspoon fennel seeds

3 plum tomatoes, cored, peeled, seeded, and finely chopped, or 1 cup (302 g) canned, drained

2 cups (480 ml) low-sodium fish broth, or bottled clam juice

freshly ground black pepper to taste

1 lb (455 g) sea bass fillet, cut into 4 pieces

spray oil

❶ Heat the oil in a skillet over medium heat. Add fennel, bell peppers, and fennel seeds; sauté until vegetables begin to soften, about 8 minutes. Add tomatoes, and cook 5 minutes more. Meanwhile, prepare the grill.

❷ Add the broth, and bring to boil; cook, uncovered, until the liquid is reduced by half, 10 to 15 minutes. Season with black pepper, and set aside, keeping warm.

❸ When the fire is ready, lightly oil the grid and grill the fish 3 to 4 minutes on each side, turning once. Season with black pepper.

❹ To serve, spoon some sauce into each of 4 warmed plates; divide fish among the plates, on top of the sauce. Garnish with chopped fresh fennel fern.

Each serving			
Calories	235	Total Fat	10 g
Protein	29 g	Saturated Fat	2 g
Carbohydrates	8 g	Cholesterol	64 mg
Dietary Fiber	3 g	Sodium	392 mg

GRILLED KEY WEST-STYLE HALIBUT

MAKES 4 SERVINGS

Garlic, oranges, scallions, and spices play an important role in Key West cuisine. If you can't find halibut, substitute grouper, monkfish, or swordfish.

1/4 cup (60 ml) fresh orange juice

1 tablespoon orange zest

1 teaspoon canola oil

3 large garlic cloves, minced

3 scallions, finely chopped

2 jalapeños, cored, seeded, and finely chopped ground allspice and nutmeg, to taste

1 to 1 1/4 lb (455 to 570 g) boneless, skinless halibut, cut into 4 equal portions

4 slices fresh pineapple

2 tablespoons finely chopped fresh mint

❶ To make the marinade, combine orange juice, zest, oil, garlic, scallions, jalapeños, allspice, and nutmeg in a bowl; mix well. Place fish in a single layer in a shallow dish. Pour marinade over the fish, and let marinate 10 to 15 minutes. Meanwhile, prepare the grill.

❷ When the fire is ready, lightly oil the grid. Grill pineapple slices 4 minutes on each side; set aside. Grill the fish about 3 minutes on each side (pineapple and fish can be grilled at the same time, if you have room); baste fish frequently with the marinade.

❸ To serve, divide fish among 4 plates, topping each serving with a slice of grilled pineapple. Sprinkle the mint over top.

HOLY HALIBUT

The name halibut means "holy fish," probably so named because it was on the table during holy days. Halibut can be very large, some weighing up to 500 pounds. The younger fish, called chicken halibut, have the finest flesh, and generally weigh two to five pounds. They are abundant in the cold waters of the North Pacific (most of the commercial catch is made there), and on both shores of the North Atlantic. A member of the flat-fish family, a halibut has two eyes on the right side of its head. Not many flatfish can claim this distinction, for the other varieties have two eyes on the left side.

Each serving			
Calories	205	Total Fat	4 g
Protein	24.5 g	Saturated Fat	0.5 g
Carbohydrates	15 g	Cholesterol	36.3 mg
Dietary Fiber	2 g	Sodium	67 mg

GRILLED GROUPER WITH HOT CORN SALSA

MAKES 4 SERVINGS

As delicious as grouper may be grilled, its taste is enhanced by the lively flavors of the hot corn salsa. The salsa can be used with other grilled fish, such as sea bass or snapper.

   spray oil
1 lb (455 g) grouper fillet, cut into 4 equal portions, rinsed and dried
1/2 cup (120 ml) fish broth or bottled clam juice
1 cup (162 g) fresh or frozen corn niblets, thawed
1/4 cup (76 g) finely chopped onion
   red pepper flakes to taste
2 tablespoons finely chopped fresh flat-leaf parsley
   juice of 1 whole lemon (3 tablespoons)
1/4 cup (57 g) each, diced: red and yellow bell peppers
   freshly ground black pepper to taste
   paprika to taste

❶ Prepare the grill. Lightly oil both sides of each piece of fish; set aside at room temperature.

❷ Heat 1 tablespoon fish broth in a skillet over medium-high heat. Add corn, onion, 1 or 2 pinches red pepper flakes, and parsley; sauté until onion is clear, about 5 minutes. Add remaining fish broth. Cook until the liquid is reduced by more than half, about 10 minutes.

❸ Stir in lemon juice, bell pepper and black pepper; keep warm over very low heat.

❹ When the fire is ready, lightly oil the grid and grill the fish about 4 minutes on each side. Serve the corn salsa on 4 plates. Place the fish on top and sprinkle paprika overall.

GROUPER IS GREAT GRILLED

There are many names for grouper, but they all belong to the sea bass family, and they thrive in warm waters. These fish can grow as long as 12 feet, and may weigh close to 100 pounds, but grouper fished for commercial use usually are less than ten pounds. The flesh is firm, which makes it a good fish to grill; if properly seasoned, it can be great on the grill. It is a flaky fish, and delicately flavored.

Each serving			
Calories	177	Total Fat	2 g
Protein	31 g	Saturated Fat	0.4 g
Carbohydrates	7 g	Cholesterol	55 mg
Dietary Fiber	0 g	Sodium	138 mg

GRILLED HALIBUT WITH BLACK BEANS AND WHITE CORN PUDDING

MAKES 4 SERVINGS

The texture and taste of black beans are excellent with grilled fish. This dish is further enhanced by a very low-fat, silky, yet crispy pudding made with white corn. Use any fresh white-meat fish, if halibut is not available.

Black Beans (recipe follows)

White Corn Pudding (recipe follows)

1 lb (455 g) boneless, skinless halibut fillet, cut into 4 pieces
spray oil

1 teaspoon finely chopped fresh thyme, or 1/2 teaspoon dried
freshly ground black pepper to taste

4 sprigs thyme for garnish

❶ Prepare Black Beans and White Corn Pudding; the Black Beans can be made one day ahead to allow the flavors to blend. (If preparing beans ahead, reheat them before serving.)

❷ Prepare the grill. Lightly spray the grid with oil. Spray oil on both sides of each piece of fish, then season with pepper and chopped thyme.

❸ When the fire is ready, add the fish, and grill about 3 minutes on each side.

❹ To serve, spoon the black beans onto 4 plates, and top each serving with a piece of grilled fish. Garnish with a sprig of thyme. Serve with White Corn Pudding on the side, if you wish.

BLACK BEANS

2 cups (544 g) canned black beans, rinsed well and drained

1 medium-size onion, finely chopped

2 tablespoons finely chopped fresh flat-leaf parsley

1 teaspoon finely chopped fresh thyme, or 1/2 teaspoon dried

1 jalapeño, seeded and finely chopped

1 bay leaf

1 cup (240 ml) low-sodium vegetable or defatted chicken broth

❶ Prepare the grill, with sections of varying heat.

❷ Combine all the ingredients in a foil baking pan, cover with foil, and put it on the grill over a moderately hot section of the fire.

❸ Cook 30 to 40 minutes, or until the beans are heated through and the onion is soft, stirring several times.

Each serving (fish and beans only)			
Calories	249	Total Fat	4 g
Protein	33 g	Saturated Fat	0.4 g
Carbohydrates	20 g	Cholesterol	36 mg
Dietary Fiber	8 g	Sodium	506 mg

WHITE CORN PUDDING

MAKES 8 SERVINGS

This creamy side dish is a delicious accompaniment for fish and many other grilled foods in this book. Use fresh white corn, although frozen white corn works well, too. Yellow corn works fine, as well, but the pudding won't be white.

3 egg whites and 1 whole egg, room temperature

2 cups (324 g) fresh or frozen white corn kernels, thawed (5 to 8 ears)

1/4 cup (151 g) all-purpose flour

salt to taste (optional)

ground white pepper to taste

2 tablespoons butter, melted

2 cups (480 ml) 1 percent fat milk

2 tablespoons finely chopped fresh basil, or 1 teaspoon dried

❶ In a large bowl, beat the egg whites and whole egg until frothy; add the corn kernels. Stir in the flour, a pinch of salt, and white pepper.

❷ Stir in butter and milk, then fold in the basil. Spray a 1 1/2-quart baking dish with oil, then set the dish in a larger pan. Pour the corn mixture into the oiled dish, then fill the larger pan with 1 inch (2 1/2 cm) warm water.

❸ Bake in a preheated 350°F (177°C) oven 1 hour, or until the custard is set. The dish can hold for about 10 minutes before serving.

Each serving			
Calories	148	Total Fat	6 g
Protein	7 g	Saturated Fat	3 g
Carbohydrates	19 g	Cholesterol	49 mg
Dietary Fiber	2 g	Sodium	106 mg

GRILLED FISH KEBABS WITH CURRIED BANANA SAUCE

MAKES 8 SERVINGS

When Helen Crimmins made this, she topped each portion with a little toasted coconut.

2 lb (900 g) skinless, boneless fish (such as swordfish, grouper, monkfish, tuna, or shark) cut into 1-inch (2 1/2-cm) cubes

1 cup (240 ml) low-fat, unsalted, chicken broth

1/2 cup (120 ml) unsweetened pineapple juice

1/2 apple, peeled, cored, and finely chopped

2 shallots, peeled and minced

1 carrot cut into small dice

1 celery rib, cut into small dice

1 small ripe banana, mashed

1 large garlic clove, minced

1 to 2 teaspoons curry powder

1/2 teaspoon ground mace

spray oil

2 tablespoons finely chopped fresh parsley

❶ Prepare the fish cubes and set aside.

❷ In a saucepan, combine broth, pineapple juice, apple, shallots, carrot, celery, banana, and garlic. Bring to a boil, reduce the heat, and simmer until the liquid is reduced by at least half, about 10 to 15 minutes.

Continued on next page

THE OMEGA-3 FATS

Based on current research, health experts suggest eating fish two or three times a week. The research shows that fish and some seafood generally are lower in cholesterol and fat, and provide the "good" fats of omega-3 fatty acids. It has been documented that omega-3 fats help prevent heart disease, according to research done on Eskimos, whose diets are rich in seafood. Other studies indicate that these fish fats may prevent cancer, and lower blood pressure, as well.

❸ Stir in the curry and mace, then mix well. Put the mixture through a food mill, or strain it through a fine sieve or several layers of cheesecloth. The sauce should be as thick as heavy cream. If the sauce is too thick, add a little broth; if it is too thin, carefully cook it over low to medium heat, uncovered, to reach desired thickness. Keep warm, being careful not to scorch.

❹ Prepare the grill. Spray the grid lightly with oil. Thread the fish cubes onto 8 skewers. When the fire is ready, grill the skewers with the cover down, turning the skewers several times to grill all sides, about 8 to 10 minutes.

❺ To serve, put 2 tablespoons warm banana sauce on each of 8 warmed plates; place 1 skewer on each plate, leaving the skewer in for the diner to remove. Before serving, sprinkle each plate with chopped parsley.

Each serving			
Calories	177	Total Fat	5 g
Protein	23.8 g	Saturated Fat	1 g
Carbohydrates	9 g	Cholesterol	44 mg
Dietary Fiber	1 g	Sodium	132.5 mg

THREE-MUSTARD HONEY GLAZED SALMON

MAKES 4 SERVINGS

While the salmon grills, brush the Three-Mustard Honey Glaze over top for delicious results. It is so easy to do, this will become a favorite. If you want to use this on a buffet, grill a whole salmon fillet, brushing it with the Three-Mustard Honey Glaze as it grills. Let it cool, then serve.

1/2 cup (120 ml) honey

1/4 cup (60 ml) grainy mustard

1/4 cup (60 ml) Dijon-style mustard

  2 tablespoons mustard seed

    spray oil

  1 lb (455 g) skinless, boneless salmon fillet, cut into 4 pieces

❶ In a small bowl, combine the honey and mustards. (This may be done ahead, and refrigerated in a jar with a tight lid. Bring to room temperature before using in step 2.)

❷ Prepare the grill. Lightly spray oil on the grid. When the fire is ready, place the salmon pieces on the grill, and immediately brush on some of the honey mixture. Grill 6 to 8 minutes, covered, basting 3 or 4 times with the honey mustard as the salmon grills; do not turn the salmon. Test for doneness by inserting a wooden skewer through the thickest part of the salmon. If it pierces easily, the salmon is done. If it flakes, it may be overdone.

CUTTING FISH INTO STEAKS

If you prefer small steaks to fillets, and if steaks are not available in the market, cut them from a whole fish. Cutting fish steaks yourself offers several advantages, such as portion control. Another advantage is that you get the head and other leftovers, which make good fish broth. Steaks can be cut from swordfish, tuna, salmon, and cod.

When grilling steaks, the skin and backbone are left in place to help keep the fish intact; they can be removed easily after grilling.

Each serving			
Calories	348	Total Fat	11 g
Protein	26 g	Saturated Fat	1.4 g
Carbohydrates	39.4 g	Cholesterol	62.4 mg
Dietary Fiber	1 g	Sodium	626.7 mg

MONKFISH WITH SPICY CITRUS SAUCE

MAKES 4 SERVINGS

1/4 cup (60 ml) frozen orange juice concentrate, thawed

    juice of 1/2 lemon (1 1/2 tablespoons)

    juice of 1 whole lime (3 tablespoons)

1/2 teaspoon hot red pepper sauce

 2 garlic cloves, minced

 1 lb (455 g) boneless, skinless, monkfish fillet, cut into 4 equal parts

 1 teaspoon arrowroot or cornstarch

 2 tablespoons lemon or orange marmalade

    spray oil

 2 tablespoons finely chopped fresh chives

 1 tablespoon finely chopped fresh thyme, or 1 teaspoon dried

    salt to taste (optional)

❶ In a medium-size bowl, combine orange juice concentrate, lemon and lime juices, hot sauce, garlic, and 1/3 cup (80 ml) water to make the marinade; mix well. Remove 1/3 cup (80 ml) of this mixture to make the sauce.

❷ Place the fish in a glass dish in a single layer; pour marinade over top. Let marinate 15 minutes at room temperature. Prepare the grill.

❸ To make the sauce, stir arrowroot into the reserved mixture; stir in the marmalade, then cook over medium heat until sauce thickens and is no longer lumpy, 3 to 4 minutes.

❹ When the fire is ready, lightly oil the grid and add the fish. Grill fish 3 to 4 minutes on each side, basting often with the marinade, not the sauce.

❺ To serve, place 1 piece of fish in the center of each of 4 warmed plates; season with salt. Spoon some of the sauce over each piece of fish, then sprinkle each with chives and thyme.

MONKFISH HAVE BIG MOUTHS

Also called angler fish, monkfish is big and ugly, with a huge mouth. If you see it at the fish market, it will probably have been beheaded and skinned. Monkfish has delicate white meat excellent for soups, chowders, and stews. If you have traveled to the Caribbean, you probably have tasted monkfish. There it is often grilled with citrus juices, in a fashion similar to what I have presented here.

Monkfish can be found in American and European waters.

Each serving (including sauce)			
Calories	174	Total Fat	2.3 g
Protein	22 g	Saturated Fat	0 g
Carbohydrates	16 g	Cholesterol	36 mg
Dietary Fiber	0.3 g	Sodium	33 mg

GRILLED SALMON KEBABS WITH SWEET AND SOUR DIPPING SAUCE

MAKES 4 SERVINGS

The soy sauce-vinegar mixture is used for both the marinade and the dipping sauce. It is good with salmon, but can be used with scallops, shrimp, swordfish, and other fish. If you plan to serve a green salad with a vinaigrette dressing, try using some of this sauce in place of the vinegar in the dressing. Mashed potatoes and grilled asparagus are good accompaniments, as well.

spray oil

1/4 cup (60 ml) each: low-sodium soy sauce and red wine vinegar

2 tablespoons sugar

1 lb (455 g) boneless, skinless salmon fillet, cut into 1-inch (2 1/2-cm) cubes

2 tablespoons finely chopped flat-leaf parsley

❶ Prepare the grill, then lightly spray the grid with oil. In a small bowl, combine soy sauce, vinegar, and sugar; mix well. If using this mixture as a dipping sauce, be sure to heat it up first.

❷ Thread the fish cubes onto 4 skewers (if using wooden ones, be sure to pre-soak them 30 minutes). Brush 2 tablespoons soy sauce mixture on both sides of the fish. When the fire is ready, put the skewers on the grill, and cook 3 minutes on each side, turning once.

❸ To serve, put a skewer on each of 4 plates, then sprinkle with parsley. Heat up the remaining sweet and sour sauce and serve it on the side.

Each serving			
Calories	205	Total Fat	7 g
Protein	24 g	Saturated Fat	1 g
Carbohydrates	11 g	Cholesterol	62 mg
Dietary Fiber	0 g	Sodium	55 mg

GRILLED SALMON STRIPS OVER LOW-FAT PUTTANESCA SAUCE

MAKES 4 SERVINGS

The word "puttanesca" is Italian and is usually a sauce for linguini. According to one source "ladies of pleasure" used the intense fragrance from the sauce to attract men. The sauce is quick and easy to make, however, I have reduced the fat content from the original recipe. Here, it is served with salmon instead of linguini, and makes a tasty dish.

1 tablespoon olive oil

1 small onion, peeled and finely chopped

3 garlic cloves, minced

1 lb (455 g) plum tomatoes, peeled and cut into 1/2-inch (1 1/4-cm) dice, or 1 (15-oz/425-g) can chopped tomatoes, drained

2 tablespoons red wine vinegar

4 pitted, cured black Italian or Greek olives, finely chopped

2 anchovies, soaked in cold water 20 minutes to remove salt

1 tablespoon capers, rinsed and drained

freshly ground black pepper to taste

1 lb (455 g) boneless, skinless salmon fillet, cut crosswise into 4 equal strips

❶ Heat the oil in a skillet, and add the onions. Cook over medium heat until they become limp, 3 to 4 minutes. Add garlic and cook 1 minute more.

❷ Add tomatoes and cook 5 minutes more, stirring several times. Add vinegar, and bring to a boil.

❸ Add olives, anchovies, and capers, and cook 1 minute. Season with a liberal amount of black pepper; keep warm. Meanwhile, prepare the grill.

❹ When the fire is ready, lightly oil the grid. Grill the salmon 3 to 4 minutes on each side, turning once.

❺ To serve, distribute the sauce among 4 warmed plates, and place a piece of salmon on top.

Each serving			
Calories	237	Total Fat	12 g
Protein	24.4 g	Saturated Fat	2 g
Carbohydrates	9 g	Cholesterol	64 mg
Dietary Fiber	2 g	Sodium	252 mg

SCALLOP AND PROSCIUTTO KEBABS WITH SCALLIONS AND SAGE

MAKES 4 SERVINGS

Sweet, tender sea scallops are grilled beautifully with the Italian flavors of prosciutto, sage, and onions. If using wooden skewers, be sure to soak them for at least 30 minutes before placing them on the grill.

  1 lb (455 g) large sea scallops (16 to 20 pieces)
  1 tablespoon olive oil
  2 garlic cloves, minced
  2 very thin slices prosciutto (about 1 oz/28 g)
  4 scallions, trimmed, washed, and cut into 12 lengths
    freshly ground black pepper to taste
 12 small sage leaves
  4 lemon wedges
    arugula or curly endive for 4
    light vinaigrette

❶ Rinse and dry the scallops. Place scallops in a bowl with oil and garlic; toss well. Let marinate 20 minutes at room temperature. Prepare the grill.

❷ Cut the prosciutto into 8 or 12 pieces, removing any visible fat.

❸ Thread each of 4 skewers by putting sage, prosciutto, and a scallion piece between each scallop.

❹ When the fire is ready, lightly oil the grid. Grill the kebabs about 3 minutes on each side, turning once.

❺ Meanwhile, toss arugula with a little vinaigrette; divide among 4 plates.

❻ To serve, place 1 skewer atop each lightly dressed salad; garnish each with a lemon wedge.

Each serving (not including salad with vinaigrette)			
Calories	172	Total Fat	5.6 g
Protein	21.3 g	Saturated Fat	1 g
Carbohydrates	8 g	Cholesterol	41.5 mg
Dietary Fiber	3 g	Sodium	279 mg

GRILLED SEA BASS WITH ITALIAN FLAVORS

MAKES 6 SERVINGS

This dish is easy to prepare, and is filled with fresh Italian flavors; use fresh herbs, if possible. Be sure your bass is really fresh, and use a wire basket when grilling the fish.

2 whole sea bass with heads and tails on (each about
    2 1/2 lb/1 1/8 kg), rinsed, and dried

1/2 cup (120 ml) fresh lemon juice

2 tablespoons olive oil

2 large garlic cloves, minced

2 tablespoons finely chopped onion

2 tablespoons each, finely chopped fresh: basil, oregano,
    and flat-leaf parsley, or 1 teaspoon each dried
    freshly ground black pepper to taste

salt to taste (optional)

❶ Make 2 cuts, about 1/2 inch (1 1/4 cm) deep on both sides of each fish. Put them in a large glass dish in a single layer.

❷ In a small bowl, blend remaining ingredients for the marinade; liberally brush the inside of each fish with the marinade. Pour the remaining marinade over both fish. Cover with plastic wrap, and leave at room temperature 15 minutes. Turn fish, cover, and marinate 15 minutes more. Meanwhile, prepare the grill.

❸ Arrange each fish in an oiled, hinged wire grill basket (or put both in one large wire basket). When the fire is ready, set the baskets on the grill, and cook, covered, 5 minutes on each side, basting often with the marinade. To test for doneness, pierce the fish with a wooden skewer. If the skewer goes through easily, the fish is cooked.

❹ Place the fish on a large platter, pouring any remaining marinade over the fish; serve immediately.

Each serving			
Calories	284	Total Fat	10.3 g
Protein	43 g	Saturated Fat	2 g
Carbohydrates	3 g	Cholesterol	195 mg
Dietary Fiber	0.2 g	Sodium	168 mg

GRILLED SALMON STRIPS WITH LEEKS AND BEET BATONS

MAKES 4 SERVINGS

- 1 lb (455 g) salmon fillet, skinned, boned, and cut crosswise into 4 strips

  spray oil

- 1/2 cup (120 ml) low-sodium chicken broth

- 4 small leeks, carefully washed and trimmed, cut in half lengthwise

  juice of 1 whole lemon (3 tablespoons)

- 1/4 cup (43 g) thinly sliced scallions

- 2 tablespoons olive oil

- 1/4 cup (60 ml) white wine vinegar

- 2 tablespoons Dijon-style mustard

- 4 small beets, cooked and peeled

- 4 small new potatoes, boiled and cut into quarters

- 4 walnut halves, coarsely chopped

1 Prepare the grill. Lightly spray the salmon strips with oil; set aside.

2 Heat chicken broth to boiling in a large skillet; add leeks and blanch 3 minutes. Drain and reserve the liquid. Set leeks aside.

3 In a large bowl, combine leek liquid, lemon juice, scallions, oil, vinegar, and mustard. Mix well and set aside.

4 When the fire is ready, oil the grid; place salmon strips and leeks on the grill. Cover and cook about 3 minutes on each side; do not overcook the salmon.

5 Slice the beets 1/4 inch (5/8 cm) thick, then cut the slices into 1/4-inch (5/8-cm) strips. Add beets and potatoes to the mixture, toss to coat.

6 To serve, divide the beet batons, potatoes, and sauce among 4 plates. Add 2 leek halves to each plate, 1 on each side of the beets. Arrange 1 salmon strip over the top of each serving, then sprinkle with walnuts and serve.

Each serving			
Calories	472	Total Fat	17 g
Protein	29 g	Saturated Fat	2.4 g
Carbohydrates	54 g	Cholesterol	63 mg
Dietary Fiber	7 g	Sodium	323 mg

GRILLED GROUPER WITH LOW-FAT SMOKED SALMON SAUCE

MAKES 4 SERVINGS

Nonfat sour cream combines with tender smoked salmon and dill in this low-fat sauce, which can accompany any fish.

1/2 cup (120 ml) nonfat sour cream

1 oz (28 g) smoked salmon, coarsely chopped

1/2 teaspoon dill weed

juice of 1 whole lemon (3 tablespoons)

freshly ground black pepper to taste

spray oil

1 lb (455 g) boneless, skinless grouper or halibut fillet, cut into 4 equal parts

2 tablespoons finely chopped chives

❶ Prepare the grill. Put the first 5 ingredients in the bowl of a food processor. Pulse several times until the salmon is well combined with the sour cream.

❷ When the fire is ready, lightly oil the grid and place the grouper on it. Grill about 3 minutes on each side. Serve with a large dollop of the sauce on top; sprinkle chives over top.

Each serving			
Calories	177	Total Fat	2 g
Protein	31 g	Saturated Fat	0.4 g
Carbohydrates	7 g	Cholesterol	55 mg
Dietary Fiber	0 g	Sodium	138 mg

SPICY-SWEET GRILLED SHRIMP

MAKES 4 SERVINGS

Lime and garlic jellies usually can be found wherever homemade preserves are sold. If not available in your area, they can be substituted by combining 1/2 cup (120 ml) apple or guava jelly with one large minced garlic clove.

1/4 cup (60 ml) lime jelly or marmalade

1/4 cup (60 ml) garlic jelly

  3 tablespoons fresh lime juice

  1 tablespoon Worcestershire sauce

  1 teaspoon minced fresh jalapeño pepper

  1 lb (455 g) shrimp (16–20 count), shelled and deveined

  spray oil

❶ In a small saucepan, combine jellies, lime juice, Worcestershire sauce, and jalapeño pepper. Cook mixture over medium heat until jellies melt, 3 to 5 minutes. Remove from heat and set aside. Place 4 (12-inch/ 30 1/2-cm) wooden skewers in a large baking dish and cover with water; let soak at least 30 minutes.

❷ Inserting the skewers from head to tail, thread 4 to 5 shrimp on each skewer, so the shrimp lay flat. Brush both sides of shrimp with jelly mixture, then place skewers on a tray; let shrimp marinate 15 minutes. Prepare the grill.

❸ When the fire is ready, lightly oil the grid, then add the skewers. Grill shrimp about 3 minutes on each side, turning once and basting with the jelly mixture. Serve skewers with remaining sauce.

THE HEAT OF PEPPERS

The jalapeño pepper is the overnight star of the culinary world. Its flavor differs from hot red peppers in the same way the flavors of red and green bell peppers differ.

The flavor of dried, ground jalapeño pepper's heat disappears sooner and therefore the pepper should be added toward the end of the cooking.

Crushed red pepper flakes are used in many recipes in this book; the *powdered form* can be substituted in dry rubs or pastes where crushed pepper may be called for. It has been said that eating hot peppers increases the metabolism, reducing the calories retained from a meal by about 10 percent.

Each serving			
Calories	220	Total Fat	1.3 g
Protein	24 g	Saturated Fat	0.3 g
Carbohydrates	28 g	Cholesterol	221 mg
Dietary Fiber	0 g	Sodium	317 mg

GRILLED SHRIMP WITH FARFALLE

MAKES 4 SERVINGS

This is another favorite of mine because of its simplicity and flavor. Don't overcook the shrimp, or they will be tough. This is garlicky, and can be hotter, depending on the amount of red pepper flakes you use. Start with about 1/4 teaspoon; you can always add more if you want, after the dish is composed.

1 lb (455 g) shrimp (16–20 count)

2 tablespoons olive oil

4 garlic cloves, minced

1/4 cup (28 g) finely chopped fresh flat-leaf parsley

pinch of red pepper flakes

1 cup (240 ml) low-sodium fish broth, or bottled clam juice

8 oz (230 g) farfalle pasta

juice of 1 whole lemon (3 tablespoons)

freshly grated black pepper to taste

❶ Peel and devein the shrimp. Rinse well and dry. Prepare the grill. When the fire is ready, place shrimp on a lightly oil grid (or skewer them, if you don't have a grid). Grill shrimp 4 to 5 minutes, turning once; set aside.

❷ Heat the oil in a large skillet over medium heat. Add garlic and sauté 2 minutes; do not let it brown. Add parsley, red pepper flakes, and broth. Bring to a boil, then reduce the heat to keep warm.

❸ Cook the pasta according to package directions. Drain well, then add to the skillet. Add the grilled shrimp and toss. Sprinkle with lemon juice and black pepper, then toss again; serve hot.

Each serving			
Calories	336	Total Fat	8.6 g
Protein	24 g	Saturated Fat	1.3 g
Carbohydrates	39 g	Cholesterol	163 mg
Dietary Fiber	2 g	Sodium	319 mg

GRILLED SHRIMP WITH LEMON AIOLI SAUCE

MAKES 4 SERVINGS

This is a good sauce for shrimp, and almost all other grilled fish. It's easy to make, and can be made ahead two or three hours. I like to cook shrimp on skewers, even if they are not to be served that way, because they are easier to turn.

1 cup (240 ml) low-fat mayonnaise

1 tablespoon low-sodium soy sauce

2 garlic cloves, minced

2 teaspoons lemon zest

2 tablespoons fresh lemon juice

1 lb (455 g) shrimp (16–20 count)
spray oil

2 tablespoons finely chopped chives
or scallions

❶ In a small bowl, combine mayonnaise, soy sauce, garlic, lemon zest, and lemon juice; mix well and refrigerate until needed. Peel and devein shrimp; rinse and pat dry.

❷ Prepare the grill and lightly spray the grid with oil. Inserting skewers from head to tail, thread the shrimp onto 4 skewers, keeping the shrimp flat. Spray shrimp with oil. When the fire is ready, put the skewers on the grill, and cook 3 minutes on each side.

❸ To serve, divide grilled shrimp among 4 plates, with a spoonful of the aioli sauce to the side. Sprinkle chives on top of the shrimp and sauce.

Serving suggestion: Serve with grilled artichokes, leeks, fennel, or a delicious ear of grilled corn.

HOW TO CLEAN SHRIMP

It is best to clean shrimp near a sink with water running. Use the tips of your fingers to carefully peel off the shell, so the shrimp is not torn or broken, especially at the tail end. With a small, sharp paring knife, make a shallow cut along the back (the curved edge) of the shrimp. Carefully pull out and discard the dark intestinal vein, which also can be grayish sometimes. Rinse your hands and the shrimp under the running water. Dry the shrimp before adding to a marinade. Discard the shrimp shells, or use them with other seafood to make fish broth.

Each serving (not including vegetables)			
Calories	266	Total Fat	13.3 g
Protein	24 g	Saturated Fat	2.4 g
Carbohydrates	12 g	Cholesterol	236 mg
Dietary Fiber	0 g	Sodium	691 mg

SKEWERED SHRIMP WRAPPED IN ZUCCHINI SLIVERS

MAKES 4 SERVINGS

If the zucchini are young and tender, they will bend easily to wrap around the shrimp. Do not peel the zucchini, as the dark green edges are important to the "look" of the dish. No salt is necessary here; instead, serve this with lemon wedges. An alternate to the corn or rice is fresh spinach, cut into 1/2-inch (1 1/4-cm) threads, lightly dressed with one teaspoon oil, two tablespoons fresh lemon juice, and a sprinkle of chopped tarragon.

1 lb (455 g) shrimp (16–20 count)

1 tablespoon olive oil

2 garlic cloves, minced

juice of 1 whole lemon (3 tablespoons)

1 teaspoon crushed fennel seeds

1/2 teaspoon red pepper flakes

3 to 4 small (1- by-6-inch/2 1/2- by-15 1/4-cm) zucchini, ends removed

2 whole tomatoes, cored, each cut into 8 chunks, or 16 cherry tomatoes

8 wooden skewers

freshly ground black pepper to taste

❶ Peel and devein the shrimp; rinse and pat dry. In a large bowl, combine shrimp, oil, garlic, lemon juice, fennel seeds, and red pepper flakes. Let marinate at room temperature 20 minutes, or longer in the refrigerator. Meanwhile, slice zucchini, lengthwise, as thinly as possible. Prepare the grill.

❷ Wrap each shrimp in 1 zucchini slice, then thread it onto 2 wooden skewers, which have been soaked in water for at least 30 minutes. (Using two skewers helps prevent the food from slipping around.) Add a piece of tomato. Repeat to make 4 servings, each with 4 wrapped shrimp and 4 tomatoes. Brush any remaining marinade over the skewers, then liberally sprinkle with black pepper.

❸ When the fire is ready, add the skewers and grill 4 to 5 minutes on each side, turning once.

Serving suggestion: Serve over hot cooked rice.

Each serving (without corn or rice)			
Calories	166	Total Fat	5 g
Protein	25 g	Saturated Fat	1 g
Carbohydrates	5 g	Cholesterol	221 mg
Dietary Fiber	1 g	Sodium	261 mg

GRILLED SHRIMP WITH PARSLEY AND PINE NUTS

MAKES 4 SERVINGS

This simple shrimp dish is delicious served over a mound of couscous. Sliced tomatoes dressed with low-fat vinaigrette can be placed attractively to the side of each serving.

1 lb (455 g) fresh shrimp (16–20 count)

1/4 cup (38 g) whole pine nuts

1 tablespoon olive oil

   juice of 1 whole lemon (3 tablespoons)

1 tablespoon each, finely chopped: fresh parsley and cilantro

2 teaspoons paprika

   hot red pepper sauce to taste

1 lemon, cut into 4 wedges

❶ Peel and devein shrimp; rinse and pat dry. Place shrimp in a large glass dish.

❷ Finely chop pine nuts. Then, in a small bowl, combine remaining ingredients, except lemon wedges. Pour marinade over shrimp; toss well to coat, and marinate 30 minutes. Prepare the grill.

❸ Thread the shrimp onto 4 skewers. When the fire is ready, grill shrimp 2 to 3 minutes on each side, turning once. Serve immediately with lemon wedges.

Each serving			
Calories	222	Total Fat	12 g
Protein	27 g	Saturated Fat	2 g
Carbohydrates	4 g	Cholesterol	221 mg
Dietary Fiber	1 g	Sodium	256 mg

GRILLED SHRIMP WITH PECAN-RAISIN CONSERVE

MAKES 4 SERVINGS

This tasty shrimp dish would be good served atop grilled potato slices. The sauce is quite spicy, but would be tamed by the potatoes. Pecans are high in calories and total fat, but they are relatively low in saturated fat, when compared to other nuts, such as brazil nuts, cashews, and macadamias.

1 lb (455 g) shrimp (16–20 count)

1/4 cup (30 g) pecan halves

1/4 cup (38 g) golden raisins

1/4 cup (60 ml) dark rum

juice of 1 whole lemon (3 tablespoons)

2 tablespoons honey

1/2 teaspoon red pepper flakes

❶ Prepare the grill. Peel and devein the shrimp; rinse and pat dry; set aside.

❷ Toast the pecans in a small, dry skillet over medium heat until they begin to color, 3 to 4 minutes; coarsely chop, then transfer to a small bowl.

❸ In the same skillet, combine raisins, rum, lemon juice, honey, and red pepper flakes. Bring to a boil, stirring constantly. Reduce the heat, and cook 2 to 3 minutes, stirring to cook off the rum. The sauce should thicken slightly. Stir in pecans, and remove from the heat.

❹ When the sauce has cooled somewhat, mix 1/3 of it with the shrimp, tossing to coat the shrimp well.

❺ When the fire is ready, place shrimp in an oiled, hinged metal basket, or skewer them. Grill 6 to 8 minutes, turning once.

❻ To serve, divide the shrimp among 4 plates; add a small spoonful of the remaining sauce to each plate. Serve immediately.

Each serving			
Calories	253	Total Fat	6 g
Protein	25 g	Saturated Fat	0.7 g
Carbohydrates	18 g	Cholesterol	221 mg
Dietary Fiber	1 g	Sodium	256 mg

JUNE GIRARD'S MUTTON SNAPPER

MOJO CRIOLLO AND SOUR ORANGE JUICE

Mojo Criollo is a Spanish-style marinade of vinegar, garlic, citric acid, onion, salt, sugar, herbs, and spices (mint, rosemary, thyme, bay leaf, and peppercorns). The mixture is packaged in bottles and can be found in Latin markets and supermarkets. June Girard makes her marinade from scratch, replacing the citric acid with lemon juice, and vinegar with wine.

If sour oranges are not available, look for Bitter Orange by Kirby in your local market.

MAKES 20 SERVINGS

This is a wonderful dish for a buffet, and it may be served hot or cold. To serve it hot, surround the fish with *al dente* broccoli, cauliflower, sliced or baby carrots, and potatoes. If served cold, add raw vegetables and a dip. If the whole fish will fit onto your barbecue grid, there is no need to remove the tail. If the fish is too large for your grid, ask your fishmonger to cut the tail off but cook it alongside the fish, then attach it when you are ready to present the fish on a platter. Cooking the tail with the body will give the same appearance to both parts when the fish is presented.

1 (15–20 lb/6.8–9 kg) whole mutton snapper, clean and scaled, tail cut off and reserved

1 cup (240 ml) sour orange juice

1 cup (240 ml) Mojo Criollo

4 large onion, peeled and sliced into rounds

1 black olive for garnish

1/2 cup (56 g) stemmed fresh parsley

lemon wedges for garnish

❶ Place fish and its tail in a large resealable plastic bag. Add orange juice and Mojo Criollo. Seal the bag, then let the fish marinate for at least 4 hours. Meanwhile, prepare the grill.

❷ Cut 3 pieces of heavy-duty aluminum foil large enough to make a tray in which the fish will fit. Stacking 2 pieces of foil, turn up the edges to make a tray. Place the onions on the foil tray spreading them out evenly over the foil. Remove the fish from the marinade and carefully place it on top of the onions. Pour 1/4 cup (60 ml) marinade over the fish. Place remaining foil on top of the fish, crimping the top and bottom edges together to seal the package.

Continued on next page

3 When the grill is ready, place the foil package on the grid. Close the grill cover and cook about 50 minutes. To test for doneness, open the package enough to stick a long wooden skewer through the thickest part of the fish. The skewer should meet no resistance and the fish should be white. If the skewer meets resistance cook a few minutes more.

4 To serve, unwrap the fish and pour off the liquid. Carefully transfer the fish to a large platter, discarding the onions. Remove the skin from one side of the body and tail. (This way, you can serve the fish directly, and when the top side of the meat has been eaten you can remove the bones to expose the meat on the bottom side.) Place an olive, or a slice in the eye socket and some parsley in the mouth of the fish. Add the tail, covering the seam with chopped parsley. Serve with lemon wedges.

Each serving			
Calories	304	Total Fat	9.6 g
Protein	47 g	Saturated Fat	1.8 g
Carbohydrates	4 g	Cholesterol	84 mg
Dietary Fiber	0.6 g	Sodium	105 mg

PEPPERED SHRIMP WITH PAPRIKA AND LEMON

MAKES 4 SERVINGS

This shrimp dish is easy and can be assembled ahead, then grilled just before serving. Serve with a crispy water chestnut side dish, directions follow. A scoop of low-fat cole slaw would complement this dish, as well.

1 lb (455 g) shrimp (16–20 count)

1 teaspoon vegetable oil

2 garlic cloves, minced

2 teaspoons paprika

1 teaspoon ground cumin

4 drops hot red pepper sauce

1 tablespoon finely chopped flat-leaf parsley

juice of 1 whole lemon (3 tablespoons)

salt to taste (optional)

❶ Peel and devein shrimp; rinse and pat dry. Place shrimp in a glass dish, and set aside.

❷ Heat oil in a skillet over medium heat, add garlic and sauté 1 minute, or until garlic begins to take on a little color. Remove from heat.

❸ Add paprika, cumin, pepper sauce, parsley, and lemon juice to the skillet; mix well. Add mixture to shrimp, toss well, and let marinate 30 minutes at room temperature, or for several hours in the refrigerator. Meanwhile, prepare the grill. Thread the shrimp onto 4 skewers.

❹ When the fire is ready, place the skewers on the grill, and cook several minutes, turning once. Serve immediately.

Serving suggestion: Crispy water chestnuts add a nice contrast in texture to this simple shrimp dish. Drain a small 16 1/2-oz can of water chestnuts in a colander; rinse and drain again; pat dry. Combine water chestnuts in a small bowl with 2 sliced scallions and 1 teaspoon oil; toss to coat all pieces with oil. Place mixture in a hinged wire basket, and grill over hot coals about 5 minutes, turning 2 or 3 times. Serve immediately.

Each serving (not including side dishes)			
Calories	133	Total Fat	3 g
Protein	24 g	Saturated Fat	0.5 g
Carbohydrates	2 g	Cholesterol	221 mg
Dietary Fiber	0 g	Sodium	256 mg

GRILLED SQUID WITH PASTA

MAKES 4 SERVINGS

Most fish markets sell whole or sliced, cleaned, squid; if you buy it whole, all that is necessary for this dish is to slice the squid. Include the tentacles for extra flavor. Cubanelle peppers (the long, thin, light green peppers) are suggested for this dish, but if you can't find cubanelles, any sweet pepper will work.

  1 lb (455 g) squid, sliced
  3 tablespoons extra-virgin olive oil, divided
      pinch of salt
      freshly ground black pepper to taste
      spray oil
  1 red onion, peeled and cut into 1/2-inch (1 1/4-cm) pieces
  2 cubanelle peppers or Italian fryers, thinly sliced
1/4 cup (28 g) each, finely chopped fresh: basil and flat-leaf parsley
12 Greek or Sicilian olives, pitted and minced
  2 garlic cloves, minced
  1 teaspoon each: balsamic vinegar and fresh lemon juice
  1 (8-oz/240-ml) bottle clam juice
  8 oz (230 g) small pasta (such as penne, radiatore, or fusilli)

❶ Rinse squid, then pat dry. Place squid in a large bowl and add 1 tablespoon olive oil, salt, and black pepper. Prepare the grill. When the fire is ready, spray a hinged, wire basket with oil; add the squid, and place the basket on the grill. Tossing frequently, cook 3 to 4 minutes. Remove squid to a large platter.

❷ Add onion, peppers, basil, parsley, olives, garlic, vinegar, and lemon juice to the squid; toss well. In a saucepan, heat clam juice to almost boiling; keep hot.

❸ Cook the pasta according to package directions, then drain. Add pasta to the squid mixture, then add the remaining 2 tablespoons olive oil, and the hot clam juice. Toss well, and season with salt and pepper. Serve warm.

Each serving			
Calories	472	Total Fat	18 g
Protein	29 g	Saturated Fat	3 g
Carbohydrates	48 g	Cholesterol	320 mg
Dietary Fiber	3 g	Sodium	774 mg

GRILLED STRIPED BASS OVER CILANTRO GAZPACHO

MAKES 6 SERVINGS

The fresh, highly seasoned vegetables mellow as they marinate, and make a tasty foundation for the charred fish.

1 (14-oz/400-g) can ready-cut tomatoes, drained

1 green bell pepper, seeded and finely chopped

1 cucumber, peeled, seeded, and finely chopped

1 medium-size onion, finely chopped

1 tablespoon olive oil

2 tablespoons balsamic vinegar

2 tablespoons finely chopped fresh cilantro

1 teaspoon sugar

   pinch of red pepper flakes

1 to 1 1/4 lb (455 to 570 g) boneless, skinless, striped bass fillets, cut into 4 pieces

   spray oil

   freshly ground black pepper to taste

❶ In a large glass bowl, combine all the ingredients, except the fish, spray oil, and black pepper; chill at least 4 hours to allow the flavors to develop.

❷ Prepare the grill. Lightly spray the grid with oil. Spray each fish piece with oil, then season with black pepper on both sides. When the fire is ready, place the fish on the grill, and cook 3 to 4 minutes on each side.

❸ To serve, place about 3 tablespoons gazpacho on each of 4 plates. Place the hot, grilled fish on top, and serve right away.

Serving suggestion: Serve half a grilled or baked potato with each portion.

Each serving (not including potato)			
Calories	135	Total Fat	4 g
Protein	15 g	Saturated Fat	0.8 g
Carbohydrates	9 g	Cholesterol	64 mg
Dietary Fiber	2 g	Sodium	166 mg

GRILLED RED SNAPPER WITH CURRIED WHITE BEANS

MAKES 4 SERVINGS

Prepare the beans first so they will be ready to put on the plate as soon as the fish comes off the grill. This is a good combination of flavors.

2 red snappers (about 2 lb/900 g each), cleaned with head and tail on

1 tablespoon finely chopped fresh oregano, or 1 teaspoon dried

freshly ground black pepper to taste

spray oil

juice of 1 whole lemon (3 tablespoons)

2 garlic cloves, peeled and cut into halves

Curried White Beans (recipe follows)

1 Rinse and dry the fish. Sprinkle the inside of the fish with oregano and pepper. Lightly spray the fish with oil. Prepare the grill, and lightly spray the grid with oil.

2 In a small bowl, combine lemon juice and garlic; press the garlic with a fork to release some juices. Discard garlic. Brush lemon-garlic juice over the fish.

3 Arrange the fish in a lightly oiled wire basket(s). When the fire is ready, grill 6 or 7 minutes on each side, basting with any leftover lemon juice. The fish should be grilled in less than 15 minutes. Serve with Curried White Beans.

Each serving (not including beans)			
Calories	158	Total Fat	2 g
Protein	32 g	Saturated Fat	0.4 g
Carbohydrates	1.6 g	Cholesterol	56 mg
Dietary Fiber	0 g	Sodium	68 mg

CURRIED WHITE BEANS

MAKES 4 SERVINGS

spray oil

1 carrot, cut into 1/4-inch (5/8-cm) dice

1 medium-size onion, cut into 1/4-inch (5/8-cm) dice

1/2 cup (60 ml) low-sodium vegetable or chicken broth, divided

2 garlic cloves, minced

1 tablespoon curry powder

2 cups (455 g) canned cannellini beans, rinsed and drained

freshly ground black pepper to taste

❶ Spray a large skillet with oil, and place over medium heat. Add carrot and onion, then sauté. When the pan becomes very dry, add 2 tablespoons broth, and cook until the liquid evaporates. Add 2 more tablespoons broth, and cook until broth evaporates again. Add garlic and curry powder. Stir well, and add the remaining broth. The entire procedure should take 6 to 8 minutes.

❷ Add the beans, and cook just to heat through. Season with pepper, then stir several times. If mixture is too thick, add a little more broth, but little or no broth should be visible.

WHITE KIDNEY BEANS, OR CANNELLINIS

If you use dried beans instead of canned, remove any debris, then put them in a large bowl, and cover with water. Soak overnight, then drain before cooking.

To cook, use 3 cups fresh water for each cup of beans. Bring to a boil in a large pot, then lower the heat, and simmer about one hour. The beans should be tender but still hold their shape. If you must add salt, sprinkle it on after the beans are cooked. One cup of dried beans will yield about 2 1/2 cups cooked.

Each serving			
Calories	129	Total Fat	1 g
Protein	6 g	Saturated Fat	0.2 g
Carbohydrates	24 g	Cholesterol	0 mg
Dietary Fiber	7 g	Sodium	292 mg

GRILLED SWORDFISH WITH MOROCCAN CHERMOULA

MAKES 4 SERVINGS

Chermoula is a spicy fish sauce that is served in Morocco. The sauce also can be used on chicken and many vegetables.

2 tablespoons olive oil

1/4 cup (28 g) each, coarsely chopped, fresh: cilantro and flat-leaf parsley

juice of 1 whole lemon (3 tablespoons)

3 large garlic cloves, peeled and cut into halves

2 teaspoons ground cumin

1 1/2 teaspoons paprika

pinch of salt (optional)

pinch of red pepper flakes

1 lb (455 g) boneless, skinless swordfish steak, about 3/4 inches (1 7/8 cm) thick, cut into 4 pieces

spray oil

❶ Place all the ingredients, except the fish, in a food processor bowl; pulse 3 or 4 times to combine.

❷ Arrange the fish pieces in a single layer in a glass dish, then pour the sauce over top. Marinate the fish for 1 hour in the refrigerator; be sure the fish is coated with the sauce and that the dish is covered with plastic wrap.

❸ Prepare and lightly oil the grill. When the fire is ready, put the fish on the grill, and brush with marinade. Grill 3 or 4 minutes on each side, basting frequently. Serve with Garlicky Mashed Potatoes, page 246.

THE GREAT FLAVOR OF CUMIN

In most countries, cumin is second only to black pepper.

Cumin is available in seed and ground form. Black cumin, also called charnushka or Russian caraway (not the cumin used in this recipe), is the tiny black seed found on top of Jewish rye bread in New York City. Charnushka also is a popular spice in Armenia, India, Israel, and Lebanon.

Each serving (potatoes not included)			
Calories	168	Total Fat	10 g
Protein	16 g	Saturated Fat	2 g
Carbohydrates	3 g	Cholesterol	30 mg
Dietary Fiber	1 g	Sodium	74 mg

SKEWERS OF SWORDFISH AND SALMON YAKITORI

MAKES 4 SERVINGS

Yakitori in Japanese means "shining broil." This means to cook the marinade, then brush it on the fish just before serving. If you use wooden skewers, be sure to soak them in cold water a minimum of 30 minutes before putting them on the grill. This preparation can be made using all swordfish, or salmon, or a combination of the two.

1/2 lb (230 g) each boneless, skinless: swordfish and salmon fillets, about 3/4 inch (1 7/8 cm) thick

 4 large scallions, trimmed, rinsed and dried

1/3 cup (80 ml) low-sodium chicken broth

1/3 cup (80 ml) sweet rice wine or dry sherry

1/3 cup (80 ml) low-sodium soy sauce

1 1/2 teaspoons cornstarch mixed with 1 tablespoon water

❶ Rinse and dry the fish, then cut each fillet into 6 chunks; put in a glass bowl, cover, and refrigerate until ready to use. Cut scallions into 16 1-inch (2 1/2-cm) long pieces. Refrigerate the scallions until ready to use.

❷ Combine broth, rice wine, and soy sauce in a small saucepan; bring to a boil. Remove from heat and remove 1/2 cup (120 ml) for marinade; set aside to cool. To make yakitori, stir cornstarch mixture into the saucepan with the remaining broth mixture. Cook over medium heat, uncovered, until it thickens, 1 to 2 minutes; set aside.

❸ When the marinade is cool, pour it over the fish pieces, tossing to coat well. Let stand at room temperature for 10 minutes. Thread scallions and fish alternately onto 4 skewers, beginning and ending with scallions. For attractive presentation, alternate 1 piece salmon with 2 pieces swordfish, then 1 piece swordfish with 2 pieces salmon, always separating fish with scallions. Brush well with the marinade.

❹ When the fire is ready, oil the grid, then grill the fish 3 to 4 minutes on each side, turning once. Transfer the skewers to a large platter and brush liberally with the thickened yakitori; serve immediately.

Serving suggestion: Serve with baked potato halves and steamed asparagus. This dish is strong, and should be complemented with a simple vegetable.

Each serving (not including potatoes and asparagus)			
Calories	190	Total Fat	6 g
Protein	25 g	Saturated Fat	1.3 g
Carbohydrates	5 g	Cholesterol	54 mg
Dietary Fiber	0 g	Sodium	755 mg

GRILLED SWORDFISH SKEWERS WITH MIRIN-SOY SAUCE

MAKES 4 SERVINGS

Japanese cooking wine is used in this simple, tasty preparation for swordfish. Serve this as an entree, as it is presented here, or as an appetizer, with each swordfish cube on a toothpick and the dipping sauce to the side.

   spray oil

4 tablespoons mirin (Japanese cooking wine)

2 1/2 tablespoons low-sodium soy sauce

1/2 teaspoon sesame oil

   pinch of red pepper flakes

1 lb (455 g) boneless, skinless, swordfish, cut into 1-inch (2 1/2-cm) cubes

1 Prepare the grill and lightly spray the grid with oil. In a small bowl, combine the mirin, soy sauce, sesame oil, and pepper flakes; stir well.

2 Thread the fish cubes onto 4 skewers (if using wooden ones, be sure to pre-soak for 30 minutes). Brush the fish with 2 tablespoons of the mirin sauce.

3 When the fire is ready, spray the fish with oil, and place the skewers on the grill. Cook 3 to 4 minutes on each side, turning once.

4 To serve, place 1 skewer on each of 4 plates, and spoon some sauce over the fish.

Serving suggestion: Serve with grilled eggplant and boiled rice.

SWEET MIRIN

Mirin is also called rice wine. It is a cooking wine, somewhat sweet, that adds a special flavor to many Oriental foods. Here, soy sauce and mirin combine to season grilled swordfish. Mirin is available in most stores where Oriental foods are found.

Good quality rice wine may also be served hot as a rather potent alcoholic beverage.

Each serving (not including eggplant and rice)			
Calories	166	Total Fat	5 g
Protein	23 g	Saturated Fat	1.3 g
Carbohydrates	2 g	Cholesterol	44 mg
Dietary Fiber	0 g	Sodium	418 mg

FIVE-SPICE GRILLED SWORDFISH

SUCCULENT SWORDFISH

Swordfish is a meaty fish that can grow to 250 pounds. It is one of the best eating fish, and probably is one of the best fish to be grilled because of its firm flesh and good taste. One great way to prepare swordfish is to cut it into cubes, then thread the cubes onto skewers to make kebabs. When I eat swordfish, I try to forget that this fish with a swordlike bill, and teeth like a buzz saw, has cost fishermen and sailors their lives.

MAKES 4 SERVINGS

When grilling with low-fat foods, it is important to use herbs and spices for additional flavor. Here is an example of how a combination of spices can enhance the taste of grilled fish. Five spices are first heated, then ground and rubbed onto the fish before grilling. It is easy to do.

1/2 teaspoon anise seeds

1/2 teaspoon coriander seeds

1/2 teaspoon cumin seeds

1/2 teaspoon dill seeds

1/2 teaspoon fennel seeds

   1 lb (455 g) boneless, skinless swordfish fillets, cut into 4 pieces

   flavored oil spray

❶ Heat a small skillet. Add the spices and, stirring frequently, toast over low heat 2 minutes, to release their flavors. Transfer spices to a mortar or spice grinder, and mash or process to grind. Transfer the powder to a large sheet of wax paper.

❷ Lightly spray oil on both sides of the fish fillets; lightly rub it in with your hands. Press each side of each fillet into the spice powder to coat it; set the fish aside on the wax paper.

❸ Prepare the grill. Lightly spray oil on the grid. When the fire is ready, grill the swordfish about 3 minutes on each side. Serve immediately.

Serving suggestion: A good accompaniment would be Garlicky Cannellini Beans with a Curly Endive Salad.

Each serving (without beans and salad)			
Calories	141	Total Fat	5 g
Protein	23 g	Saturated Fat	1.3 g
Carbohydrates	1 g	Cholesterol	44 mg
Dietary Fiber	0 g	Sodium	103 mg

GRILLED TUNA WITH CELERY BATONS AND CITRUS VINAIGRETTE

MAKES 4 SERVINGS

This is one of the easiest recipes in this book. If you like fresh tuna, try this one. The grilled celery batons are an interesting way to serve this vegetable; the healthful, refreshing citrus sauce is the perfect partner for tuna.

spray oil

1 large celery stalk, ribs separated

1 tablespoon vegetable oil

freshly ground black pepper to taste

1/2 teaspoon fennel seeds

1 to 1 1/2 lb (455 to 680 g) fresh tuna steak, 1 inch (2 1/2 cm) thick

Citrus Vinaigrette (recipe follows)

1 head leaf lettuce, trimmed

❶ Prepare the grill, and lightly spray the grid with oil. Meanwhile, wash and dry celery. Cut each rib in half lengthwise, then slice crosswise to make 4-inch (10-cm) batons. Place batons in a large bowl, then add oil and pepper and toss. Place batons on the grill so they don't fall through the grid, or put them in a grill basket. Grill about 6 minutes, turning once. Transfer to a dish, add fennel seeds and toss; cover to keep warm.

❷ While the celery is grilling, add the tuna, and grill 2 to 5 minutes, turning once. (If you want the tuna just charred at the edges and very rare in the center grill 2 to 3 minutes. Grill about 5 minutes for medium doneness. Don't overcook the tuna or it will dry out.) Remove tuna from the grill, and let cool several minutes; cut into thin slices. Meanwhile, prepare Citrus Vinaigrette.

❸ Wash and dry lettuce leaves; slice into 1/4-inch (5/8-cm) strips.

❹ Place lettuce in a large bowl. Add 2 tablespoons of the cooled citrus sauce, and toss to coat. Distribute among 4 plates, arranging lettuce mixture to one side. Place tuna slices to the side of the lettuce, and spoon remaining sauce over each serving of tuna. Do not cover tuna entirely with sauce; the grilled slices should be visible. Distribute celery batons over the lettuce and tuna.

Each serving			
Calories	206	Total Fat	9 g
Protein	27 g	Saturated Fat	2 g
Carbohydrates	2.8 g	Cholesterol	43 mg
Dietary Fiber	.70 g	Sodium	49 mg

CITRUS VINAIGRETTE

MAKES 4 SERVINGS

1 cup (240 ml) fresh orange juice

juice of 1 whole lemon (3 tablespoons)

2 tablespoons vegetable oil

1 tablespoon low-sodium soy sauce

1 tablespoon minced fresh ginger

1/2 teaspoon hot red pepper sauce

1/4 cup (28 g) finely chopped chives, scallions, or red onions

❶ Combine all the ingredients, except chives, in a saucepan.

❷ Bring to a simmer, and cook over medium heat until reduced to about half, 6 to 8 minutes.

❸ Cool to room temperature.

❹ Add chives, and toss to blend.

Each serving			
Calories	96	Total Fat	7 g
Protein	.83 g	Saturated Fat	1 g
Carbohydrates	18.3 g	Cholesterol	0 mg
Dietary Fiber	.30 g	Sodium	134 mg

GRILLED TUNA WITH RED PEPPERS, OLIVES, AND LEMON

MAKES 4 SERVINGS

These wonderful Mediterranean flavors call for a bed of pasta or couscous on which to place the grilled tuna. This is a delightful dish that you, your family, and friends will enjoy.

2 tablespoons olive oil

1 red bell pepper, cored, seeded, and cut into 1 1/4-inch (3 1/4-cm) squares

2 garlic cloves, minced

8 cured black olives, pitted, and finely chopped

2 lemons, peeled, seeded, and finely chopped

1/4 cup (28 g) finely chopped fresh flat-leaf parsley

1 tablespoon capers, drained and rinsed

    freshly ground black pepper to taste

1 lb (455 g) fresh tuna fillet, cut into 1 1/4-inch (3 1/4-cm) chunks

❶ Heat the oil in a skillet over medium heat; add bell pepper, and sauté 3 minutes, turning once or twice. Add garlic, toss well, and cook 1 minute longer.

❷ Add olives, lemon, parsley, capers and black pepper. Toss, and cook 1 minute. Remove from heat, and transfer bell pepper mixture to a bowl; cool a few minutes, then add tuna. Toss to coat well. Let marinate 20 to 30 minutes. Meanwhile, prepare the grill.

❸ Reserving excess marinade, thread bell pepper pieces alternately with tuna onto 4 skewers. When the fire is ready, grill the tuna 4 to 5 minutes, turning once.

❹ Serve over angel hair pasta or couscous (see page 120).

Each serving (without pasta or couscous)			
Calories	249	Total Fat	14 g
Protein	27	Saturated Fat	3 g
Carbohydrates	5 g	Cholesterol	43 mg
Dietary Fiber	1 g	Sodium	314 mg

GRILLED TUNA WITH DRY MUSHROOM RUB

MAKES 4 SERVINGS

In this preparation, dried mushrooms are ground and mixed with spices to add a woodsy, nutty flavor to fresh tuna. On the grill, it is divine.

1/3 oz (9 1/2 g) dried porcini mushrooms

1/2 teaspoon black peppercorns

1/2 teaspoon fennel seeds

  1 lb (455 g) fresh tuna steak, about 3/4 to 1 inch (1 7/8 to
    2 1/2 cm) thick

❶ Combine mushrooms, peppercorns, and fennel seeds in a mortar, spice grinder, or bowl of a small food processor; grind to a fine powder. Rub the powder over the tuna, pressing it into both sides.

❷ Prepare the grill. Lightly spray the grid with oil. When the fire is ready, add the tuna, and grill 3 or 4 minutes on each side, or less, if you want it rare. Remove tuna from the grill, and let stand for a few minutes; slice tuna into 8 thin pieces.

Serving suggestions: Serve with boiled or grilled new potatoes, or with a garlicky spinach salad. Garnish with fresh or grilled cherry tomatoes.

Each serving (not including salad or potatoes)			
Calories	172	Total Fat	6 g
Protein	27 g	Saturated Fat	1.4 g
Carbohydrates	1 g	Cholesterol	43 mg
Dietary Fiber	1 g	Sodium	45 mg

ANGEL HAIR PASTA

MAKES 4 SERVINGS

8 oz (230 g) angel hair pasta

1/2 cup (120 ml) white wine

reserved tuna marinade from Grilled Tuna with Red Peppers, Olives, and Lemon (page 117)

❶ Cook pasta according to package directions; drain, reserving 1 cup cooking liquid. Set pasta aside, keeping warm.

❷ Add wine to the skillet in which the pepper mixture was cooked; place over medium-high heat, and simmer to deglaze the pan. Add remaining marinade and reserved pasta cooking liquid. As soon as the liquid boils, reduce heat and add cooked pasta; toss to coat. Heat 1 to 2 minutes, to bring pasta and marinade flavors together. Divide pasta among 4 warm plates, and top with a skewer of tuna.

Each serving (pasta mixture only)			
Calories	242	Total Fat	1 g
Protein	8 g	Saturated Fat	0.2 g
Carbohydrates	45 g	Cholesterol	0 mg
Dietary Fiber	2 g	Sodium	3 mg

COUSCOUS

MAKES 4 SERVINGS

2 cups water

1 cup (193 g) couscous or 1 (6.8-oz/193-g) package couscous, minus any flavor packet that may come with it

❶ Bring water to a boil; add reserved tuna marinade.

❷ Stir in the couscous, bring to a boil again. Cover, remove from the heat, and let stand 7 minutes. Fluff with a fork, then divide among 4 warmed plates. Add a tuna skewer to each plate.

Each serving (couscous only)			
Calories	95	Total Fat	0.1 g
Protein	3 g	Saturated Fat	0 g
Carbohydrates	20 g	Cholesterol	0 mg
Dietary Fiber	1 g	Sodium	4 mg

GRILLED TUNA WITH SWEET PEPPER RELISH

MAKES 4 SERVINGS

This is an unusual combination of flavors. The relish is a bit pungent, but does not interfere with the full flavor of the tuna. Add plain crusty bread to accompany this dish.

2 each: red and yellow bell peppers

2 large ripe tomatoes, cored, peeled, and cut into 1-inch (2 1/2-cm) wedges

1/4 cup (60 ml) cider vinegar

3 tablespoons brown sugar

red pepper flakes and ground allspice, to taste

4 scallions, finely sliced

1 lb (455 g) fresh tuna fillet, cut into 4 pieces

❶ Grill bell peppers. Peel and seed peppers, then cut into 1-inch (2 1/2-cm) strips. Combine peppers and tomatoes in a bowl; set aside. Prepare the grill.

❷ Combine vinegar, sugar, pepper flakes, and allspice in a small saucepan; bring to a boil. Cook just until the sugar dissolves, about 1 minute. Spoon 1 teaspoon over tuna slices; pour remaining mixture over the peppers and tomatoes. Add scallions to the pepper mixture, then stir, and set aside.

❸ When the fire is ready, oil the grid, then grill tuna 4 to 5 minutes, turning once; if you like tuna rare, grill 3 minutes, turning once.

❹ To serve, spoon the pepper relish on each of 4 plates; place a grilled slice of tuna over each serving.

Serving suggestion: Grilled potato slices, mashed potatoes, 1/2 baked potato, or plain boiled rice would make a nice accompaniment to each serving.

Each serving (without potato or rice)			
Calories	233	Total Fat	6 g
Protein	28 g	Saturated Fat	1.5 g
Carbohydrates	17 g	Cholesterol	43 mg
Dietary Fiber	2.4 g	Sodium	58 mg

PHYLLIS ROSE'S GRILLED TUNA

SESAME SEEDS

Sesame seeds come from a very fragrant annual herb. Native to India, this plant is a popular crop in India and China, and is very important in Asian cooking. Sesame seeds have a nutty, slightly sweet flavor, and when toasted, have a taste reminiscent of almonds. These small, teardrop-shaped seeds come in shades of cream, brown, black, and red, the most common in the United States being the cream-colored variety. In the Far East, fish, poultry, and meats are rolled in black sesame seeds before the food is cooked; this creates a crunchy crust.

MAKES 4 SERVINGS

Phyllis Rose, a noted author, and my friend and neighbor in Key West, Florida, also is a great cook. In this dish, she uses fresh kingfish (which sometimes passes for tuna in Key West) and ends up with an equally good dish. The tuna does not need to marinate longer than 30 minutes.

2 tablespoons seasoned rice vinegar

1 tablespoon each: sesame oil, low-sodium soy sauce, minced fresh ginger

4 scallions, finely sliced

freshly ground black pepper to taste

1 (1-lb/455-g) piece fresh tuna steak

1 tablespoon sesame seeds

1 In a small bowl, combine vinegar, oil, soy sauce, ginger, scallions, and pepper. Place tuna in a shallow glass dish, then pour marinade over top, and marinate 15 to 30 minutes. Meanwhile, prepare the grill.

2 When the fire is ready, remove the tuna from the marinade, and coat it with sesame seeds. Place tuna on the grill and cook 4 minutes on each side, turning once (reduce cooking time for rare tuna). Baste tuna with marinade as it cooks, and season with additional black pepper.

3 To serve, remove tuna from the grill, and let sit for a couple of minutes before slicing thinly.

Each serving			
Calories	217	Total Fat	10 g
Protein	27 g	Saturated Fat	2 g
Carbohydrates	3 g	Cholesterol	43 mg
Dietary Fiber	1 g	Sodium	173 mg

GRILLED TUNA WITH POTATOES, GREEN BEANS, AND SPICY LIME SAUCE

MAKES 4 SERVINGS

I enjoyed a dish similar to this when I was visiting friends in Mougins, in southern France. The dish was served with pieces of fresh asparagus.

1 (1-lb/455-g) fresh tuna fillet, cut into 1-inch (2 1/2-cm) cubes
  spray oil
8 small new potatoes, rinsed and dried
1/2 lb (230 g) green beans, trimmed
  Spicy Lime Sauce (recipe follows)

❶ Thread the tuna cubes and the potatoes on metal skewers and lightly spray oil on both sides; set aside.

❷ Steam the beans on the stove top until crisp-tender; set aside.

❸ Prepare the grill. Lightly spray oil on the grid. When the fire is ready, grill the potatoes 20 to 30 minutes, or until tender. Remove from the grill; remove potatoes from skewers. Cut potatoes into halves. Meanwhile, prepare the sauce.

❹ While the fire is still hot, add tuna skewers, and grill about 2 minutes on each side. Remove from the grill; remove skewers.

❺ In a lightly oiled grill basket or a large cast-iron skillet; sauté beans on the grill. Add the potatoes, and toss to reheat. To serve, distribute potatoes, beans, and tuna among each of 4 warmed plates. Add a spoonful of sauce to the side of each plate.

SPICY LIME SAUCE

2 garlic cloves, minced
6 tablespoons fresh lime juice
4 tablespoons low-sodium soy sauce
1 tablespoon sesame chili oil
  pinch of red pepper flakes

Combine all ingredients and taste for spiciness. The sauce should be fiery hot; add more pepper flakes if needed. Set aside.

Each serving			
Calories	471	Total Fat	9 g
Protein	34 g	Saturated Fat	2 g
Carbohydrates	64 g	Cholesterol	43 mg
Dietary Fiber	7 g	Sodium	564 mg

CHAPTER 6
POULTRY PACKED WITH FLAVOR

INTRODUCTION

Grilling gives great flavor to all kinds of food, and it is a style of cooking used in many countries. Chicken is especially flavorful on the grill, as it absorbs the flavors of the marinades as well as the fire. Grill cooks look at chicken the way a painter looks at a blank canvas: The cook's challenge is to give low-fat poultry a new identity by mopping it, rubbing it, and immersing it in a variety of mixtures, using all the spices and herbs imaginable, and pairing it with fruits and vegetables to enhance flavor, texture, and presentation.

Grilled chicken and turkey seem to fit a casual lifestyle, and it should surprise no one that chicken and turkey are on everyone's grill. Chicken, in fact, is a main food in most countries of the world. In spite of its universal appeal and practicality, poultry with skin and dark meat is not low-fat. To meet our needs here, a few simple guidelines must be considered.

If possible, buy your poultry at a meat market, with a butcher on duty, rather than buying pre-packaged birds. This will ensure freshness, and often enable you to buy better cuts of poultry. If you must buy pre-packaged poultry, be sure to check the sell-by date for freshness. More supermarkets are offering higher-quality chickens, such as free-range, which are worth considering, even though they tend to cost more (see Chicken Buying Options on page 129).

Try to use more chicken and turkey breast meat; they are lower in fat than dark-meat cuts. The recipes in this section emphasize flavor, so there's no need to worry about preparing a bland dish. Breasts will dry out if kept on the grill too long. Keep in mind that poultry is cooked when the meat turns white, and the juices run clear when pierced with a knife or fork.

All skin and fat must be removed before grilling. To make preparation easier, buy boneless, skinless breast portions, then use scissors to snip off any remaining globs of fat—they almost always are present. Marinating and basting skinless poultry is important for adding flavor and retaining moistness. Sweeter sauces and marinades will char more quickly because of the sugar content, so use them more toward the end of the total grilling time.

Barbecued chicken, as American as apple pie, often conjures the image of crusty, juicy, fatty wings, thighs, and drumsticks, slathered in high-fat sauces. But remember, when firing up the grill, your favorite marinades, sauces, salsas, and condiments can be used just as well with low-fat cuts of poultry—turkey included—with equally delicious results.

There is no end to the possibilities for flavor when you use honey, mustard, herbs, spices, fruit, vegetables, salsas, relishes, and chutneys. In the following pages, you'll find myriad recipes showing the many wonderful ways to prepare flavorful, low-fat chicken and turkey dishes.

CHICKEN BURGERS WITH CURRY, SCALLIONS, AND APPLESAUCE

MAKES 6 SERVINGS

When making chicken burgers, start with whole, fresh chicken breasts, so you can remove any excess fat. Cut the breast meat into cubes, then grind it in your food processor by pulsing several times; do not over process.

1 lb (455 g) boneless, skinless chicken breasts, ground

1 cup (56 g) fresh bread crumbs (see note)

6 scallions, finely chopped

3 teaspoons curry powder

1 garlic clove, minced

1 cup (230 g) chunky applesauce, divided

   freshly ground black pepper to taste

   spray oil

6 sandwich rolls, split

1 In a bowl, combine ground chicken, bread crumbs, scallions, curry powder, garlic, and 2 tablespoons applesauce. Mix lightly with splayed fingers, but mix well. Gently form into 6 burgers. Put them on a plate, and liberally season with pepper; spray oil on both sides.

2 Prepare the grill. When the fire is ready, oil a wire basket. Place the burgers in the basket, and secure it so the burgers won't fall out. Put the basket on the grill, and cook 4 to 5 minutes. Turn, and grill another 4 to 5 minutes.

3 During the last few minutes of grilling, arrange the split rolls on the grill. Watch them carefully as they will burn quickly. When toasted, divide rolls among 6 plates. Add 1 burger to each, then top each with 2 tablespoons remaining applesauce. Serve immediately.

Note: To make your own fresh bread crumbs, cut the crusts off of 2 slices enriched white bread. Cut the bread into small pieces, and place them in the bowl of your food processor. Pulse several times to process into crumbs.

Each serving			
Calories	263	Total Fat	5 g
Protein	21 g	Saturated Fat	2 g
Carbohydrates	32 g	Cholesterol	42 mg
Dietary Fiber	2 g	Sodium	317 mg

CHICKEN BURGERS WITH ITALIAN ACCENTS

MAKES 6 SERVINGS

The sauce is important to this dish, so use a sauce (homemade or commercial) that you rely on. To make the sauce spicier, add a pinch of red pepper flakes; this will be very tasty with this burger.

1 lb (455 g) boneless, skinless chicken breasts, cut into 1-inch (2 1/2-cm) pieces

1 cup (56 g) fresh bread crumbs

1/4 cup (28 g) freshly grated Parmesan cheese

2 garlic cloves, halved

2 tablespoons fresh flat-leaf parsley

1 small onion, chopped into 1-inch (2 1/2-cm) pieces

1 tablespoon fresh oregano leaves, or 1 teaspoon dried

pinch of fennel seeds

1 egg white, lightly beaten

spray oil

6 sandwich rolls, split

1 cup (240 ml) spicy tomato sauce, heated

POULTRY SKIN

A 3 1/2-ounce portion of chicken breast with skin has 8 grams of fat; without skin, 4 grams of fat. A chicken leg with skin has 13 grams of fat; without skin, 8 grams of fat.

A turkey breast with skin has 3 grams of fat; without skin, 1 gram. A turkey leg with skin has 10 grams of fat; without skin, 4 grams.

A 3 1/2-ounce portion of duck with skin has 28 grams of fat; without skin, 11 grams.

To remove poultry skin, hold the skin with a paper towel, and pull it away from the meat.

Continued on next page

▼▲▼▲▼▲▼▲▼▲▼▲

WHERE DO CALORIES COME FROM?

Proteins, carbohydrates, and fats are the three food elements that produce calories. Fats produce more than twice as many calories as equal amounts of carbohydrates or proteins. It is easy to understand, therefore, that the reduction of fat is the most efficient way to reduce calories.

❶ Grind chicken. Combine chicken, bread crumbs, and Parmesan in a bowl; set aside.

❷ In the bowl of a food processor, pulse garlic to mince. Add parsley, onion, oregano, and fennel seeds; pulse several times to mince, but do not make a paste. Add garlic mixture to chicken mixture, then add egg white. With splayed fingers, lightly mix to blend well. Form the mixture into 6 burgers.

❸ Prepare the grill. When the fire is ready, arrange the burgers in a well-oiled wire basket. Spray the burgers on both sides with oil; secure the basket so the burgers won't fall out, then place the basket on the grill. Grill burgers 8 to 10 minutes, turning once. Just before burgers are done, place rolls on the grill to toast them. Transfer each roll to a plate, and add a grilled burger; top each burger with 2 tablespoons hot spicy tomato sauce.

Each serving (with 2 tablespoons sauce)			
Calories	306	Total Fat	9 g
Protein	25 g	Saturated Fat	4 g
Carbohydrates	31 g	Cholesterol	49 mg
Dietary Fiber	2 g	Sodium	621 mg

SESAME CHICKEN BURGERS

MAKES 6 SERVINGS

These tasty burgers are made more flavorful by "buttering" the rolls with Nonfat Honey-Lemon Mayonnaise on page 275.

1 lb (455 g) fresh ground chicken breasts (page 256)

1 cup (56 g) fresh bread crumbs

4 scallions, finely chopped

1 garlic clove, minced

2 teaspoons sugar

2 tablespoons plus 1 teaspoon low-sodium soy sauce, divided

2 1/2 teaspoons sesame oil, divided

6 sesame rolls, split

1/2 cup (120 ml) Nonfat Honey-Lemon Mayonnaise (page 275)

❶ Combine chicken and bread crumbs in a bowl. Add scallions, garlic, sugar, 1 teaspoon soy sauce, and 1/2 teaspoon sesame oil. With splayed fingers, lightly mix the mixture to blend well. Form into 6 burgers, and set them on a large plate.

❷ In a small bowl, combine remaining 2 tablespoons soy sauce and 2 teaspoons sesame oil. Brush this mixture over both sides of each burger, being careful not to break them. Let sit at room temperature about 10 minutes; meanwhile, prepare the grill.

❸ When the fire is ready, arrange the burgers in a well-oiled wire basket, and secure to hold the burgers in place. Place the basket on the grill, and cook 8 to 10 minutes, turning once.

❹ Just before the burgers are done, place split rolls on the grill to toast. Transfer 1 roll to each of 6 plates, and liberally spread mayonnaise over both halves of each roll. Top each roll with grilled burger, and serve hot.

CHICKEN BUYING OPTIONS

Most supermarkets offer you the following poultry options. Your first option is a bird pre-packaged by a big-name poultry producer. Those birds are processed according to USDA regulations which allow the birds to be fed hormones and antibiotics. The second option is a natural chicken, which is fed a special diet, but no antibiotics or growth hormones. The third option, free-range chickens, is probably the most natural. The chickens are allowed to move about freely and are fed grain and insects. They do not get antibiotics or hormones. These birds have a better flavor, but are more expensive.

Each serving			
Calories	268	Total Fat	5.5 g
Protein	21 g	Saturated Fat	2.2 g
Carbohydrates	32 g	Cholesterol	42 mg
Dietary Fiber	1 g	Sodium	484 mg

CHICKEN KEBABS WITH CHERRY TOMATOES AND HONEY-OREGANO SAUCE

MAKES 4 SERVINGS

This combination of chicken and tomatoes makes a pretty and flavorful dish. For more color, add broccoli or another green vegetable to the plate. A fresh spinach salad on the side would be ideal.

1 teaspoon canola oil

6 garlic cloves, peeled and each cut into 3 pieces

1 lb/455 g boneless, skinless, chicken breasts, trimmed and cut into 1 1/2-inch (4-cm) cubes

2 tablespoons honey

2 tablespoons finely chopped fresh oregano, or 2 teaspoons dried

1 jalapeño seeded and finely chopped, or a good pinch of red pepper flakes

juice of 1/2 lemon

12 cherry tomatoes, stemmed

❶ Heat the oil in a skillet; add garlic, and cook over medium heat until the garlic begins to lightly brown, about 2 minutes. Remove from the heat to cool.

❷ Place the chicken pieces in a large bowl, and add the remaining ingredients, except tomatoes. Add the garlic and oil, and toss well. Rinse and dry tomatoes. Prepare the grill.

❸ Thread the chicken onto 4 skewers, alternating with cherry tomatoes. When the fire is ready, oil the grid, and add the skewers. Grill 10 to 15 minutes, turning once or twice to grill all sides.

Each serving			
Calories	189	Total Fat	4 g
Protein	24 g	Saturated Fat	1 g
Carbohydrates	13 g	Cholesterol	63 mg
Dietary Fiber	1 g	Sodium	61 mg

GRILLED CHICKEN WITH LEBANESE FLAVORS

MAKES 4 SERVINGS

The flavors of the Mediterranean come alive in this simple preparation. You can serve the breasts whole, or sliced with a cool salad. For a refreshing, colorful salad, combine sliced cucumbers with slices of red and yellow bell peppers, roasted or raw.

4 boneless, skinless chicken breasts (about 1 lb/455 g), trimmed

juice of 1 whole lemon (3 tablespoons)

6 garlic cloves, halved

1 tablespoon paprika

2 teaspoons dried thyme

1 teaspoon ground cumin

pinch of red pepper flakes

salt to taste (optional)

❶ Rinse chicken and pat dry; place in a single layer in a shallow glass dish.

❷ In the bowl of a small food processor, combine remaining ingredients. Pulse until garlic is finely minced. Spread mixture on both sides of each chicken breast and let marinate overnight in the refrigerator. Bring to room temperature before grilling. Prepare the grill.

❸ When the fire is ready, lightly oil the grid. Put the chicken on the grill, and cook 4 minutes on each side. Remove, and season with salt.

Each serving			
Calories	141	Total Fat	3 g
Protein	24 g	Saturated Fat	1 g
Carbohydrates	4 g	Cholesterol	63 mg
Dietary Fiber	1 g	Sodium	57 mg

HONEY-HERBED CHICKEN

MAKES 4 SERVINGS

Here is another example of how to use spices, herbs, and citrus juices to create flavor for low-fat foods. You may want to add a few drops of honey on the chicken, just before serving, but this is optional, and only if you like a strong honey flavor.

3 tablespoons honey

2 tablespoons fresh lemon juice

1 tablespoon fresh orange juice

2 scallions, finely chopped

1 teaspoon each, finely chopped fresh: tarragon, thyme, and sage, or 1/3 teaspoon each dried

1 teaspoon fennel seeds, toasted and crushed

freshly ground black pepper to taste

4 small boneless, skinless, chicken breast halves, trimmed (about 1 lb/455 g total)

❶ In a large bowl, combine honey, lemon and orange juices, scallions, herbs, fennel seeds, and pepper; mix well. (Do not add more honey to the marinade, as it tends to scorch the chicken when it is on the grill.)

❷ Add the chicken, tossing to coat all sides. Let marinate 2 to 3 hours in the refrigerator. Bring to room temperature before grilling. Prepare the grill.

❸ When the fire is ready, lightly oil the grid, and add the chicken. Grill about 3 minutes on each side, turning once, and basting with marinade. Serve immediately.

Serving suggestion: Serve chicken with a romaine salad and grilled sweet potatoes (page 256). Clean and trim 1 head of romaine; cut it into quarters, lengthwise. Dress romaine with 2 or 3 tablespoons low-fat Caesar Salad Dressing (page 286).

Each serving			
Calories	178	Total Fat	3 g
Protein	23 g	Saturated Fat	1 g
Carbohydrates	15 g	Cholesterol	63 mg
Dietary Fiber	0 g	Sodium	57 mg

CHICKEN WITH SWEET BERRY SAUCE

MAKES 4 SERVINGS

This chicken dish clearly demonstrates the powerful use of herbs and spices when grilling low-fat foods. The sauce has punch and a little sweetness. Rice is the perfect accompaniment. Try Herbed Rice with Toasted Pine Nuts for a change from plain rice (page 137). Add sliced tomatoes dressed with vinaigrette, or a green salad tossed with low-fat dressing.

4 small boneless, skinless, defatted chicken breasts (about 1 lb/455 g total)

3 tablespoons finely chopped fresh thyme or 1 tablespoon dried

1 teaspoon paprika

freshly ground black pepper to taste

Sweet Berry Sauce (recipe follows)

hot, cooked rice

❶ Rinse and dry the chicken. In a small bowl, combine thyme, paprika, and pepper; rub mixture into both sides of each chicken breast. Let sit at room temperature 20 minutes, otherwise, refrigerate; bring to room temperature before grilling. Give both sides of each breast a quick spray of oil. Meanwhile, prepare the sauce.

❷ When the fire is ready, put the chicken on a lightly oiled grid. Grill about 3 minutes on each side; do not overcook, or chicken will be tough.

❸ To serve, spoon some rice in the center of each of 4 plates. Place 1 chicken breast atop each serving, then spoon the sauce over the chicken and onto the plate; do not completely cover the chicken with the sauce.

Each serving without sauce			
Calories	126	Total Fat	3 g
Protein	23 g	Saturated Fat	1 g
Carbohydrates	1 g	Cholesterol	63 mg
Dietary Fiber	0 g	Sodium	55 mg

SWEET BERRY SAUCE

1 teaspoon canola oil

2 garlic cloves, minced

2 tablespoons brown sugar

2 tablespoons white wine vinegar

1/2 cup (120 ml) dry white wine

1/2 cup (120 ml) low-sodium, defatted chicken broth

2 tablespoons blackberry preserves

1/2 teaspoon ground cumin

❶ Heat the oil in a saucepan over medium heat. Add garlic and sauté until lightly colored, 1 to 2 minutes.

❷ Add the remaining ingredients, then bring to a boil. Lower the heat to a steady simmer, and cook until reduced by half, about 6 to 8 minutes, stirring often; watch the sauce as it will reduce quickly. The sauce should be thick and syrupy.

Each serving			
Calories	80	Total Fat	1 g
Protein	1 g	Saturated Fat	0.1 g
Carbohydrates	12 g	Cholesterol	0 mg
Dietary Fiber	0 g	Sodium	69 mg

HERBED RICE WITH TOASTED PINE NUTS

MAKES 4 SERVINGS

2 cups (480 ml) low-sodium chicken broth

1 cup (181 g) uncooked long-grain rice

1/4 cup (76 g) finely chopped onion

1 tablespoon finely chopped fresh thyme, or 1 teaspoon dried

1/4 cup (38 g) toasted pine nuts

1/4 cup (28 g) finely chopped fresh flat-leaf parsley

1 Place broth in a saucepan with a tight-fitting lid; bring to a boil. Add rice, onions, and thyme. Lower the heat, cover, and simmer 20 minutes, or until the liquid is absorbed and the rice is tender. Remove from the heat, leaving the pan covered.

2 Heat a small skillet, preferably nonstick, over medium heat. Add pine nuts, and sauté, shaking the pan frequently, until they begin to color, 2 or 3 minutes. Add nuts to the rice.

3 Add parsley to rice mixture, and toss lightly.

THYME IS VIBRANT

Thyme's vibrant flavor has a special affinity for poultry and pork. French thyme has a smoky-green color, and some think a superior flavor.

Other varieties of thyme include lemon, orange, and caraway, all with different flavors. The plant is small and bushy, with dark-green leaves and purple flowers. This is a versatile herb, but use it with discretion. It also is good with fish and vegetables.

Each serving			
Calories	261	Total Fat	9 g
Protein	8 g	Saturated Fat	2 g
Carbohydrates	41 g	Cholesterol	2.5 mg
Dietary Fiber	2 g	Sodium	60 mg

GRILLED CHICKEN WITH MINTED MUSTARD SAUCE

MAKES 4 SERVINGS

Dijon mustard has become a household staple. Its impact on grilled foods is significant, often being used as an ingredient in a marinade or directly on the food to be grilled. In this recipe, Dijon-style mustard is used to make a delicious, biting sauce—perfect for chicken breasts. Adding mint to the sauce adds another dimension to its taste, and I know you'll like it. A word of caution: Since both hot sauce and black pepper are used, be careful with how much you use to begin with; you always can add more after tasting for spiciness.

2 to 3 boneless, skinless chicken breast halves (about 1 lb/455 g total), trimmed

spray oil

1/2 cup (120 ml) low-sodium, low-fat, chicken broth

1 small onion, finely chopped

1/4 cup (60 ml) Dijon-style mustard

1/4 cup (60 ml) honey

3 tablespoons finely chopped fresh mint, or 1 tablespoon dried, divided

juice of 1 whole lemon (3 tablespoons)

2 teaspoons Worcestershire sauce

1/2 teaspoon hot red pepper sauce

freshly ground black pepper to taste

4 thin slices fresh peeled papaya or orange slices, or 2 bananas, peeled and sliced lengthwise

❶ Rinse chicken breasts and pat dry; set aside at room temperature while preparing the grill and the sauce. Lightly oil the grid and the chicken; set aside.

Continued on next page

PAPAYA, A TROPICAL PRINCESS

Once rare and hard to find outside the tropics, papaya now is available in most markets year-round. It is sweet and delicious, and a good source of vitamin C. A papaya looks like a melon, with skin that is variegated with hues of green, yellow, orange, and red. Its tangerine-colored flesh is smooth as silk, and surrounds small, black seeds. The papaya is often confused with the papaw, which belongs to another fruit family. Papaya is a favorite ingredient in salsas, which pair well with grilled foods. A fresh slice or two served with grilled chicken or turkey is as tasty as can be.

2 To make the sauce, place 2 tablespoons chicken broth in a small saucepan. Bring to a boil, then add onions, and cook 3 minutes over medium heat, stirring 2 or 3 times. Add remaining broth, mustard, honey, 1 tablespoon fresh mint (or 1 teaspoon dried), lemon juice, Worcestershire, pepper sauce, and black pepper. Bring to a boil again, then lower the heat to a slow, steady simmer. Cook until broth mixture is as thick as heavy cream, about 10 minutes. Remove from the heat, keeping warm.

3 When the fire is ready, grill the breasts, about 3 to 4 minutes on each side, turning once. Remove from grill and let rest a few minutes; slice thinly.

4 To serve, divide sauce among 4 warmed plates, and arrange chicken slices over each portion of sauce. Sprinkle remaining mint over each serving, and garnish with fruit slices. Serve immediately.

TRIMMING THE FAT

Cooking on the grill is a good low-fat technique because it allows some of the fat to drip off the food as it cooks. When cooking skin-less chicken breasts, the fat content is about as low as it can get, so I add a tablespoon of oil to the marinade to help keep the breasts moist. You can elimi-nate the oil, and add a tablespoon of non-fat salad dressing, but be sure to baste the breasts often.

Each serving			
Calories	225	Total Fat	4 g
Protein	25 g	Saturated Fat	0.8 g
Carbohydrates	23 g	Cholesterol	63 mg
Dietary Fiber	1 g	Sodium	529 mg

GRILLED CHICKEN WITH SUMMER PEACH AND PLUM CHUTNEY

MAKES 4 SERVINGS

This easy-to-make chutney is the perfect companion to almost any type of grilled chicken, turkey, or pork dish. Make it ahead, and leave it in the refrigerator for up to ten days, so it will be ready when you want to grill some chicken.

1/4 cup (60 ml) Dijon-style mustard

2 tablespoons fresh lemon juice

2 tablespoons thawed apple juice concentrate

4 boneless, skinless, chicken breasts (about 1 lb/455 g total), trimmed

1/4 cup (43 g) finely sliced scallions

freshly ground black pepper to taste

Summer Peach and Plum Chutney (recipe follows)

❶ In a large bowl, combine mustard, lemon juice, and apple concentrate; mix well. Add chicken pieces, and turn to coat well. Let marinate 3 to 4 hours in the refrigerator, or 30 minutes at room temperature. Meanwhile, prepare the grill.

❷ When the fire is ready, lightly oil the grill, and season the chicken with pepper. Grill chicken about 4 minutes on each side, turning once.

❸ To serve, use a slotted spoon to place some about 1/4 cup (60 ml) chutney on each of 4 plates. Top each portion with a chicken breast, then sprinkle scallions over top.

Each serving (without chutney)			
Calories	159	Total Fat	4 g
Protein	24 g	Saturated Fat	1 g
Carbohydrates	6 g	Cholesterol	63 mg
Dietary Fiber	0 g	Sodium	437 mg

SUMMER PEACH AND PLUM CHUTNEY

MAKES ABOUT 3 CUPS

2 cups (455 g) sugar

1 cup (240 ml) white wine vinegar

2 tablespoons finely chopped fresh ginger

4 peaches, halved, seeded, and thinly sliced

4 purple or dark red plums, pitted and cut into 1/2-inch (1 1/4-cm) pieces

2 cups (190 g) blueberries, rinsed and drained

❶ Combine sugar, vinegar, and ginger in a medium-size saucepan. Bring to a boil, lower the heat, and simmer until the sugar dissolves.

❷ Add peaches, plums, and blueberries, and stir well with a wooden spoon. Remove from heat. Let the fruit marinate 1 hour. This may be made ahead several days and refrigerated.

Each tablespoon			
Calories	44	Total Fat	0.1 g
Protein	0 g	Saturated Fat	0 g
Carbohydrates	11 g	Cholesterol	0 mg
Dietary Fiber	0 g	Sodium	6 mg

ORANGE-HONEY GLAZED CHICKEN

MAKES 4 SERVINGS

In this easy-to-grill chicken recipe, I have used such fruit marm___
or lemon. If you are out of orange marmalade and have one of ___ free to
substitute.

1/4 cup (60 ml) sugar-free orange marmalade

2 tablespoons finely chopped fresh ginger

2 tablespoons each: honey, Dijon-style mustard, and white
   wine vinegar

1 tablespoon vegetable oil

2 teaspoons low-sodium soy sauce

1 large garlic clove, minced

4 boneless, skinless chicken breast halves (about 1 lb/455 g),
   trimmed

❶ Combine marmalade, ginger, honey, mustard, vinegar, oil, soy sauce, and garlic in a small, nonaluminum saucepan. Heat, stirring frequently, until the marmalade is melted, all ingredients are well blended, and the sauce has cooked down a little, 6 to 8 minutes. Cool.

❷ Rinse and dry the chicken, then place in a single layer in a large glass dish. Add the cooled marinade, being sure to coat chicken well. Cover with plastic wrap, and refrigerate for several hours. Bring to room temperature before grilling. Meanwhile, prepare the grill.

❸ When the fire is ready, oil the grid well. Shake excess marinade off chicken, letting the marinade fall back into the container, and place the chicken on the grill. Brush a liberal amount of marinade on top of each breast, as thickly as you can. Cover the grill, and cook 3 or 4 minutes. Turn the breasts, and add more marinade to the top of each. Cover the grill again; grill 3 to 4 minutes longer.

Serving suggestion: Serve hot with mashed potatoes and celery. Peel and cut 4 potatoes into 1/2-inch (1 1/4-cm) dice. Trim 3 celery ribs, remove strings, and slice thinly. Combine potatoes and celery in a large saucepan of lightly salted water; cover and bring to a boil. Boil until tender, about 15 minutes. Drain well. Add 1 tablespoon olive oil, 1 tablespoon celery seed, and a liberal amount of freshly ground black pepper. Mash by hand, and serve piping hot with the grilled chicken.

Each serving			
Calories	259	Total Fat	7 g
Protein	24 g	Saturated Fat	1.3 g
Carbohydrates	26 g	Cholesterol	63 mg
Dietary Fiber	1 g	Sodium	341 mg

ᴌᴌED CHICKEN ON A KEY WEST VERANDA

ᴍAKES 4 SERVINGS

Everyone in Key West has a grill and a veranda, or a porch, or an outside eating area. Here's a favorite of mine that I grill on my veranda. I often make a batch of this sauce, refrigerate it, and use it as I need it.

1 teaspoon canola oil

2 garlic cloves, minced

1/4 teaspoon ground cumin

2 tablespoons red wine vinegar

1 tablespoon red currant jelly, or any fruit juice concentrate

1 tablespoon fresh lemon juice

1 tablespoon Dijon-style mustard

1 teaspoon low-sodium soy sauce

ground ginger and red pepper flakes, to taste

4 small boneless, skinless, chicken breast halves, trimmed and flattened into cutlets

❶ Heat the oil in a small saucepan; add garlic, and cook over medium heat until the garlic starts to brown, 2 to 3 minutes. Add cumin, vinegar, and jelly, then cook until the jelly melts. Add lemon juice, mustard, soy sauce, ginger, and red pepper flakes. Cook, stirring until all ingredients are blended. Remove from heat to cool.

❷ Rinse and dry the chicken. Place chicken in a single layer in a glass dish. When the sauce has cooled, pour over chicken, turning to coat all sides. Cover and refrigerate 2 to 3 hours. Bring chicken to room temperature before grilling. Meanwhile, prepare the grill.

❸ When the fire is ready, oil the grid lightly, then add the chicken. Grill 4 minutes on each side, turning once. This is good with plain mashed potatoes.

Each serving (not including potatoes)			
Calories	157	Total Fat	4 g
Protein	23 g	Saturated Fat	1 g
Carbohydrates	6 g	Cholesterol	63 mg
Dietary Fiber	0 g	Sodium	194 mg

GRILLED CHICKEN WITH YOGURT AND MINT

MAKES 6 SERVINGS

Fereydoun Kia, a leading restaurateur in Buenos Aires, Argentina, cooked this for me in his home there. He cooked it over a very hard wood called *quebracho,* which means ax-breaker, as the wood is very hard. He also added a handful of fresh mint to the fire before he added the chicken. To add fresh herbs to the fire, first immerse them in water, then shake off any excess water. Instead of a *quebracho* fire, I've used both charcoal and gas grills, and both work fine. Be careful not to overcook the chicken.

1 1/2 cups (360 ml) nonfat plain yogurt

3/4 cups (84 g) finely chopped fresh mint, plus whole sprigs
    for the fire

4 garlic cloves, minced

1 teaspoon ground cumin

4 drops hot red pepper sauce

6 small boneless, skinless, chicken breast halves
    (about 1 1/2 lbs total), trimmed

❶ Combine all the ingredients in a shallow bowl, being sure to thoroughly coat the chicken. Let marinate 1 hour at room temperature, or overnight in the refrigerator; bring breasts to room temperature before grilling.

❷ Prepare the fire, and lightly oil the grid. Add the extra mint sprigs to the fire, then add the chicken to the grill. Cover and grill chicken 3 to 4 minutes on each side.

Serving suggestion: Serve with Garlic Sweet Grilled Tomatoes (page 253) or Yellow Summer Squash Grilled with Polynesian Sauce (page 258).

Each serving (not including side dishes)			
Calories	191	Total Fat	3 g
Protein	29 g	Saturated Fat	0.8 g
Carbohydrates	10 g	Cholesterol	64 mg
Dietary Fiber	3 g	Sodium	135 mg

GRILLED CHICKEN TACOS WITH CHARRED TOMATOES

MAKES 4 SERVINGS

These charred tomatoes are so delicious, you will want to use them with many other things you grill. Here, they go very well with the warmed tortillas, grilled chicken, and condiments.

> Charred Tomatoes (recipe follows)
>
> 1 lb (455 g) boneless, skinless, chicken breasts, trimmed
>
> spray oil
>
> 8 corn tortillas, warmed
>
> 4 scallions, chopped
>
> 1/4 cup (60 ml) nonfat sour cream
>
> 1 lime, quartered and seeded

❶ Prepare Charred Tomatoes, then set aside while preparing chicken tacos.

❷ Rinse the chicken, then pat dry. Spray oil on the chicken. Lightly oil the hot grid, then add chicken. Grill 3 to 4 minutes on each side. Remove from the grill to a cutting surface, and slice each breast into 1/4-inch (5/8-cm) strips.

❸ To assemble the tacos, place a heaping tablespoon of tomatoes and juice on 1 tortilla, spreading evenly. Add several chicken strips, scallions, a dollop of sour cream, and a squirt of lime juice; roll the taco. Repeat to make 8 soft tacos. Place 2 tacos on each of 4 plates, and serve immediately.

TORTILLAS AND TACOS

A tortilla is a thin, flat bread made from corn or wheat flour, and baked on a griddle.

When deep-fried, tortillas become crispy, as in tortilla chips, taco shells, and tostadas, but these are high-fat so we will focus on soft tortillas in this book.

Soft tortillas (corn and flour) can be filled with poultry, meat, beans, and vegetables, and served as soft tacos. Tortillas that are filled and rolled, then heavily sauced and baked are enchiladas. Large flour tortillas that are filled and wrapped, completely enveloping the stuffing, are burritos.

Each serving (without tomatoes)			
Calories	234	Total Fat	4 g
Protein	26 g	Saturated Fat	1 g
Carbohydrates	22 g	Cholesterol	63 mg
Dietary Fiber	0 g	Sodium	72 mg

CHARRED TOMATOES

3 large ripe tomatoes, quartered

1 medium-size onion, chopped

2 garlic cloves, minced

1 tablespoon raw sugar

1 tablespoon finely chopped cilantro

1 jalapeño pepper, seeded, and finely chopped

teaspoon olive oil

❶ Squeeze the juice and seeds from tomato quarters. Arrange tomatoes in a single layer on a double thickness of foil that is large enough to envelop them. Sprinkle with onion, garlic, sugar, cilantro, and jalapeño. Carefully sprinkle oil over the top. Enclose the packet in a Bundle Wrap (page 10). Prepare the grill.

❷ When the fire is ready, place the packet on the grid and close the cover; grill 15 minutes. Remove packet from the grill, and set aside while preparing tacos.

Each serving (tomatoes only)			
Calories	59	Total Fat	1.5 g
Protein	1 g	Saturated Fat	0.2 g
Carbohydrates	10 g	Cholesterol	0 mg
Dietary Fiber	2 g	Sodium	10 mg

GRILLED CHICKEN WITH TABBOULEH

MAKES 4 SERVINGS

This is a refreshing dish, and I like it best when red, ripe tomatoes are available. If you like, combine some fresh mint with the parsley when making the tabbouleh.

1 lb (455 g) boneless, skinless, chicken breast halves, trimmed

2 tablespoons balsamic vinegar

3 cups (710 ml) water

pinch of salt

1 cup (165 g) bulgur

2 tomatoes, cored, skinned, seeded, and finely chopped

1/4 cup (28 g) finely chopped flat-leaf parsley

juice of 1 whole lemon (3 tablespoons)

1 teaspoon canola oil

spray oil

❶ In a large, shallow dish, combine chicken and vinegar; marinate 30 minutes to 1 hour at room temperature.

❷ Bring the water to boil in a medium-size saucepan; add salt and bulgur. Cover, lower the heat to get a slow, steady simmer, then cook 10 minutes. Remove from heat, and let sit 15 minutes, covered. Drain well, then transfer to a glass bowl. Meanwhile, prepare the grill.

❸ Add tomatoes, parsley (and mint, if you wish), lemon juice, and oil to the bulgur. Toss well; set aside.

❹ When the fire is ready, spray the chicken with oil, then grill it about 4 minutes on each side, turning once, and brushing with any vinegar left in the bowl. To serve, place a large spoonful of tabbouleh on each of 4 plates; top each portion with a chicken breast.

Serving suggestion: Grilled eggplant, fennel slices, mushrooms, or any of the grilled vegetable skewers in this book go well with this dish.

BULGUR

Bulgur is a form of cracked wheat, processed by a method like that used to make converted rice. Kernels of whole wheat are steamed, then dried, and crushed into various grinds: coarse, used for pilaf; medium, for cereal; and fine, for tabbouleh.

Generally, 1/2 cup (83 g) of uncooked bulgur, cooked in one cup (240 ml) of liquid for 15 minutes, will yield 1 1/2 cups (310 g).

Be inventive in changing the flavors of tabbouleh by allowing the herbs and spices to suit your taste.

Each serving (not including vegetables)			
Calories	327	Total Fat	7 g
Protein	36 g	Saturated Fat	1.4 g
Carbohydrates	38 g	Cholesterol	63 mg
Dietary Fiber	18 g	Sodium	274 mg

GRILLED QUAIL WITH GOAT CHEESE

MAKES 4 SERVINGS

There is nothing like the distinctive taste of quail grilled over charcoal.

4 (4- to 5-oz/113- to 142-g) boneless European-style quail
    spray oil
    juice of 1/2 lemon
1 tablespoon each: Dijon-style mustard and seasoned rice vinegar
1 tablespoon finely chopped fresh tarragon, or 1 teaspoon dried
1 large garlic clove, minced
    freshly ground black pepper to taste
4 teaspoons crumbled goat cheese

❶ If you don't order the quail from one of the sources in the back of the book, ask your butcher to remove the back and breast bones, so the birds lie flat. Lightly spray them with oil. Set aside.

❷ In a small bowl, combine lemon juice, mustard, rice vinegar, tarragon, garlic, and pepper; mix well. Brush the marinade on both sides of each quail, then put them in a glass dish. Cover and refrigerate overnight, or a minimum of 3 hours. Bring to room temperature for at least 1/2 hour before grilling. Meanwhile, prepare the eggplant.

❸ Prepare the grill. Lightly spray the grid with oil. When the fire is ready, grill the quail skin side down, about 5 minutes. Turn, and grill the other side 5 minutes more.

❹ To serve, sprinkle goat cheese over top of grilled quail.

Each serving			
Calories	239	Total Fat	16 g
Protein	24 g	Saturated Fat	4.6 g
Carbohydrates	1.3 g	Cholesterol	88 mg
Dietary Fiber	.8 g	Sodium	174 mg

CURRIED CHICKEN WITH EGGPLANT AND SWEET ONION RELISH

MAKES 4 SERVINGS

This skewer features grilled chicken and eggplant, set on a fresh-tasting, mouth-watering Sweet Onion Relish, also very easy to make.

4 small boneless, skinless, chicken breasts, trimmed (1 lb/455 g total)

1 tablespoon curry powder

freshly ground black pepper to taste

1 lb (455 g) firm eggplant

Sweet Onion Relish (recipe follows)

spray oil

1/4 cup (60 ml) nonfat sour cream

4 teaspoons prepared horseradish

juice of 1/2 lemon

❶ Cut each chicken breast into 5 pieces; place in a resealable plastic bag. Add curry and black pepper. Seal the bag, and massage it carefully to coat chicken with spices. Transfer mixture to a plate.

❷ Remove the ends of the eggplant. Remove 1/2-inch (1 1/4-cm) strips of skin lengthwise from eggplant with a vegetable peeler, so the eggplant has a striped appearance. Cut crosswise into 1-inch (2 1/2-cm) slices. Cut each slice into 1-inch (2 1/2-cm) chunks (don't fret; the chunks will not be square). You should have about 25 pieces of eggplant for skewering. Prepare Sweet Onion Relish.

❸ Thread long skewers with alternating pieces of eggplant and chicken, beginning and ending with eggplant. Use 6 eggplant pieces and 5 chicken pieces to each skewer. Season with black pepper, then spray oil on both sides of each skewer.

❹ Prepare the grill. Lightly spray oil on the grid. When the fire is ready, add the skewers, and grill, turning several times to grill all sides, about 10 minutes total. Remove from grill.

Continued on next page

5 In a small bowl, blend sour cream, horseradish, and lemon juice. Place a spoonful of the horseradish sauce on each of 4 plates.

6 To serve, place a spoonful of onion relish on each plate. Lay a skewer, hot off the grill, on top. Serve immediately.

Each serving (without relish)			
Calories	175	Total Fat	3 g
Protein	25 g	Saturated Fat	1 g
Carbohydrates	12 g	Cholesterol	63 mg
Dietary Fiber	3 g	Sodium	75 mg

SWEET ONION RELISH

MAKES 4 SERVINGS

2 red onions, halved and very thinly sliced

1 dried small red pepper, halved lengthwise, or a pinch of red pepper flakes

spray oil

1/4 cup (60 ml) red wine vinegar

1/4 cup (60 ml) low-sodium vegetable broth

freshly ground black pepper to taste

salt to taste (optional)

1 Place onions and red pepper in a shallow bowl, and lightly spray oil on them.

2 In another bowl, combine vinegar, broth, and black pepper; pour vinegar mixture over onion mixture. Toss with wooden spoons (don't use your hands; the hot pepper will burn). Add a pinch of salt. Leave at room temperature 1 hour before serving.

Each serving			
Calories	32	Total Fat	0.2 g
Protein	1 g	Saturated Fat	0 g
Carbohydrates	8 g	Cholesterol	0 mg
Dietary Fiber	1 g	Sodium	65 mg

SPICY SAFFRON CHICKEN KEBABS

THE STRONG BITE OF HORSERADISH

Prepared horseradish is sold bottled in most supermarkets, and usually comes in three forms: with vinegar and salt (sodium content is surprisingly low); with beet juice, which makes it red; and as a cream sauce, which we will not use, as it is made with mayonnaise. You can make your own horseradish by grating it fresh. Fresh horseradish is considerably more pungent, so add it with discretion.

MAKES 4 SERVINGS

This is quite a spicy dish; notice the amount of hot sauce. If you would prefer less spice, decrease the amount of hot sauce. These kebabs are best served with New Potatoes on the Grill (page 243) or grilled potato slices, and a sprinkle of chopped scallions.

1/2 teaspoon saffron threads
1/2 cup (120 ml) nonfat plain yogurt
1 onion, minced
3 garlic cloves, minced
2 teaspoons hot red pepper sauce
  juice of 1 whole lemon (3 tablespoons)
1 tablespoon honey
1 teaspoon ground cumin
  pinch of ground allspice
1 lb (455 g) boneless, skinless, chicken breasts, trimmed and cut into 1 1/4-inch (3 1/4-cm) chunks

1 Combine saffron and 2 tablespoons hot water in a small bowl; let steep 5 minutes.

2 In a shallow glass dish, combine the yogurt, onion, garlic, hot sauce, lemon juice, honey, cumin, and allspice; blend well, then stir in the saffron water. Add chicken chunks, and toss to coat well. Arrange chicken in a single layer, then cover with plastic wrap, and refrigerate for 1 hour, or overnight. Remove from refrigerator 30 minutes before grilling.

3 Thread chicken onto 4 skewers. When the fire is ready, put skewers on a lightly oiled grid. Grill about 10 minutes, turning often to grill all sides. Be sure to baste with leftover marinade as often as you can, to help keep the chicken moist.

Each serving			
Calories	171	Total Fat	3 g
Protein	25 g	Saturated Fat	1 g
Carbohydrates	10 g	Cholesterol	63 mg
Dietary Fiber	1 g	Sodium	81 mg

CHICKEN KEBABS WITH HOT MANGO RELISH

MAKES 4 SERVINGS

This is a favorite of mine because the tasty relish may be made ahead, and the chicken pieces cooked just a few minutes before serving. You also may use other marinades in this book to season the chicken, then serve it with this relish.

Hot Mango Relish (recipe follows)

1 lb (455 g) boneless, skinless, chicken breasts, trimmed

2 tablespoons juice from Hot Mango Relish

1 tablespoon low-sodium tamari

spray oil

❶ Prepare relish at least 1 day ahead; store in refrigerator. Rinse chicken and pat dry; cut into 1-inch (2 1/2-cm) cubes, and put in a glass bowl. Add relish juice and soy sauce, and toss well. Let marinate for 2 hours or more.

❷ Thread chicken onto 4 skewers (if using wooden skewers, be sure to soak in water at least 30 minutes). Prepare the grill.

❸ When the fire is ready, lightly oil the grid. Spray oil on the chicken, then grill about 8 minutes, turning as necessary to grill all sides.

❹ To serve, place a spoon of relish on each of 4 plates, and top with a skewer of chicken. Pass any remaining relish. Serve immediately.

Serving suggestion: Garlicky Mashed Potatoes (page 246) will make this a complete meal.

Each serving (without relish)			
Calories	124	Total Fat	2.6 g
Protein	23 g	Saturated Fat	0.8 g
Carbohydrates	0 g	Cholesterol	63 mg
Dietary Fiber	0 g	Sodium	257 mg

HOT MANGO RELISH

MAKES ABOUT 1 1/2 CUPS (340 G)

1/4 cup (60 ml) plus 1 tablespoon water

2 tablespoons sugar

1 tablespoon mustard seeds

1 (1-inch/2 1/2-cm) piece fresh ginger, peeled and coarsely chopped

1 dried red chile, seeded, and coarsely chopped

2 garlic cloves, minced

2 tablespoons seasoned rice vinegar

1/2 large fresh mango, peeled and thinly sliced

❶ In a saucepan, combine water, sugar, mustard seeds, ginger, chile, and garlic. Bring to boil, lower the heat, and simmer just until the sugar dissolves, 3 or 4 minutes. Remove from heat, add vinegar, and stir.

❷ Put mango slices in a small container with a tight-fitting lid. Pour the chile-ginger mixture over the mango, toss well, cover, and marinate overnight in the refrigerator.

THE NEED FOR MUSTARD SEED

The traditional mustard seed is the yellow variety, which is sold in small cans and jars. Another mustard seed, which is more common in Asian, Indian, and African cooking, is the brown variety. A friend from Nepal taught me to sauté the seeds (yellow or brown) in a skillet over medium heat, with just a hint of oil, until they "burst" and release their nutty flavor.

Mustard seeds add a great flavor to salsas, sauces, marinades, and relishes.

Each serving (relish only)			
Calories	60	Total Fat	1 g
Protein	1 g	Saturated Fat	0.1 g
Carbohydrates	13 g	Cholesterol	0 mg
Dietary Fiber	1 g	Sodium	5 mg

TASTY TURKEY BURGERS

MAKES 6 SERVINGS

For added taste, dress several lettuce leaves with honey-mustard vinaigrette, then add the lettuce to the burgers.

1 lb (455 g) fresh ground turkey (page 159)

1/2 cup (28 g) fresh bread crumbs

1/2 cup (152 g) finely chopped onion

2 tablespoons finely chopped fresh flat-leaf parsley

1/4 cup (60 ml) ketchup

juice of 1/2 lemon (about 1 1/2 tablespoons)

1 teaspoon Worcestershire sauce

1 teaspoon low-sodium soy sauce

freshly ground black pepper to taste

6 sandwich rolls, split

6 lettuce leaves

honey-mustard vinaigrette, optional

1 Combine turkey and bread crumbs in a large bowl; add onion and parsley.

2 In a small bowl, combine the ketchup, lemon juice, Worcestershire, soy sauce, and pepper. Mix well, then pour over the turkey mixture. With splayed fingers, lightly mix until combined. Lightly form into 6 burgers. Put burgers on a plate, spraying oil on both sides of each.

3 Prepare the grill; spray a wire basket with oil. When the fire is ready, arrange the burgers in the basket, taking care to properly adjust the basket so the burgers don't fall out. Put the basket on the fire, and grill 4 to 5 minutes. Turn and grill 4 to 5 minutes longer.

4 Just before the burgers are done, place the split rolls on the grill; watch rolls carefully, as they grill quickly. Transfer 1 roll to each of 6 plates; top each with a grilled burger, then add lettuce leaf dressed in honey-mustard vinaigrette.

Each serving (without honey-mustard vinaigrette)			
Calories	255	Total Fat	4 g
Protein	24 g	Saturated Fat	2 g
Carbohydrates	30 g	Cholesterol	52 mg
Dietary Fiber	2 g	Sodium	457 mg

GRILLED TURKEY BURGERS WITH FAR-EAST ONION SALSA

MAKES 4 SERVINGS

Turkey burgers, popular because of the significantly lower fat content than beef, are especially delicious served with this tasty salsa.

Far-East Onion Salsa (recipe follows)

1 lb (455 g) ground turkey (see sidebar)

1/2 cup (28 g) fresh white bread crumbs

1/4 cup (28 g) finely chopped flat-leaf parsley

1/4 cup (76 g) finely chopped onions

1 egg white, beaten

freshly ground black pepper to taste

2 tablespoons low-sodium soy sauce, divided

❶ Prepare Onion Salsa and refrigerate until ready to serve.

❷ In a large bowl, combine all ingredients, except onion salsa and 1 tablespoon soy sauce. Lightly mix with splayed fingers; do not overmix. Lightly form into 4 burgers. Brush both sides with remaining 1 tablespoon soy sauce; set aside.

❸ Prepare the grill; lightly spray the grid with oil. When the fire is ready, spray the burgers with oil; grill on each side about 5 minutes.

❹ To serve, put a burger on each of 4 plates, and spoon 1/4 cup (60 ml) salsa alongside each burger.

GROUND TURKEY

For meat lovers, one of the best ways to reduce saturated fat is to use ground turkey instead of ground beef, turkey cutlets instead of beef steaks, and turkey tenders instead of sirloin tips.

For high flavor and low fat, ground turkey breast yourself making sure the turkey is fresh and skinless. If you must buy ground turkey, check the nutritional analysis on the package. Some processors add fat and skin to the ground turkey. This can make ground turkey higher is saturated fat than ground beef.

Each serving (without salsa)			
Calories	157	Total Fat	1.4 g
Protein	29 g	Saturated Fat	0.4 g
Carbohydrates	5 g	Cholesterol	77 mg
Dietary Fiber	0.4 g	Sodium	347 mg

FAR-EAST ONION SALSA

1 large sweet onion (such as Texas, Vidalia, or Maui), finely
   chopped (1 cup/304 g)

1/4 red, yellow, or orange bell pepper, finely chopped

8 snow peas, trimmed and finely chopped

3 tablespoons fresh lime juice

1 tablespoon each: low-sodium soy sauce and sesame oil

1 teaspoon sugar

   curry powder and red pepper flakes to taste

2 tablespoons toasted sesame seeds (see note)

   salt to taste (optional)

❶ Combine onion, bell pepper, and snow peas in a large bowl.

❷ In another bowl, combine lime juice, soy sauce, sesame oil, sugar, curry, and red pepper flakes. Mix well and pour over the onion mixture. Stir in toasted sesame seeds; add a pinch of salt if you wish.

❸ Cover and refrigerate until needed.

Note: To toast sesame seeds, place them in a small skillet over low heat. Toast them until lightly golden, 2 to 3 minutes, stirring frequently.

Each serving			
Calories	86	Total Fat	6 g
Protein	2 g	Saturated Fat	1 g
Carbohydrates	8 g	Cholesterol	0 mg
Dietary Fiber	1 g	Sodium	129 mg

PHYLLIS ROSE'S TURKEY BURGERS

MAKES 6 SERVINGS

My friend Phyllis Rose is an educator, writer, and excellent cook. She also makes a delicious, low-fat burger.

3 slices fresh ginger, peeled and cut into small dice

1 small onion, peeled and chopped

1 1/4 lbs (570 g) fresh turkey breast medallions

1 1/2 teaspoons Madras curry powder

1 egg white, beaten

1 cup (56 g) fresh white bread crumbs

freshly ground black pepper to taste

salt to taste (optional)

1 teaspoon tamari

1 tablespoon apple juice concentrate, thawed

spray oil

❶ Combine ginger and onion in the bowl of a food processor; chop with several pulses. Add turkey and curry powder, and pulse until turkey is chopped. Transfer to a mixing bowl.

❷ Add egg white, bread crumbs, pepper, and a pinch of salt; mix lightly by hand. Form into 6 patties. Place them on a plate, cover with plastic wrap, and refrigerate at least 30 minutes. Meanwhile, prepare the grill.

❸ In a small bowl, combine tamari and apple juice concentrate; brush the patties lightly just before grilling.

❹ When the fire is ready, spray the grid with oil. Spray oil on the patties; then grill 5 to 7 minutes on each side, basting with the tamari mixture.

Each serving (not including side dishes)			
Calories	185	Total Fat	2 g
Protein	26 g	Saturated Fat	0.5 g
Carbohydrates	15 g	Cholesterol	64 mg
Dietary Fiber	1 g	Sodium	241 mg

GRILLED QUAIL IN CITRUS MARINADE

MAKES 4 SERVINGS

A friend, and excellent chef, told me that he marinates quail and squab for three nights. As delicious as this quail may be, I think you can get by with less marinating time.

1/4 cup (60 ml) fresh orange juice

1/4 cup (60 ml) fresh lemon juice

1/4 cup (60 ml) low-sodium soy sauce

1/4 cup (60 ml) white wine

4 garlic cloves, minced

1 tablespoon plus 1 teaspoon finely chopped fresh rosemary, or 1 1/4 teaspoons dried, divided

4 (4- to 5-oz/113- to 142-g) boneless quail

spray oil

1 In a large bowl, combine orange and lemon juices, soy sauce, wine, garlic, and 1 tablespoon rosemary (or 1 teaspoon dried) for the marinade.

2 Add the quail, and turn the birds to coat them completely. Let marinate overnight, or at least 2 hours.

3 Prepare the grill. Lightly spray the grid with oil. Remove the quail from the marinade, reserving the marinade for basting, and spray oil on both sides of each bird. When the fire is ready, grill the birds 5 minutes on each side, basting often with the reserved marinade.

4 Remove the quail from the grill, and sprinkle with remaining rosemary; serve immediately.

Serving suggestion: Serve hot with Grilled Peaches with Brandied Frozen Yogurt (page 331).

Each serving (not including peaches)			
Calories	257	Total Fat	14 g
Protein	23 g	Saturated Fat	4 g
Carbohydrates	8 g	Cholesterol	83 mg
Dietary Fiber	1 g	Sodium	565 mg

GRILLED TURKEY CUTLETS WITH WATERMELON AND HONEYDEW SALSA

MAKES 4 SERVINGS

This is a refreshing dish to make during spring or summer, when the markets are full of deep-pink watermelons and pale-green honeydew melons. Sweet, crisp melons combine with pungent cilantro and tart lemons for a refreshing contrast in taste—perfect for a summer luncheon outdoors.

spray oil

4 turkey cutlets (about 1 lb/455 g)

2 tablespoons finely chopped fresh tarragon, or 2 teaspoons dried

freshly ground black pepper to taste

pinch of salt (optional)

4 teaspoons honey, warmed

8 chives

Watermelon and Honeydew Salsa (recipe follows)

❶ Prepare the grill and lightly spray the grid with oil.

❷ Dry the cutlets and spray oil on both sides of each. Rub tarragon into cutlets, coating both sides. Sprinkle liberally with black pepper, then season with salt.

❸ When the fire is ready, put the cutlets on the grill, and cook about 4 minutes on each side, or until browned.

❹ To serve, divide cutlets among each of 4 plates. Add 1/2 to 1 cup (120 to 240 ml) salsa to the side of each cutlet; do not cover the meat with the salsa. Using 1 teaspoon honey per serving, drizzle honey over the cutlets and salsa in long, thin lines. Crisscross 2 chives on top of each serving.

CHIVES

Related to onions, chives are thinner than scallions, and look more like grass, but with hollow shoots. This verdant herb forms no bulbs, so only the shoots are used. Grow chives in a pot, or in the ground near your grill, and pick them fresh when you want to use them. Using scissors, snip them into your sauces, marinades, and salsas, and use them as often as you can, snipped or whole, as a garnish. They will add a lively touch of flavor and color to any savory dish. A perennial herb, when planted in the ground, chives will return to see you the following spring.

Each serving (without salsa)			
Calories	151	Total Fat	1.2 g
Protein	27 g	Saturated Fat	0.4 g
Carbohydrates	6.5 g	Cholesterol	77 mg
Dietary Fiber	0.2 g	Sodium	227 mg

WATERMELON AND HONEYDEW SALSA

2 cups (302 g) small pieces seeded watermelon

2 cups (363 g) small pieces seeded honeydew melon

1/4 cup (28 g) finely chopped fresh chives

1/4 cup (43 g) finely chopped scallions

1 to 2 finely chopped jalapeños

2 tablespoons finely chopped fresh cilantro

1 teaspoon sugar

juice and pulp of 2 lemons

salt to taste (optional)

In a large glass bowl, combine all ingredients; cover and refrigerate until needed (no more than 1 hour). If desired, season with a pinch of salt before serving.

Each serving			
Calories	67	Total Fat	0.5 g
Protein	1 g	Saturated Fat	0.1 g
Carbohydrates	15 g	Cholesterol	0 mg
Dietary Fiber	1 g	Sodium	12 mg

GRILLED TURKEY MEDALLIONS WITH MANGO CHUTNEY

MAKES 4 SERVINGS

Prepare the chutney several days ahead, then reheat it before serving. For uniformity, chop the fruit and onion into 1/2-inch (1 1/4-cm) pieces. This chutney is very tasty with turkey medallions, cutlets, or burgers, and will complement chicken and pork, as well.

  1 lb (455 g) turkey medallions, or 4 cutlets

  spray oil

  2 tablespoons apple juice concentrate, thawed

  Mango Chutney (recipe follows)

❶ Prepare the grill, and lightly spray oil on the grid. When the fire is ready, spray oil on both sides of each turkey medallion. Place turkey on the grill and cook 3 to 4 minutes on each side, basting frequently with the undiluted apple juice, turning once.

❷ To serve, divide turkey among 4 warmed plates; add 2 tablespoons warm chutney to the side of each serving, slightly overlapping the meat.

Each serving (without chutney)			
Calories	140	Total Fat	1.1 g
Protein	27 g	Saturated Fat	0.4 g
Carbohydrates	4 g	Cholesterol	7 mg
Dietary Fiber	0 g	Sodium	52 mg

MANGO CHUTNEY

3 1/2 cups (578 g) peeled, chopped mangoes, reserve juices
2 Granny Smith apples, cored, peeled, and chopped
    zest and juice of 1 orange
2 cups (480 ml) apple cider
1 1/2 cups (425 g) sugar
1 1/2 cups (456 g) chopped onions
1/2 cup (76 g) raisins
2 tablespoons finely chopped fresh ginger
1 teaspoon red pepper flakes
1/2 teaspoon each, ground: allspice, cloves, and cinnamon
    pinch of salt

❶ Combine all ingredients in a saucepan, and bring to a boil over medium heat.

❷ Lower the heat, and simmer, partially covered, until the chutney thickens, 30 to 40 minutes.

❸ Use immediately, or store, tightly covered, in the refrigerator until needed.

Each serving			
Calories	36	Total Fat	.07 g
Protein	.2 g	Saturated Fat	.02 g
Carbohydrates	9 g	Cholesterol	0 mg
Dietary Fiber	.4 g	Sodium	.81 mg

TURKEY KEBABS WITH HERBED LEMON BUTTER

MAKES 4 SERVINGS

This is a pleasant, easy, and healthy dish. In addition to grilled tomatoes, add an ear of grilled corn to each plate.

1/2 cup (120 ml) liquid butter substitute

2 tablespoons each, finely chopped fresh: rosemary and thyme, or 2 teaspoons each dried

4 garlic cloves, minced

2 teaspoons grated orange or lemon zest

1 lb (455 g) boneless, skinless, turkey breast, trimmed and cut into 1 1/4-inch (3 1/4-cm) chunks or 1 lb (455 g) turkey medallions (16 pieces)

❶ Combine butter substitute, herbs, garlic, and zest in a bowl; mix well. Add turkey chunks, and let marinate 2 to 3 hours in the refrigerator. Bring to room temperature before grilling. Prepare the grill.

❷ Thread turkey chunks onto 4 skewers, with pieces just touching, not crammed onto the skewers.

❸ When the fire is ready, put the skewers on a lightly oiled grid. Grill 8 to 10 minutes, turning as needed to grill all sides. Baste frequently with remaining marinade.

Serving suggestion: Serve immediately with Garlic Sweet Grilled Tomatoes (page 253).

Each serving (not including tomatoes)			
Calories	153	Total Fat	1.3 g
Protein	27 g	Saturated Fat	0.4 g
Carbohydrates	6 g	Cholesterol	77 mg
Dietary Fiber	0 g	Sodium	111 mg

GRILLED CHICKEN BREAST PIECES IN SPICY ANISE SAUCE

MAKES 4 SERVINGS

Here the whole chicken breasts are chopped into smaller pieces—about three per half breast. After marinating in an unusual sauce including red chilies and dried star anise, the chicken is skewered and grilled. Dried anise stars, available in most Chinese and other specialty food shops, are inexpensive but flavorful. Throw six or eight of them on the fire and lower the grill cover for added flavor.

4 large chicken breasts (about 1 1/2 to 2 pounds)

1/4 cup dry sherry

1 tbsp peanut oil

2 tbsp soy sauce

1 tablespoon sesame oil

4 green onions, trimmed and cut into 1-inch pieces

12 dried Chinese black mushrooms

2 tablespoons grated fresh ginger

4 small whole dried red chilies

4 dried star anise

1 tablespoon sugar

   salt, optional

❶ Remove the skin from each chicken piece. Chop breasts into 2-inch pieces with breastbone in. Wash and dry well. Place in one layer in a glass, ceramic, or stainless steel dish.

❷ Mix all other ingredients and pour over chicken pieces. Marinate overnight in refrigerator, turning meat several times, or marinate at room temperature for 3 hours.

❸ When the fire is ready, remove chicken pieces from marinade and skewer them; reserve marinade. If you have extra star anise, add some to the fire. Grill, basting frequently with leftover marinade.

❹ Bring leftover marinade, if any, to boil. Distribute by spoonfuls onto 4 warmed plates. Add 1 star anise and 1 small red chili for garnish to each plate. Place grilled chicken pieces over sauce and serve.

Each serving			
Calories	361	Total Fat	9.5 g
Protein	48.5 g	Saturated Fat	1.7 g
Carbohydrates	13.7 g	Cholesterol	115 mg
Dietary Fiber	1.2 g	Sodium	720 mg

GRILLED TURKEY KEBABS WITH FRESH ORANGE AND CRANBERRY SALSA

MAKES 8 SERVINGS

Most of the alcohol in this recipe will cook off during grilling, leaving a subtle sherry flavor. If you wish, substitute one cup (240 ml) freshly squeezed orange juice for the sherry.

    1 skinless turkey breast (2 to 3 lb/1 to 1 1/2 kg), cut into
      1 1/2-inch (4-cm) cubes

    1 cup (240 ml) dry sherry

    2 tablespoons finely chopped fresh rosemary, or 2 teaspoons
      dried, crushed

    spray oil

    salt (optional) and freshly ground black pepper, to taste

    Fresh Orange and Cranberry Salsa (recipe follows)

❶ Place turkey pieces in a single layer in a large, shallow glass dish. Add sherry and rosemary, then toss well to coat. Cover and refrigerate 2 or 3 hours, tossing several times. Bring to room temperature before grilling. Meanwhile, prepare salsa and the grill.

❷ Thread turkey pieces onto 8 skewers, then lightly spray them with oil. When the fire is ready, grill skewers until turkey pieces are browned at the edges, 10 to 15 minutes, turning 2 or 3 times to grill all sides. Season with salt and pepper. Divide skewers among 8 plates, then place 2 tablespoons salsa to the side of each skewer.

Serving suggestion: Honey Grilled Onions with Cloves (page 229) would be delicious with this turkey dish.

Each serving (without salsa)			
Calories	178	Total Fat	1.4 g
Protein	34 g	Saturated Fat	0.4 g
Carbohydrates	1 g	Cholesterol	96 mg
Dietary Fiber	0 g	Sodium	65 mg

FRESH ORANGE AND CRANBERRY SALSA

MAKES ABOUT 1 CUP

1 cup (113 g) fresh or frozen cranberries

2 teaspoons grated orange zest

1 large orange, peeled, sectioned, and chopped

3 scallions, finely chopped, including green tops

2 teaspoons each, minced fresh: ginger, cilantro or flat-leaf parsley, and seeded jalapeño

salt to taste (optional)

❶ Coarsely chop cranberries in a food processor.

❷ Transfer to a bowl, and add zest and orange pieces.

❸ Add remaining ingredients and stir well; let flavors blend at room temperature at least 30 minutes, or longer if refrigerated.

❹ Use as directed.

Each salsa serving (1 tablespoon)			
Calories	20	Total Fat	0.1 g
Protein	0.4 g	Saturated Fat	0 g
Carbohydrates	5 g	Cholesterol	0 mg
Dietary Fiber	1 g	Sodium	11 mg

TURKEY KEBABS WITH PINEAPPLE AND PEPPERS

MAKES 4 SERVINGS

Turkey is a wonderful meat to grill with fruit. The natural sweetness of the pineapple enhances the taste of the turkey and peppers here.

 1 lb (455 g) turkey medallions (16 pieces)
 2 tablespoons apple juice concentrate, thawed
 2 tablespoons teriyaki sauce
12 chunks fresh pineapple, each about 1 1/2 inches (4 cm) square
 1 large bell pepper, any color, cored, seeded, and cut into
    12 (1 1/2-inch/4-cm) squares
 4 thick scallions, cut into 8 (1 1/2-inch/4-cm) pieces
    spray oil

❶ In a large bowl, combine turkey, undiluted apple juice concentrate, and teriyaki sauce. Leave at room temperature while preparing the other ingredients.

❷ Thread each skewer in this order: scallion, turkey, pineapple, pepper, turkey, pineapple, pepper, turkey, pineapple, pepper, turkey, and scallion. Spray oil on the skewers. Prepare the grill.

❸ When the fire is ready, lightly oil the grid, and add the skewers. Grill 15 to 20 minutes, turning as needed, to cook until the turkey is no longer pink. Baste with any leftover marinade while skewers are grilling.

Serving suggestion: Serve atop rice cooked with scallions and golden raisins.

Each serving (not including rice)			
Calories	206	Total Fat	1.6 g
Protein	28 g	Saturated Fat	0.4 g
Carbohydrates	19 g	Cholesterol	77 mg
Dietary Fiber	2 g	Sodium	400 mg

TURKEY AND VEGETABLE PACKETS

MAKES 4 SERVINGS

This is a tasty, simple dish to prepare, and if you place the onions in the bottom of the packet, they will caramelize while on the grill, and will add substantial taste. This sauce is made with bottled nonfat salad dressing.

  1 cup (304 g) thinly sliced onions

  1 lb (455 g) fresh turkey breast medallions (about 16 pieces)

12 broccoli florets (about 1 cup/230 g)

  1 cup (130 g) thin carrot matchsticks (about 1/4 by 2 inches/ 5/8 by 5 cm)

1/2 cup (120 ml) nonfat honey-mustard sauce (to make your own, see recipe on page 274)

  freshly ground black pepper to taste

❶ Cut 8 (12-inch/30-cm) squares of heavy-duty foil; divide them into 4 stacks of 2 sheets.

❷ Divide onions among foil, then place an equal amount of turkey to the side of the onions. Top with remaining vegetables. Pour 2 tablespoons dressing over each portion, then season with black pepper.

❸ Fold according to Bundle Wrap directions (page 10). Meanwhile, prepare the fire.

❹ When the fire is ready, set the packets on the grill, and cook about 10 minutes. When done, the turkey should no longer be pink—if left on the grill too long, the turkey will be tough. Remove carefully and serve immediately.

Each serving (without sauce)			
Calories	201	Total Fat	1.2 g
Protein	29 g	Saturated Fat	0.4 g
Carbohydrates	17 g	Cholesterol	77 mg
Dietary Fiber	3 g	Sodium	394 mg

TURKEY STRIPS WITH MUSHROOMS AND CHERRY TOMATOES

MAKES 4 SERVINGS

Turkey cutlets are easy to cut into strips and skewer. Grilling turkey this way reduces grilling time, and adds an interesting look to the skewer. Here, three skewers are served per person. Use as many wooden skewers as you have guests (or more). Be sure to soak them in water for at least 30 minutes before adding the meat and putting them on the grill.

2 teaspoons each, dried: thyme and sage

1 teaspoon cayenne pepper

2 garlic cloves, minced

  pinch of salt

4 turkey cutlets (about 1 lb/455 g), each cut lengthwise
  into 3 strips

  spray oil

12 cherry tomatoes, stemmed

12 mushrooms, capped

❶ In a small bowl, combine thyme, sage, cayenne pepper, garlic, and salt; blend well.

❷ Dry turkey strips with paper towels, then place them in a bowl, and lightly spray them with oil 2 or 3 times, making sure strips are coated. Add the herb mixture, and toss to coat. Let marinate at room temperature 45 minutes.

❸ Combine tomatoes and mushrooms in another bowl; lightly spray with oil, then toss to coat.

❹ Prepare the grill. Lightly spray the grid with oil. Thread each skewer as follows: 1 mushroom, 1 turkey strip (spear strip so it makes an "s" shape on the skewer), 1 tomato. Repeat with remaining skewers, mushrooms, turkey strips, and tomatoes. Prepare the grill.

❺ When the fire is ready, add the skewers and grill 3 to 4 minutes on each side, turning once.

Serving suggestion: Serve with Four Onions in Parchment (page 235).

Each serving (without side dish)			
Calories	156	Total Fat	1.6 g
Protein	29 g	Saturated Fat	0.5 g
Carbohydrates	6 g	Cholesterol	77 mg
Dietary Fiber	2 g	Sodium	234 mg

CHAPTER 7
MAKING THE MOST OF MEAT

INTRODUCTION

Meat and poultry are still the main courses for meals in the United States today. However, in the last ten years, the role of meat in the American diet has come under scrutiny. Nutritionists strongly recommend that we eat less meat, particularly red meat, because of the high total fat, saturated fat, and cholesterol content. But, we should not eliminate all meat from our diet because of its nutritional value. If the portions are cut to 3 1/2 to 4 ounces and lean cuts of beef are chosen, then we can have our meat and eat it, too.

Different cuts and types of meat have widely differing fat contents. (See table on page 176.) The leanest cuts are tenderloin, sirloin, and round steak; this is true of beef, lamb, pork, or veal. Buy cuts of meat from the loin and round. Even then, you will need to remove any visible fat that may be left on. Pork tenderloin has about the same fat count as chicken breast meat. Both of these cuts will require some trimming before they are cooked, as they always seem to have a little more fat on them than one would like.

Choosing lean cuts and trimming extra fat will not matter much unless you significantly reduce portion sizes. Actually, this is not difficult to do if you plan a meal that includes side dishes. Plan to include vegetables, such as a salad, potatoes, or a grain. There's much to choose from, and most can be prepared on the grill, such as artichokes, polenta, zucchini, corn, and tomatoes. Visualizing these foods on the plate will make you feel less deprived when serving a three- or four-ounce (85- or 113-g) piece of meat. When counting your calories, keep in mind that a four-ounce (113-g) piece of raw meat will cook down to three ounces (85 g).

I'll always remember an experience not long ago, when I traveled to Washington, D.C. I arrived rather late in the evening, and wanted a light meal before going to bed. Passing this request on to the maitre d' of a good hotel restaurant there, he recommended the evening's special—a 16-ounce (455-g) porterhouse steak. This sent me into shock, and from that point on, I developed a drive to counter this American red-meat syndrome, and authored the book *Vegetables—Artichokes to Zucchini,* which is available in most bookstores.

It may be next to impossible for some people to eliminate meat in their diet. But if meat is portioned and prepared properly, there is no reason to avoid it completely. I have included, therefore, some very tasty meat preparations, but keep in mind that the portions are small. Don't be surprised that three ounces (85 g) of cooked meat still has between five and ten grams of fat. But if the rest of the meal is low fat, you will get by.

COMPARING CUTS OF BEEF (3 1/2 OZ, TRIMMED AND COOKED)

Cut	Cal.	Fat (g)	Sat. fat (g)	Cholesterol (mg)
Blade roast, choice	265	15	6	106
Blade roast, prime**	318	21	8	106
Bottom round, choice	193	8	3	78
Bottom round, prime**	249	13	5	96
Eye of round, choice	175	6	2	69
Eye of round, prime**	198	8	3	69
Flank	237	13	6	71
Porterhouse steak, choice*	218	11	4	80
Sirloin, choice	200	8	3	89
Sirloin, prime**	237	12	5	89
T-Bone steak, choice*	214	10	4	80
Tenderloin, choice	212	10	4	84
Tenderloin, prime*	232	12	5	84
Tip round, prime*	200	10	4	81
Tip round, choice	180	6	2	81
Top round, choice	207	6	2	90
Top round, prime*	215	9	3	84

*trimmed to 1/4 inch of fat
**trimmed to 1/2 inch of fat
All other cuts completely trimmed of external fat.

FAT, FAT, FAT!

A gram of fat has more than double the calories of carbohydrates or protein:

1 gram of fat = 9 calories

1 gram of carbohydrates or protein = 4 calories

Our bodies store fat in a concentrated form. Fat puts on weight, and stored fat undermines good health. Animal fats, as we know, are the culprits where saturated fat is concerned. I've included some delicious meat recipes to satisfy that occasional craving. To ensure a low-fat meal, however, keep the portions small.

INVISIBLE FAT

Butter, margarine, lard, vegetable shortening, vegetable oil, and salad dressings are obviously high in fat. Most cooks are well aware of their fat content, and can easily and quickly cut back on the amount of these fats used in a recipe. But there are foods in which the fat is not so visible. Beware of the fat hidden in foods that most of us enjoy on a daily basis—these are the invisible fats.

Invisible fat can be found in egg yolks, marbled meat, cream, whole milk, chocolate, olives, nuts, coconuts, and cheese. The fat content of these foods should be calculated into the nutritional analysis of a dish, just as you would calculate the content of visible fats.

In this chapter, it is particularly important to pay close attention to the nutritional analysis of each recipe, especially when planning your menu and making decisions about foods to accompany the meat dish.

GRILLED VENISON WITH CURRANT-PEPPER JELLY

MAKES 4 SERVINGS

Venison is a relatively lean meat, compared to beef, and is delicious grilled; small steaks cut from the tenderloin are ideal for the grill.

3/4 cup (180 ml) dry red wine, divided

1/2 cup (120 ml) water

1/4 cup (76 g) chopped onion

4 black peppercorns

5 whole cloves

1 bay leaf

1 sprig rosemary

4 (1/2-inch/1 1/4 cm-thick) young venison steaks (about 1 lb/455 g total)

1/2 cup (120 ml) currant jelly

freshly ground black pepper to taste

❶ To make the marinade, combine 1/2 cup wine, water, onion, peppercorns, cloves, bay leaf, and rosemary in a shallow glass dish; mix well. Add meat, turning to coat well. Cover, and marinate overnight.

❷ Combine jelly and remaining 1/4 cup wine in a small saucepan; cook, stirring, over medium heat until jelly is melted and blended with the wine. Cook about 5 minutes, until thick as light cream. Liberally add pepper, and keep warm.

❸ Prepare the grill, and oil the grid. When the fire is ready, add the venison steaks and grill about 5 minutes on each side.

❹ To serve, divide steaks among 4 plates; spoon some currant sauce to the side of each meat portion. Do not cover the meat with the sauce.

Serving suggestion: Serve with Purée of Grilled Chestnuts (page 221).

VENISON

Venison is an integral part of American foodlore. Captain John Smith wrote in the early 1600s the Indians would store venison for winter. When the early colonists arrived, they found the woods filled with deer, and soon grilled venison over outdoor fires. Later, in the 19th century, venison was a popular meat. It was seasoned with rich marinades, for two reasons: to get the gamy flavor out, and to help preserve the meat.

Venison is one of the lowest fat meats. There are 159 calories in a 3.6 ounce piece of venison with only 3.3 fat grams and 66 milligrams of cholesterol. The same portion of ground beef contains 265 calories, 18.4 fat grams, and 85 milligrams of cholesterol.

Each serving (not including chestnuts)			
Calories	305	Total Fat	4 g
Protein	35 g	Saturated Fat	1.4 g
Carbohydrates	29 g	Cholesterol	127 mg
Dietary Fiber	1 g	Sodium	88 mg

BALSAMIC BEEF AND VEGETABLE KEBABS

MAKES 4 SERVINGS

This easy preparation is tasty and very low in fat. You can use other vegetables here, including whole mushrooms, chunks of zucchini, or yellow summer squash.

1/4 cup (60 ml) balsamic vinegar

1 tablespoon canola oil

2 tablespoons Worcestershire sauce

freshly ground black pepper to taste

1 lb (455 g) very lean beef tenderloin (filet mignon) or top sirloin

2 small- to medium-size onions, peeled and cut into quarters

1 large bell pepper, trimmed and cut into 12 (1 1/4-inch/3 1/4-cm) squares

8 whole cherry tomatoes, or 4 plum tomatoes cut into halves

4 teaspoons prepared low-sodium horseradish sauce

❶ In a small bowl, combine vinegar, oil, Worcestershire, and pepper; mix well.

❷ Cut the meat into 16 (1-inch/2 1/2-cm) cubes. Remove any visible fat, and arrange them in a single layer in a glass, ceramic, or nonaluminum dish. Marinate for at least 30 minutes. Reserve the marinade for basting.

❸ Thread 1 tomato and 1 onion piece on each of 4 skewers. Alternating meat and bell pepper. thread 4 pieces of meat and 3 pieces of pepper onto each skewer. Top each skewer with onion then tomato. Prepare the grill.

❹ When the fire is ready, add the skewers, and grill 12 minutes, turning skewers twice to grill all sides. Baste several times with remaining marinade while kebabs are grilling.

❺ To serve, place a skewer on each of 4 plates, adding a teaspoon of horseradish to the side. Season with additional black pepper.

Each serving			
Calories	269	Total Fat	13 g
Protein	25 g	Saturated Fat	4 g
Carbohydrates	12 g	Cholesterol	73 mg
Dietary Fiber	2 g	Sodium	159 mg

GRILLED FILET OF BEEF WITH CAPER MUSTARD SAUCE

MAKES 4 SERVINGS

Small, lean, beef filets are very good on the grill. After the steaks are grilled, slice the filets very thin, then arrange the slices, slightly overlapping, on each plate. This will give the appearance that more meat is on the plate than actually is being served, thus cutting calories and fat.

2 tablespoons each, nonfat: mayonnaise and sour cream

2 tablespoons finely chopped onions

2 tablespoons Dijon-style mustard

1 tablespoon capers, drained

juice of 1 whole lemon (3 tablespoons)

2 (8-oz/230-g) lean beef tenderloin (filet mignon) steaks, trimmed

1/2 teaspoon canola oil

freshly ground black pepper to taste

3 tablespoons finely chopped fresh tarragon, or 1 tablespoon dried

❶ Mix the mayonnaise, sour cream, onions, mustard, capers, and lemon juice in a glass or nonaluminum bowl until well blended. Set aside, or refrigerate until ready to use. Prepare the grill.

❷ Lightly oil both sides of each filet, then liberally season with pepper. When the fire is ready, grill the meat about 4 minutes on each side. Remove from the grill, and allow to rest 3 or 4 minutes. Thinly slice, then divide slices among 4 dinner plates.

❸ To serve, place a spoonful of Caper Mustard Sauce to the side of each meat portion; sprinkle with tarragon.

Each serving			
Calories	220	Total Fat	10 g
Protein	26 g	Saturated Fat	3 g
Carbohydrates	6 g	Cholesterol	70 mg
Dietary Fiber	1 g	Sodium	380 mg

GRILLED BEEF TENDERLOIN

MAKES 4 SERVINGS

Although the meat portions are small, they are delicious grilled with fresh herbs. Fresh herbs are available year-round in most markets. Double up, if you wish, on the Mediterranean-Style Tomatoes, suggested as an accompaniment to these beef tenderloins, or add a lightly dressed mesclun (baby greens) salad.

4 (4-oz/113-g) lean, beef tenderloin filets (see note)

   spray oil

2 teaspoons minced garlic

2 teaspoons each, finely chopped fresh: basil, rosemary, and thyme

2 teaspoons freshly ground black pepper, or to taste

❶ Spray oil on both sides of each filet.

❷ Combine garlic and herbs in the bowl of a food processor; pulse to mince. Press the mixture into each side of the filets. Liberally season filets with pepper, then marinate at room temperature while preparing the grill.

❸ When the fire is ready, oil the grill, and add the filets. Grill 3 to 4 minutes on each side, turning once. Remove filets from the grill, and let stand another few minutes.

Serving suggestion: Serve with Tomatoes in Foil with Mediterranean Flavors (page 254), or a lightly dressed green salad.

Note: Four-ounce filets may be hard to find. If so, buy 2 (8-oz/230-g) filets, each about 1 inch (2 1/2 cm) thick. Cut each filet crosswise into 4 smaller filets, each still 1 inch (2 1/2 cm) thick.

Each serving (without side dishes)			
Calories	187	Total Fat	8.6 g
Protein	24 g	Saturated Fat	3 g
Carbohydrates	2 g	Cholesterol	70 mg
Dietary Fiber	1 g	Sodium	54 mg

BEEF TENDERLOIN WITH DIJON CRUST

MAKES 4 SERVINGS

While the tenderloins are marinating, prepare grilled leeks, which are a good accompaniment to the mustard-flavored tenderloin. Or serve a lightly dressed green salad on the side.

1/4 cup (60 ml) Dijon-style mustard

1 tablespoon fresh lemon juice

2 garlic cloves, minced

1 tablespoon freshly ground black pepper, or to taste

1 teaspoon fennel seeds

4 (4-oz/113-g) lean beef tenderloin filets (see note)

❶ In a small bowl, combine mustard, lemon juice, garlic, black pepper, and fennel seeds; mix well.

❷ Spread the mustard mixture over both sides of each filet. Marinate, covered, in the refrigerator for 2 or 3 hours, or at room temperature for 30 minutes. If refrigerated, remove 20 minutes before grilling. Meanwhile, prepare the grill.

❸ When the fire is ready, oil the grid, and add the filets. Grill 3 to 4 minutes on each side, turning once, and basting with any leftover marinade. Remove filets from the grill, and let stand for several minutes.

Note: If you have trouble finding 4-oz (113-g) filets, buy 2 (8-oz/230-g) filets, each about 1 inch (2 1/2 cm) thick. Cut the filets crosswise into 4 smaller filets, each still 1 inch (2 1/2 cm) thick.

Each serving (not including side dishes)			
Calories	205	Total Fat	10 g
Protein	25 g	Saturated Fat	3 g
Carbohydrates	4 g	Cholesterol	70 mg
Dietary Fiber	1 g	Sodium	433 mg

GRILLED GARLICKY FLANK STEAK WITH SLICED TOMATOES IN HONEY-MUSTARD VINAIGRETTE

MAKES 4 SERVINGS

Flank steak is not as high in fat as one might think. It is a good cut of meat for use on the grill. Tasty and versatile, flank steak can be used in some of the beef preparations previously presented.

6 garlic cloves, minced

2 tablespoons low-sodium soy sauce

1 tablespoon honey

1 teaspoon ground cumin

4 drops hot red pepper sauce

1 (1-lb/455-g) flank steak, about 3/4 inch (1 7/8 cm) thick, trimmed

❶ In a glass or ceramic dish just large enough to hold the flank steak, combine the marinade ingredients; mix well. Place the steak in the dish and turn to coat both sides completely. Cover the dish with plastic wrap, then refrigerate for several hours, turning once. Bring to room temperature before grilling. Meanwhile, prepare the grill.

❷ Lightly spray the grid with oil. When the fire is ready, add the steak, and grill, basting frequently with the marinade, about 5 minutes on each side, turning once. Remove steak from the grill and let it rest 5 minutes or more; thinly slice it crosswise to serve.

FLANK STEAK

Flank steak comes from the belly section of the cow, below the loin. Grilled as London broil, the meat is generally marinated first, then grilled and cut diagonally into thin slices. When buying flank, choose a good grade of meat, either prime or choice. To prepare it for the grill, remove the outer membrane, as well as any fat around the steak. The butcher usually will do this for you, if you ask him. Flank steak should be brown on the outside, but still juicy and red in the middle.

Each serving (without tomatoes)

Calories	213	Total Fat	9 g
Protein	25 g	Saturated Fat	4 g
Carbohydrates	7 g	Cholesterol	59 mg
Dietary Fiber	0 g	Sodium	327 mg

SLICED TOMATOES IN HONEY-MUSTARD VINAIGRETTE

MAKES 4 SERVINGS

This is best if made about one hour before serving, left at room temperature.

1/4 cup (60 ml) seasoned rice vinegar

  1 tablespoon each: canola oil and Dijon-style mustard

  1 teaspoon honey

    freshly ground black pepper to taste

  2 large, ripe tomatoes, peeled and sliced (8 slices total)

❶ Put the vinegar in a small bowl, then whisk in oil until combined; whisk in mustard, then honey and pepper.

❷ Arrange tomato slices in a single layer in a large, shallow dish. Spoon some of the dressing over each slice. Let sit at room temperature until ready to serve.

Each serving			
Calories	59	Total Fat	4 g
Protein	1 g	Saturated Fat	0.3 g
Carbohydrates	6 g	Cholesterol	0 mg
Dietary Fiber	1 g	Sodium	104 mg

GRILLED PORK TENDERLOIN WITH MUSTARD-SPICE RUB

MAKES 4 SERVINGS

Pork tenderloin is wonderful on the grill because it has less fat than its beef and lamb counterparts. Pork tenderloin also grills quickly, about ten minutes, because it usually is sold in one-pound (455-g) portions. I always allow any meat, especially pork tenderloin to rest about five minutes before slicing. When meat is being cooked, whether on the grill or by any other method, the juices rise to the surface; resting allows the juices to be redistributed throughout the meat before it is cut.

1 large garlic clove, minced

1 tablespoon each: dry mustard, ground coriander, and paprika

1 tablespoon freshly ground black pepper

1 tablespoon canola oil

2 tablespoons cognac (optional)

1 lb (455 g) pork tenderloin, as lean as possible

❶ Combine garlic and spices in a mortar; mash with a pestle to grind. Work in the oil and cognac to make a paste. (This procedure also may be done in a small food processor.) Rub the mixture all over the pork. Cover the pork with plastic wrap, then marinate overnight in the refrigerator. Bring to room temperature 1 hour before grilling. If there is no time to marinate overnight, rub the mixture over the pork, and leave at room temperature for 1 hour before grilling.

❷ Prepare the grill, and oil the grid lightly. When the fire is ready, place the tenderloin on the grid and grill a total of 10 minutes, turning once. Watch the tenderloin to avoid excess charring. Be sure the tenderloin is at least 6 inches above the fire; if necessary, move the pork to cooler spots on the grill to avoid overcharring. Let pork rest 5 minutes or more before slicing.

Serving suggestion: Serve with mashed potatoes and the tart Cranberry Apple Conserve (page 28).

Each serving (not including side dishes)			
Calories	273	Total Fat	12 g
Protein	36 g	Saturated Fat	2.8 g
Carbohydrates	3 g	Cholesterol	107 mg
Dietary Fiber	1 g	Sodium	76 mg

LAMB CHOPS WITH RAISIN PEPPER SAUCE

MAKES 4 SERVINGS

This is a great sauce for the delectable, small lamb chops. Admittedly, not much meat, but eat slowly and savor this tasty meat and sauce preparation.

8 small loin lamb chops, trimmed

2 tablespoons garlic powder

1 tablespoon ground cumin

1 tablespoon freshly ground black pepper
Raisin Pepper Sauce (recipe follows)
spray oil

❶ Set lamb chops on a flat surface covered with wax paper.

❷ In a small bowl, combine garlic, cumin, and pepper; rub mixture into both sides of each chop. Leave the chops at room temperature while the sauce is being prepared. Meanwhile, prepare the grill and the Raisin Pepper Sauce.

❸ When the fire is ready, spray the grid or a hinged wire basket with oil. If grilling directly on the grid, spray oil on both sides of each chop, then place chops on the grid, and grill 3 minutes on each side, turning once. If using a wire basket, arrange the chops in the basket, securing it so the chops don't fall out; spray oil on both sides of the chops, then grill 3 minutes on each side, turning once.

❹ To serve, put 2 chops on each of 4 plates, then add 2 tablespoons of the raisin sauce to the side.

Serving suggestion: Plain, boiled new potatoes are a must with this dish.

LOIN LAMB CHOPS
Delicate lamb meat requires special attention when cooking it on the grill. Choose the leaner loin lamb chops, and select cuts that are fairly thick, about 1 1/2 inches. Grill them slowly over medium heat until they are well browned on the outside, with crisply charred fat on the edges. Increase the heat near the end of the grilling time to char them quickly. The meat should still be pink in the center.

Each serving (not including potatoes)			
Calories	271	Total Fat	10 g
Protein	30 g	Saturated Fat	3.3 g
Carbohydrates	14 g	Cholesterol	87 mg
Dietary Fiber	1 g	Sodium	204 mg

RAISIN PEPPER SAUCE

1 cup (240 ml) low-sodium, defatted chicken broth, divided
1/4 cup (76 g) finely chopped onions
  2 tablespoons tawny port, Marsala wine, or sweet vermouth
    pinch of red pepper flakes
    pinch of ground cumin
1/4 cup (38 g) raisins

❶ Combine 2 tablespoons chicken broth and onions in a small saucepan; cook over medium heat until onions get soft, about 3 minutes, stirring frequently.

❷ Stir in port, red pepper flakes, and cumin; sauté 1 minute.

❸ Stir in raisins and remaining broth, then simmer over medium heat, uncovered, 6 to 8 minutes, or until the liquid is reduced by one half. Set aside until ready to serve.

Each serving (1 tablespoon)			
Calories	12	Total Fat	.2 g
Protein	.3 g	Saturated Fat	.1 g
Carbohydrates	2 g	Cholesterol	.3 mg
Dietary Fiber	.2 g	Sodium	7 mg

GRILLED PORK TENDERLOIN WITH MUSTARD-MINT SAUCE

MAKES 4 SERVINGS

In this preparation, the pork can marinate overnight, and the sauce may be made ahead, as well. You'll surely enjoy this.

1 (1-lb/455-g) pork tenderloin, trimmed

spray oil

2 tablespoons low-sodium soy sauce

2 garlic cloves, minced

freshly ground black pepper to taste

Mustard-Mint Sauce (recipe follows)

❶ Wipe the tenderloin dry, and put it in a glass dish just large enough to hold the meat (a loaf pan usually will work fine). Spray the meat with oil. Add the other ingredients, coating the tenderloin completely. Cover with plastic wrap, and marinate in the refrigerator for 1 hour or overnight. Bring to room temperature before grilling. Meanwhile prepare the sauce.

❷ Prepare the grill, and lightly spray with oil. When the fire is ready, add the pork, reserving the marinade, and grill covered, 10 to 15 minutes (depending on thickness of the tenderloin), turning as needed, and basting frequently with the marinade. Remove the pork from the grill, and let rest 10 minutes before slicing.

❸ To serve, thinly slice, then place 2 slices on each of 4 plates, slightly overlapping the slices. Add a dollop of the mustard sauce to the side.

Serving suggestion: Serve with boiled new potatoes. The sauce is delicious with the potatoes, as well.

Each serving (without sauce)			
Calories	222	Total Fat	7.2 g
Protein	35 g	Saturated Fat	2.5 g
Carbohydrates	2 g	Cholesterol	107 mg
Dietary Fiber	0 g	Sodium	327 mg

MUSTARD-MINT SAUCE

1/4 cup (60 ml) nonfat mayonnaise
  2 tablespoons Dijon-style mustard
  1 teaspoon mustard seeds, or 2 teaspoons grainy mustard
    juice of 1/2 lemon (about 1 1/2 tablespoons)
  2 tablespoons finely chopped scallions
  1 tablespoon finely chopped fresh mint, or 1 teaspoon dried

To make the sauce, combine all ingredients, and mix well. Refrigerate, covered, until needed. This will keep overnight.

Each sauce serving (1 tablespoon)			
Calories	38	Total Fat	1 g
Protein	2 g	Saturated Fat	0 g
Carbohydrates	6 g	Cholesterol	0 mg
Dietary Fiber	1 g	Sodium	308 mg

GRILLED VEAL CUTLETS WITH CITRUS-HORSERADISH SAUCE

MAKES 4 SERVINGS

Citrus-Horseradish Sauce (recipe follows)

4 (4-oz/113-g) lean veal cutlets or medallions

spray oil

1 tablespoon Worcestershire sauce

freshly ground black pepper to taste

❶ Prepare the sauce and refrigerate until needed. Lay the cutlets flat on a piece of wax paper; spray oil on both sides of each cutlet. Put Worcestershire in a small bowl, then brush it on both sides of each cutlet. Season cutlets with freshly ground black pepper. Leave at room temperature while preparing the grill.

❷ When the fire is ready, spray the grid with oil; add veal, and grill 2 to 3 minutes on each side, depending on thickness. Remove cutlets from the grill, and let stand for several minutes.

❸ To serve, put a cutlet on each of 4 plates. Add a spoonful of horseradish sauce to the side.

CITRUS-HORSERADISH SAUCE

1/2 cup (120 ml) plain nonfat yogurt

2 tablespoons prepared horseradish, drained

juice of 1 whole lemon (3 tablespoons)

2 tablespoons finely chopped scallions

salt to taste (optional)

freshly ground black pepper to taste

Combine all the ingredients, put in a covered bowl, and refrigerate until needed.

Each serving (with sauce)			
Calories	278	Total Fat	15.1 g
Protein	29 g	Saturated Fat	6.05 g
Carbohydrates	11.1 g	Cholesterol	104 mg
Dietary Fiber	.3 g	Sodium	143 mg

LOIN OF VENISON IN SOUR FRUIT SAUCE

MAKES 4 SERVINGS

Venison is delicious served with a sweet-and-sour sauce.
I use seedless fruit jelly with seasoned rice vinegar.

2 shallots, peeled and finely chopped

1/4 cup (60 ml) seasoned rice vinegar, divided

1 tablespoon seedless fruit jelly, any flavor

1 tablespoon each: ketchup and low-sodium soy sauce

2 tablespoons water

1 tablespoon finely chopped fresh rosemary, or 1 teaspoon dried

1 loin of venison, trimmed, and cut into 4 small steaks (about 1 lb/455 g total)

spray oil

freshly ground black pepper to taste

❶ Combine shallots and 2 tablespoons rice vinegar in a small saucepan over medium heat; simmer until the liquid has evaporated, about 2 minutes. Add remaining vinegar, jelly, ketchup, soy sauce, water, and rosemary. Bring to boil, lower the heat, and simmer until the sauce thickens to the consistency of heavy cream, 5 to 10 minutes. Strain the sauce and return it to the pan. Set aside.

❷ Lightly spray oil on both sides of each venison piece, rubbing the oil into the meat with your fingers. Liberally season both sides of each piece with pepper.

❸ Spray the grid with oil. When the fire is ready, add the venison, and grill each side about 4 minutes.

❹ To serve, divide steak among 4 warmed plates. Reheat the sauce and spoon onto each plate, partially covering each serving of meat.

Serving suggestion: Simple mashed potatoes, or grilled new potatoes and cherry tomatoes are best with this dish.

Each serving (without accompaniments)			
Calories	205	Total Fat	3.7 g
Protein	35 g	Saturated Fat	1.4 g
Carbohydrates	6 g	Cholesterol	127 mg
Dietary Fiber	0 g	Sodium	237 mg

SPICY GRILLED PORK TENDERLOIN

MAKES 8 SERVINGS

This is surely one of my favorites. A delicious way to grill pork, this preparation can be made one or two days ahead, allowing the meat to marinate sufficiently. It only takes minutes to cook on the grill.

1 tablespoon coarsely ground black pepper

2 teaspoons each: garlic and onion powders

1 teaspoon cornstarch

1/2 teaspoon each: salt and paprika

1/2 teaspoon granulated chicken bouillon

1/2 teaspoon fennel seeds, crushed

2 (1- to 1 1/4-lb/455- to 570-g) pork tenderloins

❶ Combine all ingredients, except the pork, and mix well.

❷ Arrange 2 large sheets of plastic wrap on the counter top, each large enough to fully wrap each tenderloin. Place 1 tenderloin on each piece of plastic wrap. Carefully rub half of the spice mixture onto 1 tenderloin; use remaining mixture on the second tenderloin. Wrap each securely, and let set 30 minutes at room temperature before grilling, or refrigerate overnight, or, if you want, 2 nights. Bring to room temperature before grilling. Prepare the grill.

❸ When the fire is ready, spray the grid with oil. Grill the tenderloins, cover down, 10 to 15 minutes, turning once or twice to grill all sides; do not overcook. The inside of the pork should be pink. Remove from the grill, and let rest 4 or 5 minutes before slicing.

Serving suggestion: Serve pork slices over grilled onions or leeks, with a fresh, green salad.

Each serving (not including side dishes)			
Calories	221	Total Fat	7.3 g
Protein	35 g	Saturated Fat	2.6 g
Carbohydrates	2 g	Cholesterol	107 mg
Dietary Fiber	0.3 g	Sodium	266 mg

CHAPTER 8
A CORNUCOPIA OF GRILLED VEGETABLES

INTRODUCTION

If I had to choose one family of food to eat the rest of my life, I would choose vegetables. The variety is infinite, and vegetables can be grilled in exotic ways. Vegetables contain all the essentials of good nutrition: protein, carbohydrates, fats (but only a little), minerals, and vitamins. These elements vary in amount from one vegetable to the next, but in no other food group is there more complete nourishment. And their prize characteristic is few calories.

People today want wholesome diets that are low in fat and high in fiber. The good news is that people who concentrate on eating more fresh vegetables, fruits, and whole grains, and lower their intake of caffeine, sugar, and salt, can improve their well-being. Grilling vegetables not only opens the door to a garden path of health improvement, but also adds to the enjoyment of food.

Being a vegetarian in a mostly carnivorous society, often means second-class gastronomic citizenship. Today, however, many hosts understand—more than they did a few years ago—someone who announces a preference for a meal without meat. Not too long ago, however, a meal of vegetables meant overcooked carrots, peas, and green beans, or an oily salad of tough iceberg lettuce. Even vegetarian restaurants offered little more than sticky rice. These days, vegetables are playing a bigger role on the plates of culinary innovators. Part of the reason is probably an increased awareness of health.

Not too long ago, grills across the country were filled with thick steaks and greasy chicken wings—unfortunately, too many are still this way. But food interests have shifted, and people are grilling vegetables and fruits, and—using new seasonings, as well. We now see people trying vegetables and fruits that no one thought of grilling before—remember, many people grilled corn and perhaps eggplant, but who grilled turnip or sweet potato slices?

The concerns about grilling vegetables are similar to those brought up when broiling them: the heat is intense and, in fact, less controllable than when broiling. Experience at the grill—a great teacher—will eventually eliminate most problems. I know from my own experience, that the "mystique" of the grill is the challenge, and adds fun when grilling.

When grilling vegetables, cut the slices slightly thicker than for broiling, then spray oil on both sides, and grill. That one vegetable slice may receive many treatments, however, whether it is marinated before being grilled, or sauced just before being served. Corn, potatoes, onions, and tomatoes can be grilled successfully, and with great taste, whether they are set directly on the grill, or are wrapped in foil, one of the best wraps to use on the grill. Yet, take advantage of natural wraps, such as corn husk. Ears of corn, tied in their own husks, should be soaked in cold water for 15 minutes or so, then drained, before grilling. With special seasonings sprinkled inside the husk, grilled corn could be the epitome of grilled fare. When grilling potatoes, remove a thin strip of skin off each potato, spray them with oil, add spices and herbs—especially black pepper—then wrap them in foil and grill, or skewer the potatoes and place them directly on the grill. Grilled potatoes could even challenge corn as vegetable king of the grill.

Using spray oil on vegetables will ensure that you are using far less oil than you would, no matter how carefully you poured. Spray oils are available plain, or flavored with such seasonings as garlic, herbs, and spices. More exotic spray oils mimic the flavors of regional cuisines, such as Italian, Southwestern, Oriental, and Cajun. Any of these sprays deliver about 1/8 of a gram of fat with each spritz (1/36 of a teaspoon). It may be difficult to accept the zero fat claim on the labels of the spray-oil cans, but even if you use as many as 12 sprays on any one item, that would be equivalent to 1 1/2 grams of fat.

We dote on fish, poultry, and meat kebabs, but some of the best kebabs are neither from sea nor range. Vegetable kebabs make great accompaniments to almost any grilled food. A key point to remember is that vegetables require different cooking times on the grill. Yes, it is more attractive to thread various vegetables on the same skewer, but some may end up overcooked, while others are left semi-raw. To work around this, make several skewers each threaded with a different vegetable. Put the vegetables that need to cook the longest on the grill first, adding the quicker-cooking vegetables later, so they all will be done at the same time. Remove the vegetables from the skewers and combine them when serving. Or combine vegetables that will grill in about the same amount of time.

An excellent touch is to add herbs between the vegetable chunks on the skewers. Add a basil leaf between each cherry tomato, a mint leaf between onion pieces, or a sage leaf between chunks of swordfish. Or, sprinkle thyme, oregano, rosemary, and other herbs over the vegetables before grilling. When my herb plants are mature and strong, I prune them, then throw the stems and leaves over the coals just before I grill. If the herb branch is large enough, it can be trimmed, soaked in water, and used as a skewer. Don't use branches or wooden skewers for root vegetables, though; they need metal skewers, which heat up on the grill and help cook the inside of the dense tubers.

Vegetables are abundant, and should be more prominent on your plate and the grill. They offer added color, variety, and flavor to your plate. Grilled vegetables give a new dimension to salads, and are a delicious accompaniment to fish, poultry, meat, other vegetables, and pasta or grains.

GRILLED ARTICHOKES

MAKES 4 SERVINGS

Most people don't think of grilling artichokes; they tend to overboil them, instead. Try this method, as I know you will enjoy it. All the juices and flavors remain in the foil packet, which retains the vitamins, too.

2 large fresh artichokes, trimmed

   juice of 1 whole lemon (3 tablespoons)

1/4 cup (60 ml) defatted chicken broth or water

1 tablespoon olive oil

2 garlic cloves, minced

   freshly ground black pepper to taste

2 tablespoons finely chopped fresh flat-leaf parsley

1 Cut the artichokes in half, lengthwise, and scrape out the choke. Immediately rub the cut sides with lemon juice.

2 Cut a sheet of heavy-duty foil large enough to fully enclose 4 artichoke halves. Put the halves on the foil, cut side up, and spoon the broth over top. Sprinkle oil, garlic, and pepper over each half. Wrap the artichokes in the foil (page 10).

3 If using a gas grill, turn on one burner, leaving the second side unlit. Put the foil package on the cool side of the grill, then cover and grill 30 minutes. Move the package to the hot side, then grill 30 minutes over low heat. If using charcoal, place the package over the cool part of the grill first, then move it above the heat, when the coals are gray and ashen, to complete cooking.

4 Serve with a vinaigrette, sprinkle the parsley over the dressed artichokes.

Each serving			
Calories	67	Total Fat	3.5 g
Protein	2.7 g	Saturated Fat	0.5 g
Carbohydrates	8 g	Cholesterol	0 mg
Dietary Fiber	3.3 g	Sodium	69 mg

GRILLED ARTICHOKE HEARTS WITH BREAD CUBES AND BELL PEPPERS

MAKES 4 SERVINGS

The beauty of a kebab is that various foods can be combined, layering the flavor, then grilling and binding those flavors together. This particular kebab can be served with almost any other food.

> 2 jars low fat (6 oz each) or 1 can (14 oz) low fat marinated, quartered, artichoke hearts (see sidebar)
>
> 12 slices French or Italian bread, cut in 1 1/2-inch (4-cm) cubes
>
> 1 1/2 red bell peppers, cored, seeded and cut into 1 1/2-inch (4-cm) squares
>
> 4 tablespoons nonfat Italian dressing (see sidebar)

❶ Drain the artichokes, discard the liquid, and pat dry. Set aside.

❷ Brush the bread cubes and the pepper squares with Italian dressing.

❸ Thread each of 4 skewers as follows: Pepper square, artichoke quarter, bread cube; pepper, artichoke, bread; pepper, artichoke, bread, and pepper. Prepare the grill.

❹ When the fire is ready, oil the grid, and add the skewers. Grill 8 to 10 minutes total time, turning several times to grill all sides. Keep the bread from scorching by moving the skewer to cooler spots on the grill.

ARTICHOKES

Jarred and canned artichokes come packed in seasoned oil or water. Use the water-packed artichokes to save fat and calories. Progresso is a brand to look for. A 14-ounce (369-g) can contains six whole artichoke hearts, which can be halved for this recipe to make the required 12 pieces. Another brand, Casa Visco, packs eight or nine artichoke quarters in a mild marinade in six-ounce jars. Other brands may be available in your supermarket. Also look for nonfat Italian dressings, like those made by Kraft and Hellmann's.

Each serving			
Calories	321	Total Fat	3 g
Protein	11 g	Saturated Fat	0.7 g
Carbohydrates	62 g	Cholesterol	0 mg
Dietary Fiber	5 g	Sodium	1076 mg

GRILLED FRESH ASPARAGUS WITH RED ONION AND ORANGE VINAIGRETTE

MAKES 6 SERVINGS

If the asparagus spears are thin, they can be placed directly on a lightly oiled grill or arranged in a wire basket. If thicker—I prefer them about 1/2 inch (1 1/4 cm) or thicker—blanch them in boiling water about one minute, then drain them, and quickly immerse them in ice water, before putting them on the grill; be sure to then wipe them dry with paper towels before grilling.

1 1/2 lb (680 g) fresh asparagus, trimmed and lightly peeled

salt and freshly ground black pepper, to taste

spray oil

1/3 cup (80 ml) unsweetened apple juice

1 small celery heart, including leaves, finely chopped (about 1/4 cup/28 g)

1/4 cup (76 g) finely chopped red onion

1 tablespoon finely chopped carrot

1 tablespoon honey

2 tablespoons seasoned rice vinegar

1 tablespoon minced fresh ginger

1 teaspoon grated orange rind ·

1 Prepare the fire. When the grill is ready, oil the grid.

2 Season the asparagus (raw or blanched) with salt and pepper. When the grill is ready, oil the grid. Grill the asparagus in an oiled wire basket, or directly on the grid but be careful not to lose any asparagus between the grate openings. Grill until tender, 5 to 8 minutes, depending on the thickness of the asparagus; turn once. To test for doneness, run a wooden skewer through the asparagus spears; if the skewer goes through easily, the asparagus is cooked. Do not overcook them. Distribute among 6 plates.

3 In a small bowl, combine the remaining ingredients, mixing well. Pour vinaigrette over the asparagus.

Each serving			
Calories	49	Total Fat	0.3 g
Protein	2.8 g	Saturated Fat	0.1 g
Carbohydrates	11 g	Cholesterol	0 mg
Dietary Fiber	3 g	Sodium	9 mg

GRILLED EGGPLANT WITH TOMATO FARCE

MAKES 8 SERVINGS

Farce means a stuffing usually of meat. In this case, the "stuffing" is made with tomatoes, herbs, and spices, and is placed on top of the eggplant slice. Eggplant is cooked through when a thin wooden skewer goes through the flesh easily. Since this is a farce, the ingredients can be changed easily. I have added anchovy (after rinsing off the salt) and a tablespoon of rinsed, drained capers. I often substitute oregano for the basil. This is what is fun about a farce.

1 large, long eggplant (about 1 lb/455 g)

   salt to taste

1 tablespoon olive oil

1 (14 1/2-oz/411-g) can no-salt stewed tomatoes, drained well

1 medium-size onion, finely chopped

1 garlic clove, minced

2 tablespoons finely chopped parsley

2 tablespoons finely chopped basil, or 2 teaspoons dried

   freshly ground black pepper to taste

   balsamic vinegar to taste

❶ Cut eggplant into 1/2-inch (1 1/4-cm) slices; lightly salt slices, and put them in a colander to drain for 30 minutes. Dry the slices, removing any salt, then lightly oil them. Meanwhile, prepare the grill.

❷ When the fire is ready, add eggplant slices and grill 3 to 5 minutes on one side.

❸ While the first side is grilling, combine tomatoes, onion, garlic, parsley, basil, and pepper in a bowl; mix well. Turn over the eggplant slices on the grill, then top each with a spoonful of the tomato mixture.

❹ Put the grill cover down, and cook an additional 3 to 5 minutes. Transfer the slices to a jellyroll pan. Add a few drops vinegar to each slice, then run the slices under the broiler for 2 or 3 minutes to crisp the stuffing. Serve immediately.

Each serving			
Calories	53	Total Fat	2 g
Protein	1 g	Saturated Fat	0.3 g
Carbohydrates	9 g	Cholesterol	0 mg
Dietary Fiber	3 g	Sodium	11 mg

BLACK BEAN, ONION, AND CHEESE QUESADILLAS

MAKES 4 SERVINGS

This tasty tortilla dish is easy to make. Use the large, sweet onions from Texas, and add more than the recipe calls for, if you really go for them. This is special when served as a "vegetable" with pork tenderloin or chicken.

    8 corn tortillas

  1 (14.5-oz/411-g) can nonfat refried black beans

  1 large Texas onion, peeled and chopped

1/4 lb (115 g) low-fat Monterey Jack cheese, grated

    freshly ground black pepper, to taste

    salsa (recipe on page 29)

❶ Place 4 tortillas on a work surface, then spread each with the refried black beans.

❷ Sprinkle onion and cheese over each tortilla, then liberally season with black pepper. Top each tortilla with one of the remaining tortillas. Prepare the grill.

❸ When the fire is ready, lightly oil the grid, then add the tortillas. Grill 2 or 3 minutes on each side, turning once with a wide spatula. Remove quesadillas from the grill, and cut each into quarters. Serve warm with hot salsa.

Each serving (not including salsa)			
Calories	249	Total Fat	3 g
Protein	14 g	Saturated Fat	1.3 g
Carbohydrates	39 g	Cholesterol	6 mg
Dietary Fiber	6 g	Sodium	410 mg

GRILLED BEETS AND VIDALIA ONIONS WITH GRAPEFRUIT VINAIGRETTE

MAKES 4 SERVINGS

You may not have thought of beets as a vegetable for the grill, but they are delicious prepared this way. To make this a complete meal, grill four sea scallops per person, then add them to the beet salad. A small piece of grilled grouper or snapper, placed on top of the beet salad also is good.

3 medium-size beets, (about 1 lb/455 g), peeled

1 large Vidalia onion, peeled

spray oil

1/4 cup (60 ml) peel grapefruit sections, chopped

2 tablespoons fresh grapefruit juice

2 tablespoons extra-virgin olive oil

1 tablespoon tarragon vinegar

1 tablespoon finely chopped fresh tarragon, or 1 teaspoon dried

1 tablespoon sugar

pinch of salt and freshly ground black pepper

1/2 cup (14 g) crisp bread cubes

1 bunch arugula, rinsed

❶ Prepare the grill. Prepare beets and onions, and cut each into 1/4-inch/5/8-cm slices; spray oil on them. When the fire is ready, grill the slices in a hinged basket to keep them from falling through the grid openings. The beets will take about 15 minutes to grill both sides; the onions, about 10 minutes. When done, transfer the vegetables to a bowl; add the chopped grapefruit.

❷ In another bowl, combine grapefruit juice, olive oil, vinegar, tarragon, sugar, salt, and pepper. Mix well, and pour over the beet mixture.

❸ Just before serving, add the bread cubes, and toss lightly.

❹ To serve, arrange some arugula leaves on each of 4 plates; distribute the beet mixture over top.

Each serving			
Calories	135	Total Fat	7 g
Protein	2 g	Saturated Fat	1 g
Carbohydrates	17 g	Cholesterol	0 mg
Dietary Fiber	2 g	Sodium	59 mg

SKEWERED BOK CHOY ROLLS WITH GINGER-SESAME MARINADE

MAKES 4 SERVINGS

These Oriental green packets on skewers are tasty and fun to make. If they begin to darken while on the grill, move them to a cooler spot. These are a good addition to a grilled vegetable plate.

1/3 cup (80 ml) low-sodium soy or tamari sauce

2 tablespoons minced fresh ginger

1 tablespoon each: sesame chili oil and canola oil

1 head bok choy, about 8 leaves

1 red bell pepper, cut into 12 (1 1/4-inch /3 1/4-cm) squares

1 In a small bowl, combine the soy sauce, ginger, and oil; mix well and set aside.

2 Cut off the stem end of the bok choy; trim and separate the leaves. Rinse and dry well. Cut off the green leaves, leaving them whole. Slice the white stems into 1- to 1 1/4-inch (2 1/2- to 3 1/4-cm) pieces.

3 Brush the marinade on the leaves; fold in both sides of each leaf, then roll to make a small package.

4 Thread each of 4 skewers with white stem pieces, rolled leaves, then red pepper squares. Repeat until the skewers are full (about 3 pieces of each item on each skewer). Brush marinade over the vegetables. Prepare the grill.

5 When the fire is ready, spray the grid with oil, then add the skewers. Grill about 15 minutes, turning several times to grill all sides. Baste with any leftover marinade.

Serving suggestion: Serve with Wasabi Sauce (page 269) on the side.

Each serving (not including Wasabi Sauce)			
Calories	108	Total Fat	7 g
Protein	4 g	Saturated Fat	0.8 g
Carbohydrates	8 g	Cholesterol	0 mg
Dietary Fiber	3 g	Sodium	706 mg

GRILLED ITALIAN BREAD WITH TOMATOES AND BASIL

MAKES 4 SERVINGS

This simple, satisfying dish is even better if the bread is grilled over a small wood or charcoal fire.

2 small sweet red onions, finely chopped

2 small garlic cloves, minced

freshly ground black pepper to taste

2 tablespoons balsamic vinegar

2 tablespoons olive oil, divided

1/4 cup (28 g) finely chopped fresh basil, or 4 teaspoons dried, divided

8 medium-size ripe tomatoes

4 large slices country-style Italian or sourdough bread

1 large garlic clove, halved

❶ In a medium-size bowl, combine onions, minced garlic, pepper, and vinegar. Stir in all but 1 teaspoon oil. Add 1/2 of the basil leaves. Mix well and set aside.

❷ Slice the tomatoes as thinly as you can; season each slice with pepper. Cut the bread into 1/2-inch (1 1/4-cm) thick slices. Prepare the fire.

❸ When the fire is ready, add the bread, and grill for 2 minutes or so on each side; the goal is to toast the bread golden-brown, not scorch it. Remove the bread from the grill, and brush the remaining 1 teaspoon oil on one side of each of the 4 bread slices; quickly rub the garlic halves onto each oiled side. Arrange the bread slices on a platter or individual plates. Divide tomato slices among the 4 slices of bread; sprinkle with the remaining basil. Carefully pour the vinegar dressing over the tomatoes. Serve immediately.

Each serving			
Calories	204	Total Fat	8.4 g
Protein	5 g	Saturated Fat	1.2 g
Carbohydrates	30 g	Cholesterol	0 mg
Dietary Fiber	4 g	Sodium	178 mg

BROCCOLI, FENNEL, AND ONIONS WITH OLIVE OIL AND GARLIC

MAKES 4 SERVINGS

This unusual combination of vegetables tastes wonderful when grilled.

    1 head broccoli, cut into 2-inch (5-cm) florets
    1 fresh fennel bulb, trimmed and cut into 1/4-inch (5/8-cm) slices
    2 medium-size onions, peeled and cut into quarters
1/3 cup (80 ml) low-sodium, defatted chicken broth
    3 garlic cloves, minced
    2 tablespoons olive oil
      freshly ground black pepper to taste

❶ Prepare the vegetables, and place them in an oiled, hinged wire basket. Prepare the fire.

❷ In a medium-size bowl, combine the remaining ingredients, liberally seasoning with pepper; brush the broth mixture over both sides of the vegetables in the basket.

❸ When the fire is ready, place the basket on the grill, and cook 6 minutes on each side, basting frequently with the broth mixture.

Each serving			
Calories	136	Total Fat	7.4 g
Protein	5 g	Saturated Fat	1 g
Carbohydrates	16 g	Cholesterol	0 mg
Dietary Fiber	6 g	Sodium	77 mg

GRILLED CORN ON THE COB WITH CHILI BUTTER

MAKES 4 SERVINGS

One of the best ways to grill corn is to pull back the husks, brush seasonings onto the corn, then fold back the husks, and put the corn on the grill. The corn and seasonings will steam inside the husk, and the end result will be delicious. Don't forget to soak the corn in cool water for 15 minutes, before seasoning the corn.

1 tablespoon melted butter

1 large or 2 small garlic cloves, minced

1 teaspoon chili powder

4 ears fresh corn, unshucked

❶ Combine butter, garlic, and chili powder in a small bowl; mix well and set aside.

❷ Soak unshucked corn in cool water for 15 minutes. Drain corn, then carefully pull back the husks without removing them at the stem end. Carefully remove the silks. Brush the chili butter onto each ear, then smooth husks back over the corn. You may tie kitchen string around the ears of corn to secure the husks, but it is not necessary. Prepare the grill.

❸ When the fire is ready, grill the corn in one of two ways:
a) Wrap each ear in foil and then put on the grill; close the cover, and grill about 30 minutes, turning every 10 minutes or so.
b) Or put the ears directly on the grill, and cook 15 to 20 minutes, turning once. Watch carefully to make sure the husks do not catch fire.

Each serving			
Calories	162	Total Fat	4.6 g
Protein	4 g	Saturated Fat	2 g
Carbohydrates	32 g	Cholesterol	8 mg
Dietary Fiber	4 g	Sodium	57 mg

GRILLED CORN WITH SPICY TOMATO SAUCE

MAKES 8 SERVINGS

This can be served as a side dish or as a salad.

4 cups (648 g) grilled corn kernels (4 to 6 ears)

2 tomatoes, cored, peeled, seeded, and coarsely chopped

1 small onion, peeled and coarsely chopped

2 tablespoons ketchup

1 tablespoon each: vegetable oil and seasoned rice vinegar

1 teaspoon paprika

1/2 teaspoon chili powder

❶ Grill the corn (page 211, eliminating seasonings); cut off the kernels and put them in a bowl; set aside.

❷ Combine the remaining ingredients in the bowl of a food processor; pulse several times to blend. Do not liquefy—the sauce should be chunky. Pour sauce into the bowl with the corn, stir well. May be served at room temperature.

Each serving			
Calories	119	Total Fat	3 g
Protein	3 g	Saturated Fat	0.4 g
Carbohydrates	24 g	Cholesterol	0 mg
Dietary Fiber	3 g	Sodium	64 mg

GRILLED BRUSSELS SPROUTS WITH CUMIN, CURRY, AND FENNEL

MAKES 4 SERVINGS

Try this recipe for Brussels sprouts, even if you don't like them. The flavor is exciting and exotic.

24 fresh Brussels sprouts, trimmed

    spray oil

  1 tablespoon olive oil

  1 teaspoon ground cumin

  1 teaspoon curry powder

1/2 teaspoon fennel seeds

❶ Cut an "x" in the stem end of each Brussels sprout; place in a bowl, and cover with lightly salted cool water. Let sit 1 hour, then drain. Prepare the fire.

❷ Thread 6 Brussels sprouts onto each of 4 skewers. Spray oil on both sides of each sprout.

❸ When the fire is ready, spray oil on the grid and add the skewers. Grill about 6 minutes on each side, longer if the Brussels sprouts are large; turn once.

❹ Meanwhile, combine remaining ingredients in a small saucepan; cook, stirring, over moderate heat for several minutes to allow flavors to develop. Brush the spice mixture over the sprouts as they come off the grill.

Each serving			
Calories	83	Total Fat	4 g
Protein	4 g	Saturated Fat	0.5 g
Carbohydrates	11 g	Cholesterol	0 mg
Dietary Fiber	6 g	Sodium	30 mg

GRILLED CELERY, FENNEL, ONION, AND BELL PEPPER

MAKES 4 SERVINGS

A great combination of vegetables, the foil packet allows the smoky flavors of the grill to penetrate the food. Serve these vegetables with grilled chicken or turkey, or as a first course. As a vegetarian main dish, serve it over cooked rice.

2 celery hearts, trimmed, and quartered lengthwise

1 fennel bulb, trimmed and cut lengthwise into 8 pieces

1 large onion, peeled and cut into 8 wedges

1 large red, yellow, or orange bell pepper, seeded and cut into 8 strips

spray oil

juice of 1 whole lemon (3 tablespoons)

1/3 cup (80 ml) vegetable or defatted chicken broth

salt and freshly ground black pepper, to taste

1 tablespoon honey

1 Combine all the vegetables in a bowl; spray them with oil, then add lemon juice and broth. Toss well. Add a dash of salt and a liberal amount of black pepper; lightly toss again.

2 Using a large sheet of heavy-duty foil make a Bundle Wrap (page 10). Lightly spray oil on the foil. Transfer all the vegetables and juices to the foil; pour the honey over top. Fold the ends of the foil, leaving the packet partially open. Punch several holes in the sides of the package, high enough so the juices don't ooze out. Prepare the fire.

3 When the fire is ready, carefully set the package on the grid. Close the cover and grill 20 to 30 minutes, or until the vegetables are tender. Test for doneness with a wooden skewer. Check several times to see if the package needs to be moved to a cooler spot on the grill. When done, serve immediately.

Each serving			
Calories	62	Total Fat	0.3 g
Protein	2 g	Saturated Fat	0 g
Carbohydrates	15 g	Cholesterol	0 mg
Dietary Fiber	4 g	Sodium	197 mg

GRILLED EGGPLANT WITH CHILI-SOY MARINADE

MAKES 4 SERVINGS

The eggplant is delicious because the marinade is quite heavy with onions and garlic. More marinade can be added to each slice after the first side is cooked. The flavor is great, and will complement many dishes. I often add a slice or two of this eggplant to the side of a salad.

2 tablespoons chili oil

1 tablespoon each: low-sodium soy sauce and seasoned rice vinegar

2 garlic cloves, minced

1/2 medium-size onion, minced

1 eggplant (1 lb/455 g)

1 In a bowl, combine the chili oil, soy sauce, rice vinegar, garlic, and onion; set marinade aside.

2 Rinse and dry the eggplant. Remove the ends but do not peel. Slice no thicker than 1/2 inch (1 1/4 cm).

3 When the fire is ready, brush the marinade on both sides of each slice. The eggplant soaks up the marinade, so be frugal; you need enough to cover the slices, and still have some left over. Grill about 5 minutes on each side, turning once and basting with additional marinade. Grill the second side with the cover down. Test for doneness with a wooden skewer; if the skewer penetrates easily, the slice is done. To avoid scorching the eggplant, move the slices around the grill or right into an oven at 275°F/135°C when done. Then enjoy!

Each serving			
Calories	109	Total Fat	7.2 g
Protein	2 g	Saturated Fat	1 g
Carbohydrates	11 g	Cholesterol	0 mg
Dietary Fiber	4 g	Sodium	131 mg

FEDELINI PASTA WITH GRILLED PEPPERS AND ZUCCHINI

MAKES 8 SERVINGS

Fedelini is a dried, fine pasta, narrower than spaghetti, but larger than angel hair. It is a favorite of mine.

- 6 tablespoons extra-virgin olive oil
- 3 tablespoons seasoned rice vinegar
- freshly ground black pepper to taste
- 4 (1-by-6-inch/2 1/2-by-15 1/4-cm) zucchini, rinsed, ends removed, and cut in half lengthwise
- 1 large red onion, trimmed and cut into 1/2-inch (1 1/4-cm) slices
- 2 large garlic cloves, minced
- 2 large red, yellow, or orange bell peppers, grilled, peeled, and seeded, or use prepared roasted peppers (see note)
- 1 cup (235 g) finely chopped fresh or canned tomatoes
- 1 1/2 cups (360 ml) vegetable or defatted chicken broth
- 1 lb (455 g) fedelini or other thin pasta
- 1/4 cup (28 g) each, finely chopped fresh: basil and flat-leaf parsley
- red pepper flakes (optional)
- 8 thin slivers Romano cheese, or 1/2 cup (57 g) freshly grated

◆ To make the dressing combine oil, vinegar, and black pepper in a large, shallow bowl. Add zucchini, onion, and garlic, adding more pepper as desired. Toss well, and marinate 30 to 40 minutes. Drain the vegetables, reserving the dressing. Prepare the grill.

Continued on next page

FRESH TOMATO SAUCE
MAKES ABOUT 2 CUPS (480 ML)

Another marvelous way to serve pasta or grilled vegetables is with this versatile sauce.

- 1 teaspoon olive oil
- 3 tablespoons red wine vinegar
- 1 small onion, peeled and finely chopped
- 1 garlic clove, minced
- 1 lb (455 g) ripe tomatoes, cored, peeled, seeded, and chopped, or 1 (16-oz/455-g) can chopped tomatoes, drained
- pinch of sugar
- freshly ground black pepper to taste

In a large glass bowl, combine all the ingredients, seasoning liberally with pepper. Taste and adjust the seasoning with more vinegar, if you wish.

❷ When the fire is ready, spray the grid with oil. Place zucchini and onion in a hinged wire basket, then grill about 4 minutes on each side. When done, remove from the grill to cool; cut into 3/4-inch (1 7/8-cm) pieces.

❸ Put the reserved dressing in a large saucepan. Add zucchini, onion, bell peppers, tomatoes, and broth; bring to a boil, then turn the heat off, and let sit while preparing pasta.

❹ Cook the pasta according to package directions until *al dente*. Drain well, then add pasta to vegetable mixture. Add basil, parsley, and red pepper flakes; toss over low heat to blend well, 2 to 3 minutes.

❺ To serve, divide among 8 plates, and add a sliver of Romano to the top of each serving, or pass the cheese, and let people add their own.

Note: To save time, buy prepared roasted peppers, available in 6 1/2-oz (184-g) jars or 7-oz (200-g) cans.

Each serving			
Calories	365	Total Fat	13.3 g
Protein	12 g	Saturated Fat	2.7 g
Carbohydrates	49 g	Cholesterol	5 mg
Dietary Fiber	3 g	Sodium	154 mg

GRILLED CHINESE CABBAGE

MAKES 4 SERVINGS

Chinese cabbage is known in the United States as either Napa cabbage, which looks like romaine lettuce, or bok choy, which looks like a cross between Swiss chard and celery, and also may be called Chinese mustard cabbage. Napa cabbage is crispy and juicy, with a more delicate flavor than other cabbages; the leaves have a slightly bitter taste, but its white stalks are sweeter.

1 small to medium-size head Napa cabbage, trimmed, and quartered lengthwise

1 tablespoon each: sesame chili oil, mustard seeds, and fresh lemon juice

1/2 teaspoon sugar

pinch of salt

freshly ground black pepper to taste

❶ Prepare the cabbage; mix remaining ingredients in a small bowl. Brush the chili oil mixture over the cut sides of each cabbage quarter, using all of the mixture. Prepare the grill.

❷ When the fire is ready, place the cabbage on the grill, cut side down. Grill, with the cover down, about 12 minutes, or until lightly browned. Turn cabbage over, and cook about 12 minutes more. Test for doneness with a wooden skewer; the cabbage should be tender before taking it off the grill.

Each serving			
Calories	60	Total Fat	4.4 g
Protein	2.5 g	Saturated Fat	0.5 g
Carbohydrates	4 g	Cholesterol	0 mg
Dietary Fiber	2 g	Sodium	38 mg

GRILLED GARLIC BULBS WITH ITALIAN BREAD

MAKES 4 SERVINGS

Garlic becomes soft and sweet when grilled; the taste is quite different from raw garlic. Oil, salt, and pepper add more flavor as the garlic cooks. Grilled garlic is a natural companion to bread. Spread the garlic on the bread slices, and enjoy it simply with fresh tomato slices.

4 whole garlic bulbs

1 teaspoon unsalted butter, melted

1 tablespoon olive oil

juice of 1 whole lemon (3 tablespoons)

4 sprigs fresh thyme, or 1 teaspoon dried

salt and freshly ground black pepper to taste

4 (1/2-inch/1 1/4-cm) slices Italian bread

1 Remove papery skins from garlic bulbs, leaving the bulbs whole. With a sharp knife, slice off the top quarter of each bulb to expose the top of the cloves.

2 Cut 4 sheets of heavy-duty foil, each about 12 inches (30 cm) square. Place 1 garlic bulb in the center of each piece of foil. In a small bowl, combine butter, oil, and lemon juice. Brush butter mixture on the cut end of each bulb. Place 1 herb sprig across each bulb; season with salt and pepper, then wrap the bulbs in the foil, see Bundle Wrap (page 10). Prepare the grill.

3 When the fire is ready, place the packets over the fire, and grill for 30 to 40 minutes. Remove from the grill, open the packets, and allow the bulbs to cool.

4 Grill the bread slices on both sides until golden.

5 Place 1 piece of bread on each of 4 plates; position 1 garlic bulb to the side of each piece of bread. Instruct guests to squeeze the pulp out of each clove and onto the bread. (Alternatively, lay a whole bulb on its side, then press on it to squeeze the pulp from the bulb all at once. Repeat with remaining 3 bulbs, scooping the pulp into a bowl to be passed with the bread.)

Each serving			
Calories	150	Total Fat	5.5 g
Protein	4 g	Saturated Fat	1.3 g
Carbohydrates	22 g	Cholesterol	3 mg
Dietary Fiber	1 g	Sodium	188 mg

PURÉE OF GRILLED CHESTNUTS

MAKES 4 SERVINGS

Chestnuts have an earthy flavor, and are an excellent accompaniment to most grilled meats and poultry. My grandmother had to cook two pounds of these because my grandfather would eat a pound as they came off the grill. He would cover them first with a towel and let them cool for a half hour or so that they would be easier to peel. He was right, that is the best way to unpeel chestnuts.

1 lb (455 g) chestnuts

1 teaspoon vegetable oil

1 tablespoon white wine vinegar

1 onion, peeled and halved

2 large celery ribs, cut into 3-inch (7 1/2-cm) lengths

   freshly ground black pepper to taste

1 tablespoon olive oil

❶ Cut an "x" on the flat side of each chestnut. Place them in a foil pan with the vegetable oil and toss to coat. Prepare the grill.

❷ When the fire is ready, place the foil pan on the grill and close the cover; grill about 30 minutes, or until the shells and underskins may be removed easily.

❸ Combine shelled chestnuts in a saucepan with vinegar, onion, and celery; add just enough water to cover. Bring to boil, lower the heat to a slow, steady simmer, and cook, covered, until chestnuts are very tender, about 30 minutes. Drain, discarding celery and onions. Return chestnuts to the saucepan and add pepper and olive oil; mash with a potato masher. Serve warm.

Each serving			
Calories	235	Total Fat	5.7 g
Protein	2 g	Saturated Fat	0.8 g
Carbohydrates	44 g	Cholesterol	0 mg
Dietary Fiber	6 g	Sodium	20 mg

EGGPLANT ROLLS IN HERBED SAUCE

MAKES 4 SERVINGS

Make the sauce the night before serving. The grilled eggplant rolls marinate in the sauce thirty minutes before serving. This may be served as an appetizer, side dish, or buffet item.

2 small eggplants, about 1 1/4 lb
1 teaspoon canola oil
1 tablespoon olive oil
1/4 cup (60 ml) red wine vinegar
1 anchovy, rinsed 2 or 3 times
2 garlic cloves, minced
1/4 cup (28 g) finely chopped flat-leaf parsley
2 tablespoons finely chopped red onion
2 tablespoons drained capers, rinsed
    freshly ground black pepper to taste

1 Prepare the grill. Wipe the eggplant clean and cut off the ends; do not peel. Stand each eggplant on one end, and cut lengthwise into 1/4-inch (5/8-cm) slices. Lightly brush canola oil on both sides of each slice, then grill until tender, 6 to 10 minutes, turning once. Do not char them, or they will break when you roll them. Remove the slices as they grill, rolling each one; set rolls on a large platter.

2 In a small bowl, combine olive oil, vinegar, and anchovy; mix with a fork, breaking up the anchovy and blending it into the mixture. Add remaining ingredients, then pour over eggplant rolls.

3 Let marinate at room temperature about 30 minutes before serving.

Each serving			
Calories	128	Total Fat	5.3 g
Protein	3 g	Saturated Fat	0.7 g
Carbohydrates	21 g	Cholesterol	1 mg
Dietary Fiber	7 g	Sodium	205 mg

SKEWERED MUSHROOMS IN SESAME-SOY MARINADE

MAKES 4 SERVINGS

This is a tasty dish that can accompany almost any other grilled food. It is excellent as an appetizer or first course, also.

1 lb (455 g) medium-size white button or cremini mushrooms

2 tablespoons finely chopped chives, parsley, or scallions

1 tablespoon each: low-sodium tamari and sesame oil

2 garlic cloves, minced

2 scallions, coarsely chopped

1/2 teaspoon ground ginger

juice of 1 whole lemon (3 tablespoons)

❶ To make the sesame-soy marinade, combine the tamari and sesame oil, minced garlic, chopped scallions, ground ginger, and lemon juice in the bowl of a small food processor; pulse to purée. Transfer marinade to a large glass bowl.

❷ Do not peel or wash the mushrooms. Instead, wipe them clean, then cut off and discard the thick end of the stems. Put the mushrooms in the bowl with the marinade, tossing well. Let mushrooms marinate several hours, refrigerated; bring them to room temperature before adding to the grill. Meanwhile, prepare the grill.

❸ When the fire is ready, thread mushrooms onto 4 skewers running the skewers through the caps and out the stems. Place skewers on a lightly oiled grid, and cook 10 to 15 minutes, turning to grill all sides. Baste with any leftover marinade.

❹ Sprinkle with chives before serving.

SESAME OILS

Three of my favorite oils to cook with are all sesame oils. One is dark, with a nutty, somewhat strong flavor. It is made from roasted sesame seeds, and is available in stores where Chinese and Japanese ingredients are sold. This oil can be used for flavoring and sautéing, but a little bit goes a long way. The second is paler, and not quite as strong in taste as the roasted sesame oil. This can be used in wok cooking. It, too, is available in markets selling Asian foods. The third type is a sesame chili oil. Sesame oil and chili oil are combined with a fiery result; it should be used with discretion. Any of these oils will help create great-tasting grilled foods.

Each serving			
Calories	71	Total Fat	4 g
Protein	3 g	Saturated Fat	0.6 g
Carbohydrates	8 g	Cholesterol	0 mg
Dietary Fiber	2 g	Sodium	133 mg

PENNE PASTA WITH GRILLED CORN AND LEEK SAUCE

MAKES 4 SERVINGS

The smoky flavors of the grilled vegetables seep into the pasta sauce and make this a tasty dish, while the grilled corn and leeks add texture.

spray oil

2 leeks (about 1 inch/2 1/2 cm thick), cleaned and thinly sliced crosswise

2 cups (604 g) chopped tomatoes

2 garlic cloves, minced

1/4 cup (28 g) finely chopped fresh basil, or 4 teaspoons dried

1 teaspoon sugar

1/2 teaspoon fennel seeds

freshly ground black pepper to taste

2 ears fresh corn, in husks

1/2 lb (230 g) penne pasta, cooked

1/4 cup (29 g) freshly grated pecorino cheese

❶ Cut 2 (18-inch/45 3/4 cm-square) sheets of foil and stack them; lightly spray oil on the top side.

❷ Discard the dark green portion of each leek. Put leeks, tomatoes, garlic, basil, sugar, fennel seed, and pepper in the center of the foil. Make a Bundle Wrap (page 10); don't fret if there are gaps at the top of the packet.

❸ Peel back the husks on the corn, exposing the silk without removing the husk. Remove the silk, and smooth husks back over the corn; immerse in water for 10 minutes.

❹ Prepare the grill. Lightly spray the grid with oil. When the fire is ready, place the foil packet and the corn on the grid. Grill about 20 minutes, turning the corn every 5 minutes or so. Remove from grill.

❺ Transfer contents of the foil packet to a large bowl. Cut the kernels off the cobs, and add them to the bowl. Add the cooked pasta and toss well. Season with black pepper, and serve, passing the cheese on the side.

Each serving			
Calories	339	Total Fat	3.9 g
Protein	12 g	Saturated Fat	1.4 g
Carbohydrates	67 g	Cholesterol	7 mg
Dietary Fiber	6 g	Sodium	108 mg

HERBED PORTOBELLO MUSHROOMS WITH MASCARPONE

MAKES 4 SERVINGS

People often confuse portobellos and porcini mushrooms, as their flavor is quite similar. Portobellos are meatier than porcino, and have large spreading caps that are deep brown in color. Portobellos are cultivated, and often are more readily available than porcinos. Like most mushrooms, portobellos are delicate, so they should be used within 24 hours.

8 large fresh portobello mushrooms, wiped clean, stems removed
   spray oil
   juice of 1/2 lemon (1 1/2 tablespoons)
2 garlic cloves, minced
1 tablespoon each, finely chopped: basil and oregano, or
1 teaspoon each dried
1/3 cup (80 ml) low-sodium vegetable or defatted chicken broth
   freshly ground black pepper to taste
2 oz (57 g) mascarpone cheese, divided into 8 pieces

❶ Prepare the mushrooms, and lightly spray oil on both sides.

❷ Combine lemon juice and garlic in a small saucepan over medium heat; sauté garlic 1 to 2 minutes. Add herbs, broth, and pepper. Bring to a boil, then remove from heat.

❸ Liberally brush each mushroom with the herb mixture, especially on the undersides, where the mixture will be absorbed. Roll the mascarpone pieces into 8 balls; set aside.

❹ Prepare the grill. Lightly spray the grid with oil. When the fire is ready, add the mushrooms, grill, right side up, 6 to 8 minutes, with the grill cover down. Turn the mushrooms over, and add 1 cheese ball to the center of each, where the stem was removed. Close the cover again, and grill about 6 minutes longer. Remove mushrooms from the grill, and serve hot.

Each serving			
Calories	78	Total Fat	4.4 g
Protein	4 g	Saturated Fat	3 g
Carbohydrates	7 g	Cholesterol	11 mg
Dietary Fiber	1 g	Sodium	89 mg

SHIITAKE MUSHROOMS WITH WINE GLAZE

MAKES 4 SERVINGS

Mushrooms all grill beautifully. Be sure to select firm mushrooms that are clean and unblemished, with no gray spots. It is not necessary to peel them; instead, brush or wipe them lightly, then trim the stems. For the different types of mushrooms, see page 234.

1 cup (240 ml) low-sodium, defatted chicken broth

1/2 cup (120 ml) dry white wine

    freshly ground black pepper to taste

1 lb (455 g) large, fresh shiitake mushrooms

1 tablespoon olive oil

2 garlic cloves, halved

1 Combine chicken broth and wine in a saucepan over high heat; boil until mixture is reduced by 2/3, 5 to 10 minutes. Stir in the pepper and set aside.

2 Trim mushrooms and cut stems so the caps will lie flat on the grilling grid. Put mushrooms in a glass dish in a single layer.

3 Heat the oil in a skillet, and add the garlic; sauté until garlic begins to turn golden, about 3 minutes. Discard the garlic, reserving the oil; cool. Pour oil over the mushrooms and toss; use your hands to coat the mushrooms with oil. Prepare the grill.

4 When the fire is ready, add the mushrooms, and grill 2 minutes or longer on each side. When ready to serve, brush the wine glaze over the mushrooms.

Each serving			
Calories	117	Total Fat	3.6 g
Protein	2 g	Saturated Fat	0.5 g
Carbohydrates	17 g	Cholesterol	0 mg
Dietary Fiber	2 g	Sodium	20 mg

SKEWERED OKRA

MAKES 4 SERVINGS

Always popular in the South, okra is now available in many supermarkets and green grocers in other parts of the country. It is an essential ingredient in Creole cooking. Okra has a unique texture, and its flavor tastes like a cross between egg-plant and asparagus. Okra combines well with other vegetables, especially corn, tomatoes, and bell peppers. It also can be added to the Garlic Sweet Grilled Tomatoes dish on page 253.

20 okra pods (about 1 lb/455 g)

1 tablespoon olive oil

2 garlic cloves, peeled and halved

   pinch of red pepper flakes

❶ Rinse and dry the okra. Trim the stems, and thread 5 pods onto each of 4 skewers; set aside.

❷ In a small pan, heat oil over medium heat; add garlic, and sauté until golden. Remove the pan from the heat, and discard the garlic, reserving the oil; add red pepper flakes. Brush the flavored oil over the okra, coating well. Prepare the grill.

❸ When the fire is ready, place the skewers on the grill, and cook for about 15 minutes, or until they are tender and lightly charred, turning as needed.

Each serving			
Calories	49	Total Fat	3.5 g
Protein	1 g	Saturated Fat	0.5 g
Carbohydrates	4 g	Cholesterol	0 mg
Dietary Fiber	1 g	Sodium	3 mg

HONEY GRILLED ONIONS WITH CLOVES

MAKES 4 SERVINGS

I love onions on the grill; they can be used in so many ways. Add them to a green salad; use them as a side dish with other vegetables, grilled chicken, or pork; and surely add them to the many grilled fish recipes in this book.

4 large white onions, peeled

spray oil

4 tablespoons honey

2 garlic cloves, minced

1 tablespoon finely chopped fresh oregano, or 1 teaspoon dried

1 teaspoon ground cloves

freshly ground black pepper to taste

❶ Cut 2 sheets of foil, each 12 by 18 inches (30 by 45 cm) and stack them.

❷ Cut onions into 1/4-inch (5/8-cm) slices; spray each side of each slice with oil.

❸ Stack 1/3 of the onion slices on the foil. Drizzle half of the honey, half of the garlic, half of the oregano, and half of the cloves over the onions. Grind some fresh pepper over top.

❹ Place another third of the onions on top, then add remaining honey, garlic, oregano, and cloves. Top with remaining onion slices, then wrap foil around onions, using the Drugstore Wrap (page 10). Prepare the grill.

❺ When the fire is ready, place the packet on the grill. Grill 10 minutes, then turn the packet and grill the second side 10 minutes more. Cool a few minutes before carefully opening the packet.

Each serving			
Calories	126	Total Fat	0.4 g
Protein	2 g	Saturated Fat	0.1 g
Carbohydrates	31 g	Cholesterol	0 mg
Dietary Fiber	3 g	Sodium	7 mg

GRILLED PEPPER, ONION, AND SMOKED MOZZARELLA SANDWICHES

MAKES 4 SERVINGS

This is perfect for a luncheon. Just add a green salad, and some fruit for dessert. The combination of grilled peppers with onions and mozzarella is superb.

2 red bell peppers

1 large onion, peeled and cut into 1/4-inch (5/8-cm) slices

1/2 lb (230 g) smoked mozzarella, thinly sliced

4 (1/2-inch/1 1/4-cm) slices Italian bread

2 tablespoons olive oil

2 garlic cloves, minced

❶ Prepare the grill. Grill the peppers. Peel and seed the peppers, then slice the flesh into 2-inch (5-cm)-wide strips; set aside. Grill onion slices, and set aside; they may be grilled with the peppers.

❷ Grill bread slices lightly on 1 side. Remove bread to a work surface.

❸ In a small bowl, combine oil and garlic; brush oil mixture onto the grilled sides of each bread slice. Divide peppers, onions, and cheese among slices of bread; return bread to the grill. Do not put the bread slices over direct heat. Close the cover, and heat until cheese melts, 3 to 5 minutes.

Each serving			
Calories	350	Total Fat	22 g
Protein	16 g	Saturated Fat	11.3 g
Carbohydrates	22 g	Cholesterol	41 mg
Dietary Fiber	2 g	Sodium	542 mg

GRILLED EGGPLANT WITH BASIL AND GARLIC SAUCE

MAKES 4 SERVINGS

This simple dish is typical of the way eggplant is often grilled in Italy. I have enjoyed it many times, and I think you will also. If you refrigerate the Basil and Garlic Sauce, you will have to bring it to room temperature before serving it.

3 cloves garlic, chopped

1/4 cup (20 g) fresh basil leaves

4 walnuts, chopped

2 tablespoons olive oil

1 eggplant (about 1 lb/455 g)

2 tablespoons flour

salt and freshly ground black pepper, to taste

spray oil

1 Combine garlic, basil, and walnuts in a mortar; pound with a pestle, slowly incorporating the oil. (Alternatively, blend in the bowl of a small food processor.) Set aside.

2 Wipe the eggplant clean and remove the stalk end; slice a piece off the other end so the eggplant can sit upright. Cut the eggplant crosswise into 1/2-inch (1 1/4-cm) slices. Lightly salt the slices, then put them in a colander for 20 to 30 minutes to drain. Wipe the slices dry with paper towels. Prepare the grill.

3 When the fire is ready, spray the grid with oil. Lightly dust the slices with flour, salt, and pepper; spray oil on one side of each slice. Put the oiled sides on the grill, and spray the top sides with oil. Grill each side about 4 minutes. To test for doneness, run a small wooden skewer through each slice; if the skewer penetrates easily, the eggplant is cooked.

4 Serve hot with a dollop of Basil and Garlic Sauce.

Each serving			
Calories	146	Total Fat	10 g
Protein	3 g	Saturated Fat	1.2 g
Carbohydrates	13 g	Cholesterol	0 mg
Dietary Fiber	4 g	Sodium	138 mg

GRILLED FENNEL SLICES WITH SMOKED MOZZARELLA

MAKES 4 SERVINGS

Combining fennel and mozzarella creates a wonderful marriage of Mediterranean flavors. Smoked mozzarella is preferred, but if you can't find it, regular mozzarella will do.

4 (1/2-inch/1 1/4-cm) slices fresh fennel (1 large or 2 small bulbs)

1/2 cup (120 ml) low-sodium, defatted chicken broth

1 teaspoon olive oil

4 very thin slices smoked mozzarella

freshly ground black pepper to taste

❶ Prepare the fennel, placing the 4 slices in a skillet. Add broth, and bring to a boil over medium heat. Lower the heat, and simmer until almost tender, about 5 minutes. Remove the slices, and place on paper towels. Brush both sides of each slice with a little oil. Prepare the grill.

❷ When the fire is ready, place the fennel slices in a hinged wire basket and place on the grill; cook 3 minutes on each side, turning once.

❸ Just before removing the fennel slices from the grill, carefully add a slice of mozzarella to each. Within seconds, the cheese should begin to melt. Remove the fennel from the grill, and season with pepper; serve immediately.

Each serving			
Calories	77	Total Fat	4.8 g
Protein	5 g	Saturated Fat	2.7 g
Carbohydrates	5 g	Cholesterol	10 mg
Dietary Fiber	2 g	Sodium	143 mg

GRILLED FRESH FIGS AND CREMINI MUSHROOMS

MUSHROOMS

The most popular mushroom varieties include:

(a) White and Off-white Buttons: A light, earthy flavor.
(b) Brown Buttons: A stronger flavor; frequently labeled cremini.
(c) Cèpes: An intense flavor; also known as bolete and porcini.
(d) Chanterelles: Strong flavor; shaped like trumpets.
(e) Enokis: Mild and sweet; small caps, long, thin stems.
(f) Portobellos: Hearty flavor; large, flat tops and long, thick stems.
(g) Shiitakes: Rich flavor; large umbrella-shaped caps; brown-black color, Also called golden oak, black, and forest mushrooms.

MAKES 4 SERVINGS

My grandfather's favorite foods were figs and mushrooms. He had his own fig tree on a fire escape landing in a New York City apartment. He loved eating them fresh, but on outings and picnics, he would grill them with mushrooms.

4 fresh figs
8 cremini mushrooms, stems trimmed
　spray oil
1/3 cup (80 ml) red wine
2 garlic cloves, minced
　salt to taste (optional)
　freshly ground black pepper to taste

❶ Clean the figs and mushrooms with a damp towel and set aside.

❷ In a small skillet, heat wine and garlic over medium-high heat, reducing wine until slightly thickened, 3 to 5 minutes. Remove from the heat.

❸ Thread 2 mushrooms, alternating with 1 fig, on each of 4 skewers. Brush with the wine mixture to coat. Season with salt and pepper. Prepare the grill.

❹ When the fire is ready, lightly oil the grid, and add the skewers. Grill, turning 2 or 3 times, 15 to 20 minutes. Serve warm.

Each serving			
Calories	62	Total Fat	0.3 g
Protein	1 g	Saturated Fat	0.1 g
Carbohydrates	12 g	Cholesterol	0 mg
Dietary Fiber	2 g	Sodium	3 mg

FOUR ONIONS IN PARCHMENT

MAKES 4 SERVINGS

Combine different kinds of onions for a lively taste. The grilling procedure is different here, but it works extremely well with this recipe.

4 medium-size yellow onions, peeled

1 large red onion, peeled

4 scallions, thinly sliced

8 shallots, peeled and cut into halves

1 tablespoon olive oil

freshly ground black pepper to taste

salt to taste (optional)

❶ Cut each yellow and red onion into 8 wedges.

❷ Divide all onion pieces among 4 sheets of parchment paper, each about 11 by 16 inches (28 by 40 1/2 cm). Add oil, lots of pepper, and salt to each packet. Secure the packages (page 10). Prepare the grill.

❸ When the fire is ready, lay a double fold of foil on the grid, then place the parchment packets on top. Close the grill cover. Cook the onions until they are tender, about 20 minutes. Serve them directly from the packets.

Each serving			
Calories	115	Total Fat	3.7 g
Protein	3 g	Saturated Fat	0.5 g
Carbohydrates	20 g	Cholesterol	0 mg
Dietary Fiber	3 g	Sodium	11 mg

ITALIAN-STYLE STUFFED BELL PEPPERS

MAKES 4 SERVINGS

This makes an entire meal with the addition of a small green salad. To shorten the grilling time, you may parboil the peppers, but I don't think the extra step is necessary. It is important here to grill the peppers over indirect heat. Serve with any of the salsas or sauces in this cookbook that you prefer.

   4 large red bell peppers

   1 teaspoon olive oil

   1 small onion, chopped

1/2 cup (76 g) pine nuts

   2 garlic cloves, minced

   2 tablespoons finely chopped fresh flat-leaf parsley

   1 tablespoon finely chopped fresh oregano, or 1 teaspoon dried

   1 cup (230 g) cooked cannellini beans

   2 1/2 cups (140 g) fresh Italian bread crumbs

1/2 cup (120 ml) white wine

   2 tablespoons freshly grated Parmesan cheese

      pinch of red pepper flakes

❶ Rinse and dry the peppers. Slice the tops off, reserving them, and discard the seeds and ribs; be careful not to puncture the skin. Set aside.

❷ Heat the oil in a skillet over medium heat. Add onions, and cook until soft, about 4 minutes. Add pine nuts and garlic, and cook 2 minutes longer. Remove from the heat.

❸ Add parsley, oregano, beans, bread crumbs, wine, cheese, and red pepper flakes; toss lightly to combine. Fill the peppers with the bread crumb mixture. Put the tops back on the peppers, then tie with string, or secure each with a small steel skewer. Prepare grill.

❹ When the fire is ready, place peppers on the grid. Grill, with the cover down, for 50 to 60 minutes, moving the peppers to cooler spots as needed, and keeping them from charring too much.

Each serving			
Calories	559	Total Fat	21 g
Protein	23 g	Saturated Fat	3 g
Carbohydrates	73 g	Cholesterol	3 mg
Dietary Fiber	9 g	Sodium	1,140 mg

GRILLED PEPPERS WITH WALNUT STUFFING

MAKES 8 SERVINGS

Cubanelle peppers are four to five inches long, with a tapered end. When fully mature, the color can range from yellow or light green to red. They have more flavor than bell peppers, which are a viable substitute if cubanelles are not available. These stuffed peppers are great as a first course atop a bed of field greens, with dry toast on the side. Or serve them as a vegetable with grilled fish or meat.

8 red cubanelle peppers, cut into halves lengthwise and seeded, or 6 large red bell peppers cut into thirds lengthwise and seeded

1 tablespoon olive oil

1 (14.5-oz/411-g) can chopped tomatoes, drained

4 anchovies, soaked in water 15 minutes, drained and finely chopped

1/4 cup (28 g) chopped fresh basil, or 4 teaspoons dried

4 shallots, peeled and minced

2 tablespoons capers, rinsed and drained

2 tablespoons freshly grated Parmesan cheese

1/4 cup (32 1/2 g) chopped walnuts

freshly ground black pepper to taste

❶ Lightly coat peppers with oil, inside and out. Arrange peppers, cut side up, on a work space; set aside.

❷ In a small bowl, combine tomatoes, anchovies, basil, shallots, capers, cheese, and walnuts; mix well. Divide mixture among the pepper halves. Prepare the grill, and lightly oil the grid.

❸ When the fire is ready, place the pepper halves to the edges of the hottest part of the fire. With the cover down, grill about 20 minutes; occasionally check to see that bottoms of peppers are not being scorched. Remove from grill, and serve hot, warm, or at room temperature.

Each serving			
Calories	83	Total Fat	4.7 g
Protein	3 g	Saturated Fat	0.7 g
Carbohydrates	8 g	Cholesterol	3 mg
Dietary Fiber	2 g	Sodium	277 mg

VEGETABLE SAUCE

MAKES ABOUT 1 CUP (240 ML)

Another great way to serve grilled peppers and grilled vegetables in general is with this hearty sauce.

1 teaspoon olive oil

4 small beets, trimmed and rinsed

2 large carrots, trimmed and cut into 1-inch (2 1/2-cm) square chunks

1 tablespoon tamari

1 tablespoon finely chopped fresh oregano, or 1 teaspoon dried

1/2 teaspoon paprika

vegetable broth or water (optional)

❶ Coat beets and carrots with oil in a large bowl. Thread beets on one skewer, and the carrots on another. When the fire is ready, lightly oil the grid. Add the skewers; grill 20 to 30 minutes, remove and cool.

❷ In a food processor, combine beets, carrots, any oil remaining in the bowl, tamari, oregano, and paprika; pulse to liquefy. If the sauce is too thick, thin with vegetable broth. This sauce may be served warm or at room temperature.

Each tablespoon			
Calories	13	Total Fat	0.3 g
Protein	0.4 g	Saturated Fat	0 g
Carbohydrates	2 g	Cholesterol	0 mg
Dietary Fiber	0.5 g	Sodium	63 mg

PEAS AND WATER CHESTNUTS WITH MINT AND GINGER

MAKES 6 SERVINGS

These seem like unlikely ingredients for grill cooking, but nicely flavored in a foil packet, these vegetables render a surprisingly delicious side dish.

1 (10-oz/284-g) package frozen green
   peas, thawed

1 (8-oz/230-g) can water chestnuts, packed in
   water, (whole or sliced)

1 small head Boston or Bibb lettuce, cut into
   thin strips

1/4 cup (28 g) finely chopped fresh mint

6 scallions, thinly sliced

1 tablespoon finely chopped candied ginger

1 teaspoon sugar

1 Combine all the ingredients in a bowl and mix well.

2 Place the mixture in the center of a sheet of heavy-duty foil, about 18 inches (45 3/4 cm) square, and secure it with a Bundle Wrap (page 10). Prepare the grill.

3 When the fire is ready, place the packet on the grill, and cook 15 to 20 minutes. The foil will get very hot, so remove the package with either oven mitts or the help of a spatula.

Each serving			
Calories	94	Total Fat	0.5 g
Protein	5.3 g	Saturated Fat	0.03 g
Carbohydrates	18 g	Cholesterol	0 mg
Dietary Fiber	7 g	Sodium	76 mg

GRILLED POLENTA WITH CHARRED ONIONS AND FENNEL

MAKES 8 TO 9 APPETIZER SERVINGS OR 4 TO 5 MAIN-COURSE SERVINGS

This is a terrific dish that is light enough to be served as an appetizer, yet hearty enough to make a meal, depending on serving sizes. In areas where polenta is hard to find, cornmeal makes a perfect substitute. I use them interchangeably.

    spray oil
1/4 teaspoon fennel seeds
  1 large onion, finely chopped
    white wine
  2 cups (480 ml) low-sodium vegetable or chicken broth
  1 cup (240 ml) cold water
  1 cup (151 g) polenta or yellow cornmeal
  4 teaspoons olive oil, divided
1/4 cup (29 g) freshly grated pecorino cheese
    freshly ground black pepper to taste
    salsa

❶ Lightly spray a skillet with oil; add fennel seeds, and cook 2 minutes over medium heat. Add onions, and sauté until they soften and turn translucent, about 5 minutes. If needed, add 1 or 2 tablespoons white wine, broth, or water to keep onions from sticking to the pan. Cook off the liquid, then set aside.

❷ In a medium-size saucepan, bring 2 cups broth to a boil. In a small bowl, combine polenta and 1 cup water; whisk to blend (this keeps the polenta from lumping). Pour polenta mixture into simmering broth, and whisk constantly until the mixture thickens and leaves the sides of the pan. Remove from the heat. Stir in 2 teaspoons olive oil, cheese, pepper, and onion mixture, mixing well.

Continued on next page

❸ Lightly spray an 8-by-8-by-2-inch (20 1/4-by-20 1/4-by-5-cm) glass dish with oil. Add the polenta mixture, using a rubber spatula to push polenta into the corners of the dish and smooth the surface. Cool to firm, at least 1 hour, or refrigerate overnight. Slice polenta into 9 squares; brush lightly with remaining 2 teaspoons oil. Bring to room temperature, about 20 minutes. Prepare the grill.

❹ When the fire is ready, spray the grid with oil, then add the polenta squares. Grill 3 to 4 minutes on each side, or until each side is browned; use a stainless steel spatula to turn the polenta.

❺ Season with additional black pepper, and serve 2 tablespoons of sauce on the side of each square.

Each serving			
Calories	202	Total Fat	8.4 g
Protein	6 g	Saturated Fat	2.3 g
Carbohydrates	28 g	Cholesterol	9 mg
Dietary Fiber	3 g	Sodium	142 mg

NEW POTATOES ON THE GRILL

MAKES 4 SERVINGS

This is a basic recipe that can be altered in many ways. To begin with, you can add a sprinkling of your favorite herb as the potatoes come off the grill. The grilled potatoes can be cut into halves, then dressed with a light vinaigrette, or used in potato salad. To shorten the grilling time, parboil the potatoes, but I don't think that is necessary.

16 small new potatoes

 1 teaspoon olive oil

freshly ground black pepper to taste

salt to taste (optional)

❶ Wash and dry the potatoes. Put them in a bowl, add the oil, and toss well. Prepare the grill.

❷ Thread 4 potatoes onto each of 4 metal skewers; when the fire is ready, place the skewers on an oiled grid. With the cover down, grill 20 to 30 minutes, depending on the size of the potatoes. When tender, remove potatoes from grill.

❸ Divide skewers among 4 plates, and season potatoes with pepper and a little salt.

Each serving			
Calories	137	Total Fat	1.3 g
Protein	5 g	Saturated Fat	0.2 g
Carbohydrates	26 g	Cholesterol	0 mg
Dietary Fiber	3 g	Sodium	6 mg

GRILLED NEW POTATOES AND GREEN BEANS WITH PESTO

MAKES 6 SERVINGS

Pesto is a popular and tasty condiment, and is delicious here, served on the side with grilled potatoes and green beans.

2 cups water

1 lb (455 g) fresh green beans, rinsed and trimmed

12 small new potatoes (about 1 1/2 lb/680 g)

   spray oil

2 1/2 cups (280 g) tightly packed basil leaves

1/4 cup (28 g) coarsely chopped flat-leaf parsley

2 tablespoons olive oil

1/3 cup (80 ml) low-sodium vegetable broth

2 large garlic cloves, peeled and halved

1/4 cup (45 g) pine nuts

1/4 cup (35 g) freshly grated Parmesan cheese

❶ Bring water to boil in a large pot; insert a steamer basket. Place the beans in the basket, and steam until almost tender, about 8 minutes. Transfer beans to a bowl of ice water to stop the cooking. Drain beans, and cut them into halves.

❷ Prepare the grill. Thread 3 new potatoes onto each of 4 metal skewers. Spray the potatoes and the grid with oil. When the fire is ready, place skewers on the grill. Turning as needed, grill 20 to 30 minutes, or until potatoes are tender. Remove potatoes from the grill and the skewers; set aside. When cool enough to handle, cut each potato in half. Set aside.

❸ To make the Pesto, combine basil, parsley, olive oil, broth, garlic, pine nuts, and Parmesan in the bowl of a food processor. Pulsing 4 or 5 times, process until blended and of sauce consistency. Transfer to a small bowl.

❹ While the fire is still hot, place a hinged wire basket on the grill; lightly oil the basket, then add potatoes and beans. Place the basket on the grill, and heat, tossing frequently, 4 to 5 minutes. Remove from grill, and divide mixture among 4 plates. Serve along with the Pesto, or add a spoonful of Pesto to each plate, to the side of the potatoes.

Each serving			
Calories	231	Total Fat	9.6 g
Protein	8 g	Saturated Fat	2 g
Carbohydrates	32 g	Cholesterol	4 mg
Dietary Fiber	6 g	Sodium	102 mg

GARLICKY MASHED POTATOES

MAKES 5 CUPS OR 10 SERVINGS

This is not a recipe for the grill, but it goes so well with so many grilled foods, that it has to be included in this book. The potatoes can be made a day ahead, put in a foil-covered dish, and reheated on the grill.

2 1/2 lb (1 1/8 kg) large red-skinned potatoes, peeled and cut into 3/4-inch (1 7/8-cm) cubes

8 garlic cloves, halved

1/2 cup (120 ml) skim milk

1/2 cup (120 ml) nonfat sour cream

1 teaspoon olive oil

1/2 teaspoon each: salt and white ground pepper, or to taste

❶ Place potatoes and garlic in a saucepan; add water to cover. Bring to a boil, and cook over medium heat until potatoes are tender, about 15 minutes. Drain well, and return potatoes and garlic to the same pan. Put the pan over the warm burner to dry the potatoes, 1 to 2 minutes; remove from the heat.

❷ Meanwhile, slowly heat milk, sour cream, and olive oil in a small saucepan, stirring constantly, about 2 minutes. Add milk mixture to the potatoes. Season with salt and pepper, then mash the mixture to reach desired consistency. Keep warm until ready to serve.

Each serving			
Calories	111	Total Fat	0.6 g
Protein	3 g	Saturated Fat	0.1 g
Carbohydrates	24 g	Cholesterol	0.2 mg
Dietary Fiber	1 g	Sodium	127 mg

SPICY GRILLED POTATO WEDGES

MAKES 4 SERVINGS

These potato wedges go well with most dishes in this book.

1 1/2 lb (680 g) large baking potatoes, peeled and cut into 1-inch (2 1/2-cm) wedges

1 teaspoon each: paprika and dried thyme

1/2 teaspoon cayenne pepper

1 Cook the potato wedges in simmering water until they are a little more than half way done, 10 to 15 minutes. Drain and dry well; cool. Place cooled potatoes in a large bowl.

2 Combine remaining ingredients in a small bowl, mixing well; sprinkle over potatoes, tossing to coat well. Prepare the grill.

3 When the fire is ready, lightly oil a wire basket; put the potatoes in the basket. Place the basket on the grill. With the cover down, grill 10 to 15 minutes, turning several times, until fork-tender. Serve immediately.

Each serving			
Calories	119	Total Fat	0.3 g
Protein	3 g	Saturated Fat	1 g
Carbohydrates	28 g	Cholesterol	0 mg
Dietary Fiber	2 g	Sodium	7 mg

GRILLED RADICCHIO HALVES WITH BUTTER, OIL, AND GARLIC

MAKES 4 SERVINGS

A member of the chicory family, radicchio looks like a purplish-red small head of cabbage, but also can be shaped like romaine lettuce. Much of the radicchio sold in this country comes from Italy (it is a favorite in the cities of Treviso and Verona), and is fairly expensive, even when produced domestically.

2 small heads radicchio, trimmed and halved through the stem end

1 tablespoon each: butter and olive oil

2 garlic cloves, peeled and halved

pinch of salt

freshly ground black pepper to taste

1 Rinse and drain the radicchio halves; set aside.

2 In a small skillet or saucepan, heat butter and oil over medium heat. When hot, add garlic, and sauté until lightly golden. Remove the pan from the heat, discarding the garlic halves. Brush the butter-oil mixture over the cut sides of the radicchio. Season with the salt and pepper. Prepare the grill.

3 When the fire is ready, spray the grid with oil; place the radicchio, cut side down on the grid. Grill about 5 minutes, turn the radiccho, then grill 5 minutes more, or until tender. Test for doneness with a wooden skewer.

Each serving			
Calories	84	Total Fat	6.5 g
Protein	2 g	Saturated Fat	2.3 g
Carbohydrates	6 g	Cholesterol	8 mg
Dietary Fiber	0 g	Sodium	230 mg

GRILLED RUTABAGA SLICES

MAKES 4 SERVINGS

Rutabagas look like turnips, but are a separate species. However, they are said to be a cross between a turnip and a wild cabbage. The name comes from the Swedish word "rotabagge" meaning "round root." The flesh is firm, usually yellowish, and somewhat sweet. Rutabagas are delicious on the grill, and are low fat, even when lightly brushed with a little butter.

  2 rutabagas (about 2 lb/900 g total)

    spray oil

  1 tablespoon butter, softened

    pinch of salt

    freshly ground black pepper to taste

    paprika for garnish

  2 tablespoons finely chopped chives

❶ With a sharp paring knife, remove the wax and skin from each rutabaga. Slice into 1/3-inch (7/8-cm) rounds, then spray oil on both sides of each slice. Prepare the grill.

❷ When the fire is ready, spray oil on the grid. Place the slices on the grill, and cook, with the cover down, about 8 minutes on each side. To test for doneness, run a wooden skewer through several slices; if tender, remove from the grill.

❸ Place slices in a large bowl. Add butter, salt, pepper, paprika, and chives; toss carefully to combine. Serve hot.

Each serving			
Calories	108	Total Fat	3.4 g
Protein	3 g	Saturated Fat	1.9 g
Carbohydrates	19 g	Cholesterol	8 mg
Dietary Fiber	6 g	Sodium	251 mg

SHALLOTS IN BOURBON AND BUTTER

MAKES 4 SERVINGS

Shallots often grow in pairs. To use them, cut or break them apart, then treat them as individual shallots, if each one is bigger than a clove of garlic.

24 shallots, trimmed and peeled

1/3 cup (80 ml) bourbon

1 tablespoon butter

1 teaspoon brown sugar

pinch of each: salt and freshly ground black pepper

❶ Place shallots in a large bowl.

❷ Combine bourbon, butter, and sugar in a small saucepan. Place over medium heat, and cook just enough to melt the butter and dissolve the sugar. Pour the mixture over the shallots; toss well.

❸ Cut 2 (18-inch/45 3/4-cm) squares of heavy-duty foil, stacking them to make a double thickness. Transfer shallots and sauce onto the foil; use a rubber spatula to get all the sauce out of the bowl. Make a Bundle Wrap (page 10). Prepare the grill.

❹ When the fire is ready, place the foil packet on the grill, away from the direct heat. Close the cover, and grill 30 to 40 minutes, stirring several times to make sure the shallots don't scorch.

Serving suggestion: Serve with other vegetables, fish, poultry, or meat.

Each serving			
Calories	129	Total Fat	3 g
Protein	2 g	Saturated Fat	1.8 g
Carbohydrates	14 g	Cholesterol	8 mg
Dietary Fiber	1 g	Sodium	215 mg

GRILLED SHALLOTS WITH PORT WINE AND PARSLEY

MAKES 4 SERVINGS

Shallots are wonderful cooked this way, and will caramelize, with the help of the wine. This preparation is a nice accompaniment to poultry and meat.

20 shallot cloves, peeled and trimmed

4 baby or small carrots, trimmed and quartered lengthwise

1/4 cup (60 ml) port wine

1/4 cup (28 g) finely chopped flat-leaf parsley

1 tablespoon butter, cut into bits

1 tablespoon Worcestershire sauce

❶ Cut 2 (18-inch/45 3/4-cm) squares of heavy-duty foil, stacking them to make a double thickness. Place all the ingredients on the foil, tossing to blend well. Make a Bundle Wrap (page 10). Prepare the grill.

❷ When the fire is ready, place the package on the grill, away from direct heat; cook about 40 minutes, or until tender.

❸ To test for doneness, open the package and insert a wooden skewer into a shallot; the skewer should meet no resistance. When done, transfer the contents of the package carefully to a bowl. Serve hot.

SHALLOTS

A member of the onion family, shallots have a mild taste, and a thin, golden skin, the color of Spanish onions. They are divided into cloves, usually two to four cloves to one shallot. They keep well for several weeks in the refrigerator, either in the vegetable drawer, or in a covered jar. Shallots are imported from France, but also are grown domestically, mostly in New York and New Jersey.

Each serving			
Calories	102	Total Fat	3 g
Protein	2 g	Saturated Fat	1.8 g
Carbohydrates	16 g	Cholesterol	8 mg
Dietary Fiber	1 g	Sodium	8 mg

GARLIC SWEET GRILLED TOMATOES

MAKES 4 SERVINGS

This is very tasty, and couldn't be more simple to prepare. A little sugar is added to soften the tartness of the tomatoes, while the basil and garlic add lots of flavor. You'll find many uses for this dish.

3 large ripe tomatoes

2 garlic cloves, minced

2 tablespoons raw sugar

1 tablespoon finely chopped fresh basil

freshly ground black pepper to taste

1 teaspoon olive oil

1 Wash and dry the tomatoes; core, and cut each into 4 wedges. Squeeze the juice and seeds from each wedge.

2 Arrange the tomatoes in one layer on a double sheet of foil, large enough to envelop them. Sprinkle garlic, sugar, basil, a liberal amount of pepper, and oil over the tomatoes. Enclose by making a Bundle Wrap (page 10). Prepare the grill.

3 Place the packet on the grill, then close the cover and cook 15 minutes. Juices will form in the packet as the tomatoes cook; pour the juice over the tomatoes as they are being served.

Each serving			
Calories	65	Total Fat	1.6 g
Protein	1 g	Saturated Fat	0.2 g
Carbohydrates	13 g	Cholesterol	0 mg
Dietary Fiber	2 g	Sodium	13 mg

TOMATOES IN FOIL WITH MEDITERRANEAN FLAVORS

MAKES 4 SERVINGS

This is one of my favorite dishes. It's easy, fresh, and full of flavor. Add it to cooked pasta, too.

4 large tomatoes

salt to taste

1 garlic clove, minced

1 cup (80 g) fresh basil leaves, loosely packed (reserve 4 leaves for garnish)

2 tablespoons pine nuts

2 tablespoons freshly grated Parmesan cheese

pinch of red pepper flakes

1 tablespoon olive oil

1 Wash and core the tomatoes. Cut an opening in the top of each tomato, large enough for about 1 tablespoon filling. Cut a very thin slice off the bottoms, so tomatoes will sit upright. Sprinkle a pinch of salt inside each tomato, then invert the tomatoes to drain about 15 minutes.

2 In the bowl of a small food processor, combine garlic, basil, pine nuts, Parmesan cheese, red pepper flakes, and oil. Using the pulse button, blend the basil mixture, but do not overprocess; the filling should be coarse. Turn the tomatoes upright and fill the cavities with the basil filling.

3 Cut 1 (18-inch/45 3/4-cm) square heavy-duty foil; place tomatoes on foil, and close the packet, Bundle Wrap style (page 10). Prepare the grill.

4 When the fire is ready, add the packet, and close the cover. Grill 15 to 20 minutes. Remove from the grill, and serve immediately, with a basil leaf garnishing each tomato; spoon juices onto each tomato.

Each serving			
Calories	144	Total Fat	8 g
Protein	7 g	Saturated Fat	1.6 g
Carbohydrates	14.5 g	Cholesterol	2.5 mg
Dietary Fiber	6 g	Sodium	255 mg

GRILLED TURNIP SLICES WITH HORSERADISH

MAKES 6 SERVINGS

Some people don't like turnips, but after they've tasted turnips prepared this way, they change their minds. Turnips take on a different flavor when grilled, and they couldn't be easier to prepare.

1 lb (455 g) turnips

1 tablespoon canola oil

freshly ground black pepper to taste

1 1/2 tablespoons prepared horseradish

❶ Clean and trim the turnips, and put them in a saucepan with water to cover. Bring to boil, lower the heat, and simmer until they are crisp-tender. Timing here is dependent on the size of the turnip, but to test for doneness, insert the tip of a sharp knife into the turnip—if it meets a little resistance, remove from the heat and drain; cool. Cut the turnips into 1/2-inch (1 1/4-cm) slices; lightly brush them with oil. Prepare the grill.

❷ When the fire is ready, grill the slices about 2 minutes on each side, or until they show grill marks. Remove from the grill with a spatula to a plate. Top each slice with a dab of horseradish.

Each serving			
Calories	35	Total Fat	2.3 g
Protein	1 g	Saturated Fat	0.2 g
Carbohydrates	4 g	Cholesterol	0 mg
Dietary Fiber	2 g	Sodium	41 mg

GRILLED SWEET POTATOES WITH PINEAPPLE JAM

MAKES 4 SERVINGS

Whether you have eaten grilled sweet potatoes before or not, you should try this recipe. You will be surprised how tender the potatoes are. One trick is to keep them from scorching; all you have to do is move the slices to a part of the grill where the heat is less intense. The touch of sweetness from the jam adds a great taste to the potatoes when served with composed salads, fish dishes, and especially other grilled vegetables.

2 large sweet potatoes (1 to 1 1/2 lb)

1 tablespoon canola oil

   freshly ground black pepper to taste

   salt to taste (optional)

1/4 cup (60 ml) pineapple or other jam

2 tablespoons apple juice concentrate, thawed (optional)

1 Peel the sweet potatoes, and cut crosswise into 1/4-inch (5/8-cm) slices. Lightly brush each slice with oil; season with pepper and salt. Prepare the grill.

2 When the fire is ready, lightly spray oil on the grid. Add potato slices, and grill until lightly browned, 3 to 4 minutes on each side, turning once.

3 Meanwhile, combine jam and apple juice concentrate in a small saucepan over medium heat. Stirring to blend, heat mixture until jam and concentrate are melted; set aside.

4 As they are done, remove potato slices from the grill, and place in a large bowl. Add the jam mixture and toss lightly to coat each slice. Keep warm until ready to use.

Each serving			
Calories	146	Total Fat	3.5 g
Protein	1 g	Saturated Fat	0.3 g
Carbohydrates	28 g	Cholesterol	0 mg
Dietary Fiber	2 g	Sodium	8 mg

GRILLED HONEY-ORANGE ACORN SQUASH

MAKES 4 SERVINGS

This vegetable grills beautifully, and is kept moist by the addition of citrus juice and honey, added during the last few minutes of grilling. The juice and honey also add considerable taste. The squash develops a smoky flavor, and will melt in your mouth.

  2 medium-size acorn squash (1 1/2 lb), halved

  1 teaspoon canola oil

1/4 cup (60 ml) honey

1/4 cup (60 ml) fresh orange juice

  2 tablespoons finely chopped scallions

    freshly ground black pepper to taste

❶ Lightly brush some oil over the squash halves, inside and out. Prepare the grill.

❷ When the fire is ready, lightly oil the grid. Place squash, cut side down, on the grid. With the cover down, grill 20 minutes; turn, and grill 20 minutes longer. Five minutes after turning the squash halves, add 1 tablespoon each of honey and orange juice to the center of each half. When done, a wooden skewer should penetrate the squash flesh easily. Serve hot.

Each serving			
Calories	160	Total Fat	3.6 g
Protein	1 g	Saturated Fat	0.3 g
Carbohydrates	34 g	Cholesterol	0 mg
Dietary Fiber	5 g	Sodium	6 mg

YELLOW SUMMER SQUASH GRILLED WITH POLYNESIAN SAUCE

TO MAKE YOUR OWN POLYNESIAN SAUCE

Combine 1 cup chopped fresh peeled peaches (or canned peaches), two tablespoons light corn syrup, two tablespoons white wine vinegar, and a pinch each of cinnamon, red pepper flakes, and freshly ground black pepper in a saucepan.

Cook over medium heat for 10 minutes, or until the peaches are cooked.

Transfer peach mixture to the bowl of a food processor, and pulse to mince.

Use as directed above. Makes about 1 1/4 cups sauce.

MAKES 4 SERVINGS

Polynesian, a prepared sauce found in most supermarkets, is often used to baste spareribs and poultry. The sauce is made of peaches or apricots, corn syrup, vinegar, and spices; it has a sweet-and-sour taste. Here, the sauce is used with just-picked summer squash, and it is simply delicious.

2 medium-size yellow squash, rinsed and cut
 into 1/4-inch (5/8-cm) slices
1/4 cup (60 ml) prepared Polynesian sauce
 freshly ground black pepper to taste

1 Prepare the grill. Oil a wire basket.

2 When the fire is ready, secure the squash slices in the basket, and place on the grill.

3 Cook 3 to 4 minutes, then turn the basket.

4 Open the basket and brush the sauce on each squash slice.

5 Close the basket and the grill cover, and grill until the slices are done, 3 to 4 minutes. Serve hot.

Each serving			
Calories	28	Total Fat	0.15 g
Protein	1 g	Saturated Fat	0.03 g
Carbohydrates	7 g	Cholesterol	0 mg
Dietary Fiber	1 g	Sodium	40 mg

TOFU-TOMATO KEBABS IN SOUR CREAM SAUCE

MAKES 4 SERVINGS

These healthy ingredients create a wonderful and unique kebab. The tasty, tangy, low-fat sauce adds just the right touch.

1 lb (455 g) extra-firm tofu, cut into 1-inch (2 1/2-cm) cubes

8 cherry tomatoes

1 large bell pepper, cut into 1 1/4-inch (3 1/4-cm) squares

1 large red onion, cut into 8 chunks

8 medium-size mushrooms, wiped clean and trimmed

Sour Cream Sauce (recipe follows)

❶ Combine tofu and vegetables in a large bowl. Prepare the Sour Cream Sauce, then add it to the vegetables; toss gently to coat. Cover tightly, and refrigerate overnight, or for at least 4 hours.

❷ Thread the tofu and vegetables among 4 skewers. (If you plan to use wooden skewers, be sure to soak them in water at least 30 minutes.) Prepare the grill.

❸ When the fire is ready, add the vegetables, and grill about 15 minutes, turning every 5 minutes or so to grill all sides. Brush the sauce on the vegetables as they grill, saving some to serve with the vegetables once they come off the grill.

Note: One piece of tofu about 2 1/2 by 2 3/4 by 1 inch (6 1/3 by 7 by 2 1/2 cm) has 86 calories, 9.4 grams of protein, and 5 grams of fat; only 0.8 grams of the fat is saturated, and it has no cholesterol.

TOFU

Also called bean curd, tofu is made from soybean milk, which is collected after the beans are cooked and mashed. The soy milk is mixed with *nigari*, a mineral, derived from sea salt, used to curdle the milk. The curds are then pressed into neat, shimmering, puddinglike blocks.

Tofu blocks are available in extra firm, firm, and soft consistencies. Extra-firm tofu generally is best for the grill.

While tofu is bland, the good news is that it will absorb any flavor in which it is cooked. Tofu will take on the flavors of marinades and sauces, as well as the smoky flavors of the grill.

Buy tofu in sealed and dated airtight packages. Store unused tofu in fresh water, in a tightly covered container.

Each serving (not including sauce)			
Calories	195	Total Fat	10 g
Protein	20 g	Saturated Fat	1.5 g
Carbohydrates	12 g	Cholesterol	0 mg
Dietary Fiber	2 g	Sodium	22 mg

SOUR CREAM SAUCE

1/3 cup (80 ml) nonfat sour cream

1/3 cup (80 ml) plain nonfat yogurt

2 tablespoons chopped fresh herbs (such as chives, tarragon, or thyme)

salt to taste

freshly ground black pepper to taste

Combine all ingredients in a bowl; blend with a rubber spatula. Taste, and adjust seasonings with salt and pepper. Use immediately, or refrigerate for later use.

Each serving			
Calories	11	Total Fat	0 g
Protein	1 g	Saturated Fat	0 g
Carbohydrates	2 g	Cholesterol	0 mg
Dietary Fiber	0 g	Sodium	10 mg

VEGETABLES IN A MUFFULETTA SANDWICH

MAKES 12 SERVINGS

Three grilled vegetables in a large tasty sandwich.

1 large round loaf Italian or French bread

1 tablespoon olive oil

1/2 cup (120 ml) red wine vinegar

1 anchovy, rinsed 2 or 3 times in water, dried

4 garlic cloves minced, divided

1/4 cup (29 g) fresh grated Parmesan cheese

1 tablespoon finely chopped basil, or
   1 teaspoon dried

2 large white onions, cut into 1/4-inch (5/8-cm)
   slices

2 small eggplants

4 large red bell peppers

spray oil

freshly ground black pepper to taste

❶ Spray onion slices with oil. When the fire is ready, place onions in a grill basket, and grill 6 to 10 minutes, basting frequently with half of the vinegar, and turning once. Season with black pepper.

❷ Slice bread in half lengthwise; reserve the top. Hollow out the bottom half. In a small bowl, combine olive oil, half of the vinegar, anchovy, and half of the garlic; mix well, mashing anchovy into the sauce. Brush onto the bread halves.

❸ Spread half of the onions on the bottom of the bread. Arrange eggplant on top of the onions. Sprinkle the cheese over top. In a small bowl, combine grilled peppers with remaining garlic and basil; mix well. Layer the pepper mixture over the cheese, then top with the remaining onions.

❹ Replace the top of the bread; wrap the loaf tightly with plastic wrap; refrigerate for 3 hours. Remove about 20 minutes before serving. Cut the loaf into 12 wedges.

GRILLED BELL PEPPERS

Wipe the peppers clean, then grill them until the skins are charred on all sides. Put them in a brown paper bag, close the end of the bag, and set aside to cool for ten minutes. Shake the bag to loosen the skins. Peel the skins and discard the seeds, ribs, and cores.

GRILLED EGGPLANT

Wipe eggplants clean, then cut off the ends. Stand each on one end, and cut, lengthwise, into 1/4-inch (5/8-cm) slices. Lightly spray the slices with oil. Place on grill, and cook 6 to 10 minutes, turning once. Season with black pepper.

Each serving			
Calories	148	Total Fat	3 g
Protein	5 g	Saturated Fat	0.9 g
Carbohydrates	27 g	Cholesterol	2 mg
Dietary Fiber	4 g	Sodium	230 mg

GRILLED VEGETABLES WITH LEMON-MAYONNAISE SAUCE

MAKES 6 SERVINGS

12 artichoke heart quarters

12 cherry tomatoes, stemmed and rinsed

3 zucchini (each 1 by 6 inches/2 1/2 by 15 1/4 cm)

2 yellow or red bell peppers, cored, seeded, and cut into 1 1/2-inch (4-cm) squares

juice of 1 whole lime

1 tablespoon olive oil

1 teaspoon finely chopped fresh thyme, or 1/2 teaspoon dried

freshly ground black pepper to taste

1/4 cup (60 ml) nonfat mayonnaise

3/8 cup (89 ml) nonfat sour cream

juice of 1 whole lemon (3 tablespoons)

4 drops hot red pepper sauce

freshly ground black pepper to taste

❶ To make the lemon-mayonnaise sauce, combine mayonnaise, sour cream, lemon juice, and hot sauce in a small bowl; mix until smooth. Season with black pepper. Store in refrigerator until ready to use.

❷ In a large bowl, combine the vegetables. Add lime juice, oil, and black pepper; toss well to mix.

❸ Thread the vegetables onto 6 skewers. Wooden skewers should be soaked in water for 30 minutes before threading.

❹ When the fire is ready, lightly oil the grid; add vegetables, and grill until they are cooked, about 15 minutes, turning 2 or 3 times. Use any leftover oil-lime juice mixture to baste the vegetables while they are grilling.

❺ Serve a skewer on each plate with a teaspoonful of sauce on the side.

PREPARING THE ARTICHOKE HEARTS

Artichoke hearts can be fresh, frozen, or canned. Fresh artichoke hearts will need to be cooked before being placed in the marinade; they can be steamed or grilled. Thaw frozen artichokes before marinating, and canned artichokes should be drained, rinsed, and drained again before marinating. The smoky grilled vegetables are delicious with the cold sauce on the side.

Each serving (entire recipe)			
Calories	84	Total Fat	2.6 g
Protein	3 g	Saturated Fat	0.4 g
Carbohydrates	14 g	Cholesterol	0 mg
Dietary Fiber	4 g	Sodium	110 mg

VEGETABLES EN BROCHETTE WITH OREGANO AND LEMON

MAKES 4 SERVINGS

Zucchini may be used in place of the yellow squash, but use small, young ones, about 1 by 6 inches (2 1/2 by 15 1/ 4 cm) in size.

2 yellow summer squash, rinsed and cut into 12 chunks

1 large tomato, cored and cut into 8 chunks

1/2 large green bell pepper, cored, seeded and cut into 8 pieces

1 tablespoon each: balsamic vinegar and honey

1 tablespoon finely chopped fresh oregano, or 1 teaspoon dried

    freshly ground black pepper to taste

1 lemon, cut into 4 wedges, and seeded

❶ Prepare the vegetables and set aside in a large bowl.

❷ Combine vinegar, honey, oregano, and pepper in a small bowl; blend well. Pour mixture over the vegetables, and toss well.

❸ Thread each of 4 skewers as follows (if using wooden skewers, be sure to soak them in water for at least 30 minutes): squash, tomato, pepper, squash, pepper, tomato, and squash. Prepare the grill.

❹ When the fire is ready, lightly oil the grid, and place the skewers on top. Grill 4 minutes on each side or longer, depending on size of squash, turning once. Serve each skewer with a lemon wedge.

Each serving			
Calories	34	Total Fat	0.2 g
Protein	1 g	Saturated Fat	0 g
Carbohydrates	8 g	Cholesterol	0 mg
Dietary Fiber	1 g	Sodium	6 mg

GRILLED GARLIC AND LEMON SAUCE

MAKES ABOUT 3/4 CUP (180 ML)

Grilled garlic becomes soft, with a less "biting" taste than raw garlic. It is a wonderful addition to sauces. Try it with any kind of grilled potatoes. It is delicious with asparagus, turnip, tofu, and the many varieties of vegetable kebabs included in this book.

  2 large bulbs garlic
1/3 cup (80 ml) low-sodium vegetable broth, divided
      freshly ground black pepper to taste
      juice of 1 whole lemon (3 tablespoons)
  1 tablespoon olive oil

❶ Cut off the tops of each garlic bulb to expose the cloves; place them on a sheet of foil large enough to wrap them. Sprinkle 2 tablespoons broth over garlic, then season with black pepper; make a Bundle Wrap (page 10). Prepare the grill.

❷ When the fire is ready, place the packet over a cooler spot on the grill, moving the packet around as needed. Grill about 1 hour, or until the cloves are soft. Remove from the grill and let cool.

❸ When cool enough to handle, squeeze the soft pulp from each clove into the bowl of a food processor. Add lemon juice, oil, 2 tablespoons broth, and pepper. Process, pulsing until the mixture is blended.

❹ Add more broth to reach desired consistency. Serve sauce cold or at room temperature. It will keep overnight in refrigerator.

Each tablespoon			
Calories	26	Total Fat	1.8 g
Protein	0.5 g	Saturated Fat	0.2 g
Carbohydrates	3 g	Cholesterol	0 mg
Dietary Fiber	2 g	Sodium	42 mg

WATER CHESTNUTS AND PEPPERS IN FOIL WITH FAR EAST FLAVORS

MAKES 8 SERVINGS

The chestnuts retain their crunch while gaining a lot of flavor from the other ingredients.

2 (8-oz/230-g) cans water chestnuts, drained

1 orange or red bell pepper, cored, seeded, and cut into 1/2-inch (1 1/4-cm) dice

1 tablespoon each: low-sodium tamari and sesame chili oil

2 teaspoons sugar

8 scallions, thinly sliced

2 garlic cloves, minced

❶ Dry the water chestnuts with paper towels, and place them in a large bowl. Add remaining ingredients and toss well.

❷ Cut a piece of heavy-duty foil about 18 inches (45 3/4 cm) square; place vegetable mixture in the center. Enclose the packet Bundle Wrap style (page 10). Prepare the grill.

❸ When the fire is ready, place the packet on the grill, and close the cover; cook 20 minutes. Using oven mitts, carefully remove packet from the grill. Divide vegetables among 8 plates, and pour the sauce in the packet over the vegetables when serving.

Each serving			
Calories	54	Total Fat	2 g
Protein	1 g	Saturated Fat	0.3 g
Carbohydrates	10 g	Cholesterol	0 mg
Dietary Fiber	2 g	Sodium	107 mg

JICAMA AND PEPPERS IN FOIL

MAKES 4 SERVINGS

Jicama, often referred to as the Mexican potato, has grown in popularity recently in the United States. It is a white-fleshed tuber that varies in size from less than one pound to more than four pounds. With a thin, light-brown skin, jicama looks like a large turnip, and is very crisp. It can be eaten raw, but also is delicious grilled, either in thin slices, chunks, or cut like shoestring potatoes. When choosing jicama, look for hard tubers; they should feel heavy for their size. Do not purchase jicama with brown and scruffy skin. Remove the thin skin with a vegetable peeler or a sharp paring knife. Store cut jicama pieces in the refrigerator in a container of water.

- 1 jicama (1 to 2 lb/455 to 900 g) peeled
- 1 red or yellow bell pepper, cored and seeded, then cut into 1/4-inch (5/8-cm) strips
- 1 tablespoon low-sodium tamari
- 1 tablespoon sesame chili oil
- 2 teaspoons sugar
- 8 scallions, trimmed and sliced
- 2 garlic cloves, minced

1 Cut the jicama into 1/2-inch (1 1/4-cm) slices; cut slices into 1/2-inch (1 1/4-cm) strips; dry with paper towels. Combine jicama and pepper strips with remaining ingredients in a large glass bowl; toss well.

2 Make a double-foil package, large enough to enclose the vegetables; cut foil about 18 inches (45 3/4 cm) square. Place jicama mixture in the center of the foil, and secure using a Bundle Wrap (page 10). Prepare the grill.

3 When the fire is ready, place the package on the grill and, with the cover down, cook about 20 minutes.

THE KOHLRABI ALTERNATIVE

Kohlrabi, also called cabbage turnip, is a funny-looking nobby bulb, with a lovely green color. It tastes like a daikon, broccoli, and turnip rolled into one. The smaller bulbs seem to have more flavor. You may use kohlrabi in recipes calling for jicama. Peel off the tough peel, then slice as directed in the recipe.

Each serving			
Calories	116	Total Fat	3.6 g
Protein	2 g	Saturated Fat	0.5 g
Carbohydrates	20 g	Cholesterol	0 mg
Dietary Fiber	9 g	Sodium	135 mg

GRILLED ZUCCHINI BOATS WITH FONTINA CHEESE

MAKES 4 SERVINGS

Zucchini is a good vegetable for the grill, as there are many ways to prepare it. Here is a special one, with extra flavor from fontina cheese and sage.

4 (1-by-6-inch/2 1/2-by-15 1/4-cm) zucchini, washed and ends removed

spray oil

2 garlic cloves, minced

1 teaspoon dried sage

4 oz (113 g) fontina cheese, grated

freshly ground black pepper to taste

❶ Cut zucchini in half lengthwise; remove seeds and the center of each zucchini half with a melon baller, leaving a 1/4 inch (5/8 cm) thick shell. Bring a large pot of water to a boil; add zucchini halves, and cook 1 to 2 minutes, just to tenderize them. Drain well, dry, and spray oil on both sides of each half.

❷ In a small bowl, combine garlic, sage, fontina, and pepper; mix well.

❸ Prepare the grill. Lightly spray the grid with oil. When the fire is ready, add the zucchini boats, cut side down, and grill about 3 minutes, or until lightly brown. Remove zucchini from the grill to a plate, cut side up.

❹ Carefully fill each zucchini half with the cheese mixture. Return filled zucchini halves to the grill, cut side up, and close the cover. Grill until the bottoms are browned and the cheese has melted, 3 to 5 minutes. Season with more pepper, and serve immediately.

Each serving			
Calories	117	Total Fat	9 g
Protein	8 g	Saturated Fat	5.4 g
Carbohydrates	2 g	Cholesterol	33 mg
Dietary Fiber	0.3 g	Sodium	228 mg

ZUCCHINI PACKETS ON THE GRILL

MAKES 4 SERVINGS

People seem to like packets of grilled foods, and this preparation is one of the easiest; it's tasty, too. Grilling zucchini this way allows for a good bit of variation. Consider the following suggestions as you prepare the packets: add a spoonful of finely chopped onions; substitute chopped basil or tarragon for the oregano; add two whole cherry tomatoes to each packet; add a few drops of balsamic vinegar or lemon juice to each.

4 (1-by-6-inch/2 1/2-by-15 1/4-cm) zucchini, rinsed

spray oil

4 teaspoons finely chopped fresh oregano, or 1 teaspoon dried

garlic powder to taste

freshly ground black pepper to taste

salt to taste (optional)

❶ Cut 4 (12-inch/30-cm) squares of foil.

❷ Cut ends off zucchini, then cut each into 1/4-inch (5/8-cm) slices. Divide zucchini slices among 4 sheets of foil.

❸ Spray with oil. Sprinkle 1 teaspoon fresh oregano over each. Sprinkle garlic powder, pepper, and salt over top. Prepare the grill.

❹ Make a Drugstore Wrap (page 10). When the fire is ready, place the packets on the grill (ideally, 5 inches above the heat source). Grill 20 minutes, turning every 5 minutes. Carefully remove packets from the grill—use a stainless steel spatula or oven mitts. Place each packet on a plate, then serve, allowing diners to open their own packets.

WASABI SAUCE
MAKES 1 CUP
(240 ML)

Try this hot sauce on just about any grilled vegetable.

1/4 cup (38 g) wasabi powder

1/4 cup (60 ml) seasoned rice vinegar

1 tablespoon Dijon-style mustard

1/4 cup (60 ml) water

1/4 cup (60 ml) low-fat sour cream

❶ Combine wasabi powder, vinegar, and mustard in the bowl of a food processor. With the machine running, add water.

❷ Add sour cream, and process, using the pulse button, until sauce is smoothly blended.

Each serving			
Calories	4	Total Fat	0.1 g
Protein	1 g	Saturated Fat	0 g
Carbohydrates	1 g	Cholesterol	0 mg
Dietary Fiber	0 g	Sodium	0.5 mg

GRILLED ZUCCHINI AND EGGPLANT LASAGNE

MAKES 6 SERVINGS

This is an excellent way to combine vegetables with pasta. The vegetables develop a smoky flavor on the grill, and combined lasagne-style, the dish actually has more flavor. You will enjoy this, and will want to repeat it.

   1 lb (455 g) zucchini (1 by 6 inch/2 1/2 by 15 1/4 cm each)

   2 red, yellow, or green bell peppers roasted or 1 (12-oz/340-g) jar roasted peppers

   1 eggplant (about 1 lb /455 g)

   2 tablespoons olive oil

1/3 cup (38 g) freshly grated Parmesan cheese

   2 tablespoons finely chopped fresh basil, or 2 teaspoons dried

   1 tablespoon finely chopped fresh oregano, or 1 teaspoon dried

   2 garlic cloves, minced

      freshly ground black pepper to taste

   1 quart (1 L) low-sodium vegetable broth

   8 sheets instant no-boil lasagne (see note)

❶ Rinse and dry the zucchini and eggplant. Slice off the ends of the zucchini and slice lengthwise into 1/4-inch (5/8-cm) strips. Do the same with the eggplant. Slice roasted bell peppers into 2- to 3-inch (5- to 7 1/2-cm) wide strips. If using jarred peppers, drain and set aside. Brush all vegetables with the olive oil. Prepare the grill.

❷ When the fire is ready, add eggplant and zucchini slices to a lightly oiled grid; grill until tender when pierced with a wooden skewer, turning once. The eggplant will take a little longer than the zucchini: about 3 to 4 minutes on each side for the zucchini, 4 or 5 minutes for the eggplant. Set aside.

Continued on next page

3 In a small bowl, combine the cheese, herbs, garlic, and pepper. Stir well and set aside.

4 In a 6-by-12-by-2 inch baking pan, pour 1/2 cup broth into the bottom, then top with 2 sheets lasagna pasta, side-by-side. Cover with the grilled eggplant, then sprinkle 1/3 of the cheese mixture over top. Place 2 more pasta sheets over the eggplant, then pour 1 cup broth over the pasta; place grilled peppers over the broth. Add another third of the cheese mixture on top of peppers. Add 2 more pasta sheets and another cup of broth; arrange zucchini over top. Add the last third of the cheese mixture, then top with remaining 2 sheets of pasta and remaining broth. Sprinkle liberally with pepper. Bake in a 375° preheated oven for 30 minutes, or until the pasta is cooked through. To test, run a wooden skewer through the lasagne layers; if it penetrates easily, the pasta is cooked. The lasagne also should be bubbling. Remove from the oven and let sit for 10 minutes. Serve hot.

Note: No-boil lasagne is a new product that can be found in the dried pasta section of your supermarket. It works well and tastes surprisingly good, too.

Each serving			
Calories	373	Total Fat	9 g
Protein	15 g	Saturated Fat	2.6 g
Carbohydrates	60 g	Cholesterol	8 mg
Dietary Fiber	6 g	Sodium	183 mg

ARUGULA PESTO FOR VEGETABLE KEBABS

MAKES ABOUT 1 CUP (240 ML)

3 cups (240 g) tightly packed arugula with stems,
rinsed and drained

2 tablespoons fresh lemon juice

1 tablespoon olive oil

2 teaspoons seasoned rice vinegar

1/2 teaspoon hot red pepper sauce

Put the arugula in the bowl of a food processor. Chop, using the pulse button; do not liquefy. Add lemon juice, oil, vinegar, and hot sauce; pulse just to incorporate. Transfer to a glass bowl, and refrigerate until ready to use.

Each tablespoon			
Calories	4	Total Fat	0.3 g
Protein	0.1 g	Saturated Fat	0 g
Carbohydrates	0.3 g	Cholesterol	0 mg
Dietary Fiber	0 g	Sodium	1 mg

CURRIED YOGURT SAUCE

MAKES ABOUT 1 3/4 CUPS (420 ML)

1 1/2 cups (360 ml) low-fat or nonfat plain yogurt

2 tablespoons grated horseradish or bottled horseradish, drained

2 teaspoons curry powder

1 tablespoon fresh lemon juice

Combine all ingredients in a bowl; whisk until well blended. If the curry flavor is too pronounced, add a little more yogurt until you reach the desired taste.

Each tablespoon			
Calories	10	Total Fat	0.1 g
Protein	1 g	Saturated Fat	0 g
Carbohydrates	2 g	Cholesterol	0.3 mg
Dietary Fiber	0.1 g	Sodium	13 mg

HOT MUSTARD SAUCE

MAKES ABOUT 1 1/4 CUPS (300 ML)

Very low in calories and fat, this sauce has many uses. A teaspoonful will go alongside a variety of vegetable skewers, as well as grilled asparagus, potatoes, or turnip slices.

1 cup (240 ml) low-fat or nonfat cottage cheese

1 tablespoon skim milk

2 tablespoons grated horseradish or bottled horseradish, drained

1 tablespoon dry mustard

❶ Combine cottage cheese and skim milk in the bowl of a food processor until smooth. (Alternatively, combine cheese and milk in a large bowl, then whip with a wire whisk.)

❷ Add horseradish and mustard, then whip to blend. Store in refrigerator until ready to use.

Each tablespoon			
Calories	15	Total Fat	0.4 g
Protein	2 g	Saturated Fat	0.1 g
Carbohydrates	0.9 g	Cholesterol	1 mg
Dietary Fiber	0.1 g	Sodium	60 mg

HONEY-MUSTARD SAUCE

MAKES ABOUT 1/4 CUP (60 ML)

This sauce has many uses. Try it on plain grilled eggplant slices, leeks, scallions, onions, asparagus, artichokes, and potato slices.

2 tablespoons apple juice concentrate, thawed

1 tablespoon honey

2 teaspoons each: olive oil, seasoned rice vinegar, and
    Dijon-style mustard

In a small bowl, combine all ingredients; whisk until incorporated. Store in the refrigerator, in a tightly covered jar, until ready to use.

Each tablespoon			
Calories	43	Total Fat	2 g
Protein	0.2 g	Saturated Fat	0.3 g
Carbohydrates	7 g	Cholesterol	0 mg
Dietary Fiber	0.1 g	Sodium	53 mg

LOW-FAT PESTO

MAKES ABOUT 1 3/4 CUP (420 ML)

  2 garlic cloves, peeled and halved

  2 cups (224 g) tightly packed fresh basil leaves

  2 tablespoons pine nuts

  1 tablespoon olive oil

1/2 cup (120 ml) low-sodium vegetable broth

1/2 cup (57 g) freshly grated Parmesan cheese

In the bowl of a food processor, combine garlic, basil, pine nuts, olive oil, and broth. Process until smooth, scraping down sides. Add the cheese, and process just to incorporate. Use this sauce within 4 to 5 hours, before it turns brown.

Each tablespoon			
Calories	41	Total Fat	2 g
Protein	3 g	Saturated Fat	0.7 g
Carbohydrates	3 g	Cholesterol	3 mg
Dietary Fiber	2 g	Sodium	92 mg

NONFAT HONEY-LEMON MAYONNAISE

MAKES ABOUT 1 CUP (240 ML)

    juice of 1 whole lemon (3 tablespoons)

  1 tablespoon each: honey and Dijon-style mustard

  1 large garlic clove, minced

1/2 cup nonfat mayonnaise

    freshly ground black pepper to taste

In a small bowl or food processor, combine lemon juice, honey, mustard, and garlic; blend well. Add mayonnaise and pepper, and blend just enough to incorporate.

Each tablespoon			
Calories	28	Total Fat	0.2 g
Protein	0.2 g	Saturated Fat	0 g
Carbohydrates	6 g	Cholesterol	0 mg
Dietary Fiber	0.1 g	Sodium	168 mg

LOW-FAT ORANGE-SAFFRON SAUCE

MAKES ABOUT 1 1/2 CUPS (360 ML)

    2 tablespoons each: dry white wine and fresh orange juice
    1/2 teaspoon saffron threads
    1 1/2 teaspoons fresh orange zest
    4 oz (120 ml) egg substitute
    2 garlic cloves, minced
    1 cup (240 ml) nonfat mayonnaise

❶ Combine wine and orange juice in a small saucepan over medium heat; add saffron. Stir until saffron is absorbed, 2 to 3 minutes. Add zest, then remove pan from the heat and cool, 10 to 15 minutes; set aside.

❷ Combine egg substitute and garlic in the bowl of a food processor; blend by pulsing several times. Add mayonnaise and the wine mixture. Continue blending with 3 or 4 more pulses, or until the sauce is well combined. Store in the refrigerator up to 24 hours.

Each tablespoon			
Calories	45	Total Fat	3 g
Protein	1 g	Saturated Fat	0.5 g
Carbohydrates	3 g	Cholesterol	4 mg
Dietary Fiber	0 g	Sodium	97 mg

TARTAR SAUCE

MAKES ABOUT 1 1/2 CUPS (360 ML)

    1 cup (240 ml) low-fat mayonnaise
    juice of 1 whole lemon (3 tablespoons)
    2 tablespoons each, finely chopped: flat-leaf parsley, dill pickles, capers, and red onions
    1 tablespoon each: Dijon-style mustard and teriyaki glaze
    freshly ground black pepper to taste

Combine all the ingredients in a medium-size bowl; cover and refrigerate up to 2 days.

Each tablespoon			
Calories	27	Total Fat	2 g
Protein	0.2 g	Saturated Fat	0 g
Carbohydrates	2 g	Cholesterol	3 mg
Dietary Fiber	0 g	Sodium	109 mg

WHITE WINE MARINADE WITH FENNEL AND ROSEMARY

MAKES 1 1/4 CUP (300 ML)

Use to marinate vegetables one hour before grilling, and to baste vegetables, even those on skewers, while on the grill.

1 cup (240 ml) dry white wine

2 tablespoons olive oil

2 garlic cloves, minced

1 tablespoon finely chopped fresh rosemary, or 1 teaspoon dried

1/2 teaspoon fennel seeds

    freshly ground black pepper to taste

In a jar with a tight-fitting lid, combine all ingredients; shake well to blend.

Each tablespoon			
Calories	26	Total Fat	2 g
Protein	0.1 g	Saturated Fat	0.2 g
Carbohydrates	0.3 g	Cholesterol	0 mg
Dietary Fiber	0.1 g	Sodium	1 mg

YOGURT AND CUCUMBER SAUCE

MAKES ABOUT 1 1/2 CUP (360 ML)

1 1/4 cups (300 ml) plain yogurt

1/4 cup (28 g) finely chopped cucumber

1 tablespoon chopped fresh fennel

1 teaspoon dried dill weed

In a medium-size bowl, combine all ingredients, blending well. Refrigerate until ready to use. Double the amount of cucumber, if you like cucumber.

Each tablespoon			
Calories	11	Total Fat	0.6 g
Protein	1 g	Saturated Fat	0.4 g
Carbohydrates	1 g	Cholesterol	2 mg
Dietary Fiber	0 g	Sodium	8 mg

YOGURT, GARLIC, AND CHIVE SAUCE

MAKES 1 TO 2 CUPS (240–480 ML)

This sauce is wonderful with grilled eggplant and many other grilled vegetables.

1 to 2 cups (240–480 ml) low-fat or nonfat plain yogurt
1 tablespoon garlic powder
2 tablespoons finely chopped chives
1 tablespoon fresh lemon juice

Combine 1 cup (240 ml) yogurt, garlic, and chives in a medium-size bowl. Whisk until well blended. Taste and adjust ingredient amounts; if garlic is too strong, add more yogurt until you reach the desired garlic taste. Stir in lemon juice.

Each tablespoon (based on 1 cup [240 ml] low-fat yogurt)			
Calories	12	Total Fat	0.2 g
Protein	1 g	Saturated Fat	0.2 g
Carbohydrates	2 g	Cholesterol	1 mg
Dietary Fiber	0 g	Sodium	11 mg

YOGURT, LEMON, AND SCALLION SAUCE

MAKES 1 1/4 CUP (300 ML)

This is a wonderful sauce to serve cold with grilled new potatoes.

1 cup (240 ml) plain yogurt
1/4 cup (43 g) finely chopped scallions
juice of 1 whole lemon (3 tablespoons)
freshly ground black pepper to taste

In a small bowl, combine ingredients, blending well. Refrigerate until ready to use.

Each tablespoon			
Calories	11	Total Fat	0.5 g
Protein	0.6 g	Saturated Fat	0.3 g
Carbohydrates	1 g	Cholesterol	2 mg
Dietary Fiber	0.1 g	Sodium	7 mg

LOW-FAT YOGURT MUSTARD SAUCE

MAKES ABOUT 1 CUP (240 ML)

The mustard and rice vinegar add distinctive flavors to this sauce. Serve cold and the sauce will keep, refrigerated, up to two days.

1 tablespoon Dijon-style mustard

1/2 tablespoon seasoned rice vinegar

2 scallions, sliced

　freshly ground black pepper to taste

1 (8-oz/240-ml) carton low-fat yogurt (1 percent fat or less), divided

1/3 cup (21 g) finely chopped fresh fennel leaves

1 teaspoon canola oil

❶ Combine mustard, vinegar, scallions, pepper, 2 tablespoons yogurt, and fennel in the bowl of a food processor; blend, pulsing until smooth.

❷ Add remaining yogurt, and blend well. Add oil, and pulse just enough to incorporate. Taste and adjust seasoning with pepper; serve, or refrigerate until ready to use.

Each tablespoon			
Calories	14	Total Fat	0.6 g
Protein	1 g	Saturated Fat	0.2 g
Carbohydrates	1 g	Cholesterol	1 mg
Dietary Fiber	0.1 g	Sodium	35 mg

CHAPTER 9
FRESH SALADS FROM THE GRILL

INTRODUCTION

Revel in nature's abundance of seasonal produce now available in markets or at roadside stands. Vegetables, fruits, and grains are the basis of a diet that can reduce many health risks. Fresh produce is a nutritious and delicious food choice any time of the day. This chapter indulges in tempting grilled salads, easy ways to enjoy a low-fat diet and good health.

High-fat foods should be replaced by foods that are low-fat and nutritious as well. Think of fresh produce as the focus of your meal. This will decrease your fat intake while increasing the important nutrients in your diet.

Remember the general rule: the darker green the leaves, the more nutritious the salad green. Leaf and romaine lettuces, for example, have up to six times as much vitamin C as iceberg lettuce. Arugula has four times the vitamin C as romaine. If you vary the greens in your salad, you will enhance the nutritional content, as well as the taste and texture.

The health benefits of salads are directly related to the low calorie count, with the added benefit of high nutrients. Notice how two cups (3 1/2 oz/99 g) of lettuce greens compare:

	CALORIES	VITAMIN C (IN MG)	CALCIUM (IN MG)
Arugula	23	91	309
Chicory	23	24	100
Leaf	18	18	68
Watercress	11	43	120

Restaurants are including more salads on their menus, and some offer low-fat selections. Vegetable-only salads contain essentially no fat. Regular dressings can add 20 to 50 grams of fat, so low-fat dressings are a must to dress healthy salads.

Another growing trend in restaurants is the use of small amounts of grilled chicken, turkey, fish, and pork in salads. Note, however, that not all chicken is low fat. For example, one chicken wing contains seven grams of fat; avoid it. Battered and deep-fried chicken breasts may have 15 to 20 grams of fat.

When planning healthy menus, it's a challenge to create a meal low in fat but high enough in calories to keep one energized until the next meal. In this chapter, I've done this by adding grilled chicken, turkey, fish, or pork, to the greens, vegetables, and fruit, and dressed each with a low-fat dressing. Who can resist the tempting simplicity of a plateful of mixed greens? This chapter proves that a salad can be a satisfying main course, as well as the new celebrity of the grill world.

LOW-FAT SALAD DRESSINGS

When making low-fat salad dressings at home, keep in mind several principles:

❶ Cut the amount of oil by at least half; add cooked-down fruit juices, which not only will concentrate the flavor, but also will nicely balance the tartness of the vinegar in the dressing.

❷ Use a little—with emphasis on "little"—strong-flavored food, such as soy sauce, Parmesan or goat cheese, peppercorns, red pepper flakes, or chiles for extra flavor.

❸ Toast spices, such as fennel seeds, before adding them to the salad dressings. To toast spices add them to a hot skillet for a minute or two, until they begin to pop. Toasted spices release flavors that otherwise would go unnoticed.

❹ Purées made from grilled vegetables will add concentrated flavor, providing substantial foil for the acid in the dressing. Purées also add body.

CAESAR SALAD WITH SLICED GRILLED CHICKEN OR PORK TENDERLOIN

MAKES 6 SERVINGS

Here is a fairly low-fat Caesar salad and dressing that will adapt to many variations. I like to top the salad with a small amount of sliced grilled chicken breast or pork tenderloin, to create a main-course salad entree; it's easy to do and very satisfying. If you don't want to add the meat, add some sliced apples, instead.

2 slices white bread, crusts removed, cut into 1/2-inch (1 1/4-cm) cubes

spray oil

1 large head romaine lettuce, washed and drained

1/2 cup (120 ml) Low-Fat Caesar Salad Dressing (recipe on page 286)

1/4 cup (29 g) freshly grated Parmesan cheese

1 teaspoon capers, rinsed and drained (optional)

❶ Place the skillet over medium heat, then spray it 1 or 2 times with oil. When the skillet is hot, add the bread cubes and lightly brown them, tossing frequently, 4 to 5 minutes. Cool the bread cubes.

❷ Dry lettuce leaves with paper towels, then cut into bite-size pieces. Place the lettuce in a large mixing bowl. Add the bread cubes and the dressing; toss lightly. Add the Parmesan and toss again; garnish with capers.

Each serving			
Calories	69	Total Fat	2.6 g
Protein	3 g	Saturated Fat	1.1 g
Carbohydrates	9 g	Cholesterol	4 mg
Dietary Fiber	0.4 g	Sodium	342 mg

GRILLED CHICKEN AND SPINACH SALAD WITH CRANBERRY DRESSING

MAKES 4 SERVINGS

Cranberries add color and zing to this low-fat dressing. If you can't find dried cranberries, use golden raisins or currants. Substitute grilled turkey for the chicken, if you wish. Serve with slices of Italian or French bread, sprayed with oil, then grilled.

4 boneless, skinless chicken breast halves, trimmed (about 1–1 1/2 lbs/455–682 g)

spray oil

freshly ground black pepper to taste

1 (10-oz/284-g) package fresh spinach, large stems removed

1/2 cup (120 ml) cranberry juice cocktail

3 tablespoons each: sugar and red wine vinegar

1/4 cup (38 g) dried cranberries

1/4 cup (76 g) finely chopped red onion

1 teaspoon low-sodium soy sauce

1 cup (112 g) thinly sliced celery hearts

❶ Spray chicken breasts with oil, then season liberally with pepper. Prepare the grill.

❷ Place the spinach in a large salad bowl.

❸ In a small saucepan, combine cranberry juice, sugar, vinegar, cranberries, and onions. Bring to a boil, then cook just until the sugar is dissolved, 1 to 2 minutes. Remove from heat, and add soy sauce. Rub about 2 tablespoons cranberry juice mixture onto both sides of each chicken breast; marinate at room temperature, about 20 minutes. Set remaining dressing aside.

❹ When the fire is ready, spray the grid with oil. Add chicken breasts, and cook about 4 minutes on each side; do not overcook, or the chicken will be tough.

❺ Pour reserved dressing over spinach, then toss lightly. Divide among 4 plates, then place chicken breast atop each, and sprinkle celery hearts over top.

Each serving			
Calories	196	Total Fat	2.8 g
Protein	24 g	Saturated Fat	0.8 g
Carbohydrates	19 g	Cholesterol	63 mg
Dietary Fiber	1 g	Sodium	135 mg

LOW-FAT CAESAR SALAD DRESSING

MAKES 1 1/2 CUPS (360 ML)

This amount will keep two or three days in the refrigerator. Use 1/2 cup dressing for a salad that serves six.

1 bulb of garlic

1/3 cup (80 ml) low-sodium vegetable or chicken broth

1/4 cup (76 g) finely chopped onion

2 anchovies, rinsed well and dried, or 1 teaspoon anchovy paste

1 tablespoon Dijon-style mustard

juice of 1 whole lemon (3 tablespoons)

2 tablespoons red wine vinegar

3 tablespoons olive oil

freshly ground black pepper to taste

salt to taste (optional)

❶ Peel the garlic cloves and place them in a small saucepan. Cover with water, then bring to a boil; lower the heat and simmer 10 to 15 minutes until the cloves are soft. Drain the water off, then mash by hand, or place them in the bowl of a food processor, pulsing 3 or 4 times to purée. If making the dressing by hand, transfer purée to a mixing bowl, otherwise, leave purée in food processor.

❷ Add broth, onion, anchovies, mustard, lemon juice, and vinegar. Blend with additional pulses, or, if mixing by hand, blend with a whisk or fork.

❸ With the motor running, or while whisking, add the oil slowly; process until the mixture is blended. Add pepper and salt (keep in mind that the anchovies are salty). If you refrigerate the dressing, be sure to bring it to room temperature before adding to the salad.

Each tablespoon			
Calories	20	Total Fat	2 g
Protein	0.3 g	Saturated Fat	0.3 g
Carbohydrates	1 g	Cholesterol	0 mg
Dietary Fiber	0.1 g	Sodium	30 mg

GRILLED CHICKEN SALAD WITH PINEAPPLE DRESSING

MAKES 4 SERVINGS

This is a pleasant salad, with flavorful fruit juices, in which chicken, turkey, or pork can be added. If you want it spicier, add a minced, fresh, seeded jalapeño or a light sprinkling of red pepper flakes.

1/2 cup (120 ml) unsweetened pineapple juice

1/4 cup (60 ml) unsweetened apple juice

2 tablespoons fresh lemon juice

1/4 cup (60 ml) white wine vinegar

1 tablespoon Dijon-style mustard

1 tablespoon finely chopped candied ginger

1 garlic clove, minced

freshly ground black pepper to taste

1 lb (455 g) boneless, skinless chicken breasts, trimmed

2 tablespoons each, finely chopped: scallions, celery hearts, and red bell pepper

2 tablespoons drained, crushed pineapple

spray oil

4 radicchio leaves, or other suitable lettuce

❶ In a small bowl, combine pineapple, apple, and lemon juices with vinegar, mustard, ginger, garlic, and black pepper. Pour half of the mixture in a shallow glass dish; reserve the remaining dressing in a container with a tight-fitting lid.

Continued on next page

❷ Place chicken in the shallow glass dish, turning to coat all sides with the dressing; marinate in the refrigerator 2 hours. Add scallions, celery, bell pepper, and crushed pineapple to the remaining dressing mixture; refrigerate until ready to dress the salad.

❸ Prepare the grill; lightly spray it with oil. Remove the chicken from the marinade, and lightly spray oil on both sides. When the fire is ready, place the chicken on the grill, and grill each side about 4 minutes, basting with leftover marinade. Cool just long enough to cut the grilled chicken into 1-inch (2 1/2-cm) cubes. Transfer chicken to a large bowl, then add the dressing mixture; toss well.

❹ To serve, arrange the radicchio leaves on each of 4 plates or a large platter; top each leaf with the chicken salad. Grind more black pepper on top of each portion.

Each serving			
Calories	171	Total Fat	3 g
Protein	24 g	Saturated Fat	0.8 g
Carbohydrates	11 g	Cholesterol	63 mg
Dietary Fiber	1 g	Sodium	156 mg

GRILLED PINEAPPLE AND HERBED COTTAGE CHEESE

MAKES 4 SERVINGS

This may be served as a side salad or an appetizer. It also may take the place of a vegetable, especially if grilled pork or chicken is being served. Grilling the pineapple and adding herbs to the cottage cheese make this special, with lots of flavor and few calories or fat grams.

1/2 cup (113 g) low-fat cottage cheese

3 tablespoons buttermilk

1 teaspoon each, finely chopped fresh: basil, oregano, and garlic

1 teaspoon paprika

freshly ground black pepper to taste

4 (1/2-inch/1 1/4-cm) slices fresh cored pineapple

4 sprigs fresh mint

❶ Combine cheese, buttermilk, herbs, and spices in the bowl of a food processor or a blender; process until smooth. Refrigerate until needed.

❷ Prepare the grill, and lightly spray the grid with oil. When the fire is ready, add the pineapple slices, and grill 6 minutes on each side.

❸ To serve, place pineapple slices, hot off the grill, on each of 4 plates, spooning a dollop of cottage cheese in the center of each ring. Snip fresh mint over each serving.

Each serving			
Calories	69	Total Fat	1 g
Protein	4 g	Saturated Fat	0.4 g
Carbohydrates	13 g	Cholesterol	4 mg
Dietary Fiber	1 g	Sodium	108 mg

MEDITERRANEAN PASTA SALAD WITH GRILLED CHICKEN

MAKES 4 SERVINGS

Orzo, rice-shaped pasta, is a wonderful addition in salads. Meaning "barley" in Italian, orzo is slightly smaller than a pine nut. Great in soups, it is an especially nice alternative to the more traditional rice. It is found in almost every supermarket.

1 cup (170 g) uncooked orzo

2 lemons

2 tablespoons Dijon-style mustard

1 tablespoon each: olive oil and honey

2 chicken breast halves, boneless and skinless (about 1/2 lb/230 g)

1 small cucumber, peeled, seeded, and chopped (about 1 cup/112 g)

4 small plum tomatoes, peeled, seeded, and chopped

1/2 cup (152 g) chopped red onion

6 cured olives, pitted and chopped

1/4 cup (28 g) finely chopped fresh mint, basil, or thyme

4 large lettuce leaves (for garnish)

1/4 cup (28 g) crumbled feta cheese, or cubed smoked or plain mozzarella

❶ Cook the orzo according to package directions. Drain and run under cool water; drain well, then set aside. Remove the zest from 1 lemon; squeeze the juice from both. You should have about 6 tablespoons juice.

Continued on next page

2 In a small bowl, combine zest, lemon juice, mustard, oil, and honey; whisk until smooth, then set aside. Transfer 1/4 of the mixture to a large bowl; add chicken and marinate for at least 30 minutes. Prepare the grill.

3 When the fire is ready, add chicken breasts and grill 4 minutes on each side. Remove chicken from grill, cool slightly, then slice into thin strips.

4 In a salad bowl, combine orzo, cucumber, tomatoes, onion, olives, and mint; pour dressing over top. Add grilled chicken strips, then toss lightly but thoroughly. Separate chicken strips out of mixture.

5 To serve, place 1 lettuce leaf on each of 4 plates. Spoon the pasta mixture onto each leaf. Sprinkle cheese over top, then arrange the chicken slices on top.

Each serving			
Calories	333	Total Fat	8.3 g
Protein	20 g	Saturated Fat	2.3 g
Carbohydrates	46 g	Cholesterol	38 mg
Dietary Fiber	4 g	Sodium	451 mg

GRILLED ARTICHOKE SALAD WITH SLICED CUCUMBERS

MAKES 4 SERVINGS

This combination will make an excellent side salad. If you want this as an entree, double the ingredients, or add a few slices of grilled chicken breast to each portion.

2 (12-oz/340-g) jars marinated artichoke hearts
1 cucumber, ends removed
1 teaspoon hazelnut oil
2 tablespoons balsamic vinegar
2 teaspoons seasoned rice vinegar
   spray oil
1/4 cup (32 1/2 g) chopped toasted hazelnuts
   freshly ground black pepper to taste

❶ Drain artichoke hearts, reserving liquid. Thread artichokes on each of 4 skewers; set aside. Peel the cucumber, leaving some skin on, then slice thinly. Keep cool by combining cucumber slices in a bowl with several ice cubes.

❷ In a large bowl, combine hazelnut oil and vinegars; set aside and prepare the grill.

❸ When the fire is ready, place the skewers on a lightly oiled grid. Grill 3 or 4 minutes on each side, basting with the artichoke liquid. Remove skewers from the grill, and artichokes from the skewers; place artichokes in the bowl with the dressing. Drain cucumbers and add to the dressing; toss lightly but well. Distribute mixture among 4 salad plates. Dot each with chopped hazelnuts, and season with black pepper.

CALIFORNIA ARTICHOKES

Almost all American artichokes come from the Monterey area in California, the setting of many John Steinbeck novels. If you look closely at the leaves of an artichoke, you will see lightly browned edges. This means they've experienced the touch of frost; it is not an indication of quality. Artichokes, trimmed and cooked plain, have about 50 calories each and six to eight grams of carbohydrates. They also are rich in minerals and vitamins.

Each serving			
Calories	141	Total Fat	6 g
Protein	5 g	Saturated Fat	0.5 g
Carbohydrates	21 g	Cholesterol	0 mg
Dietary Fiber	11 g	Sodium	113 mg

GRILLED CHICKEN AND FARFALLE SALAD WITH TOMATO-HERB DRESSING

MAKES 4 SERVINGS

Pasta and grilled poultry are naturally good combined; fresh-tasting, filling, and healthful. Substitute grilled turkey for the chicken in this recipe, if you wish. This dish is easy to double or triple, if you need to serve a larger group of people.

1 lb (455 g) boneless, skinless chicken breasts, trimmed
　　spray oil

1/4 cup (60 ml) plus 2 tablespoons barbecue sauce, divided

1/2 lb (230 g) farfalle pasta, cooked and drained

1 cup (240 ml) no-salt tomato juice

2 tablespoons each: balsamic vinegar and olive oil

2 garlic cloves, minced

1 small onion, finely chopped

1/4 cup (28 g) finely chopped flat-leaf parsley

1 tablespoon each, finely chopped fresh: basil, oregano, and thyme, or 1 teaspoon each dried

　　freshly ground black pepper to taste

　　pinch of red pepper flakes

❶ Rinse the chicken, then pat dry with paper towels; spray oil on both sides of each portion. Prepare the grill. Lightly spray the grid with oil.

❷ When the fire is ready, place chicken on the grid and grill each side about 4 minutes. Halfway through cooking, baste both sides with 1/4 cup (60 ml) barbecue sauce. When the chicken is done, remove from the grill to cool. When cool enough to handle, cut into 1-inch (2 1/2-cm) cubes.

❸ Place pasta in a large bowl or platter; add chicken cubes.

❹ In a small bowl, combine remaining ingredients, including 2 tablespoons barbecue sauce; pour over pasta and chicken. Toss well and serve. This is delicious served at room temperature.

Each serving			
Calories	413	Total Fat	11 g
Protein	31 g	Saturated Fat	2 g
Carbohydrates	47 g	Cholesterol	63 mg
Dietary Fiber	3 g	Sodium	258 mg

GRILLED CHICKEN SALAD WITH SPICY YOGURT DRESSING

MAKES 8 SERVINGS

- 1 cup (240 ml) plain low-fat yogurt
- 1 tablespoon Dijon-style mustard
- 2 teaspoons finely chopped red bell pepper
- 2 tablespoons each, finely chopped: flat-leaf parsley and chives
- 1 teaspoon each: curry powder, celery seeds, fresh lemon juice, and grated horseradish or prepared horseradish, drained

  dash of each: paprika, garlic powder, and hot red pepper sauce or red pepper flakes

  freshly ground black pepper to taste
- 2 lb (900 g) boneless, skinless chicken breasts, trimmed

  spray oil

  leaf lettuce (optional)

  honeydew or cantaloupe slices (optional)

❶ Make the dressing first so the flavors will blend. In a large bowl, mix all ingredients except chicken, spray oil, lettuce, and melon slices. Cover and refrigerate 1 to 3 hours.

❷ Prepare the grill and coat the grid lightly with oil. Rinse and dry the chicken, then coat it lightly with oil. When the fire is ready, add chicken to the grill and cook 3 to 4 minutes on each side; don't overcook. Remove from the grill and let cool.

❸ Cut chicken into 1-inch (2 1/2-cm) cubes, then add to the bowl with the dressing. Let marinate 1 hour, covered, in the refrigerator. Remove from the refrigerator 10 to 15 minutes before serving; toss again.

❹ To serve, divide chicken mixture among 8 plates lined with lettuce or spoon the salad onto 8 plates garnished with thin slices of ripe honeydew or cantaloupe.

Each serving			
Calories	147	Total Fat	3.4 g
Protein	25 g	Saturated Fat	1.1 g
Carbohydrates	3 g	Cholesterol	65 mg
Dietary Fiber	0.3 g	Sodium	125 mg

GRILLED SQUASH AND CORN SALAD WITH LIME JUICE

MAKES 4 SERVINGS

This light salad may be used as an appetizer or a side dish with grilled meat or poultry. However, you can turn it into an entree by adding a small amount of sliced, grilled chicken, turkey, or other poultry, or cubes of grilled chicken or beef.

2 ears fresh corn

1 tablespoon olive oil

4 (1-by-5-inch/2 1/2-by-12 3/4-cm) zucchini, rinsed, ends removed, and sliced in half lengthwise

2 large red onions, peeled and cut into 1/2-inch (1 1/4-cm) slices

2 tablespoons fresh lime juice

1 tablespoon rice vinegar

1 small fresh jalapeño, seeded and minced

1 tablespoon minced fresh cilantro or flat-leaf parsley

❶ Remove the silks from each ear of corn without removing the husks. Smooth the husks over the corn and tie with a string, to secure. Place the ears in a pan of water for 10 minutes. Meanwhile, prepare the grill. Drain the corn, then grill about 10 minutes, turning several times. Remove from grill and cool. When cool enough to handle, remove husks and cut off the kernels; set aside.

❷ Lightly brush olive oil over the zucchini and onions. Secure them in an oiled hinged wire basket, and grill, covered, until tender and lightly charred, about 10 minutes, turn once. As the vegetables grill, transfer cooked pieces to a dish.

❸ In a small bowl, combine corn kernels, lime juice, vinegar, jalapeño, and cilantro; toss well.

❹ To serve, distribute 2 or 3 onion slices onto each of 4 plates. Arrange 2 zucchini halves over each serving of onions, then spoon the corn mixture over each.

Each serving			
Calories	103	Total Fat	4 g
Protein	2 g	Saturated Fat	0.6 g
Carbohydrates	16 g	Cholesterol	0 mg
Dietary Fiber	2 g	Sodium	10 mg

GRILLED TURKEY SALAD WITH RASPBERRIES AND MANGOES

MAKES 4 SERVINGS

Fruit combines well with grilled meats, as we have seen elsewhere in this book. Here, a fruit marinade flavors the turkey, while fresh and colorful fruit is added to the salad.

1/3 cup (80 ml) seedless raspberry jam

1/4 cup (60 ml) seasoned rice vinegar

3 tablespoons honey

1 tablespoon extra-virgin olive oil

   freshly ground black pepper to taste

1 lb (455 g) turkey breast, cut into 1-inch (2 1/2-cm) cubes

2 hearts romaine lettuce, cut into 1-inch (2 1/2-cm) slices, rinsed, and spun dry

1 bunch arugula, trimmed, rinsed, and spun dry

1 star fruit, rinsed and sliced very thin

1 tablespoon finely chopped tarragon, or 1 teaspoon dried

1 cup (142 g) fresh raspberries

1 cup (165 g) sliced fresh mango

❶ In a small saucepan, combine the jam, vinegar, honey, olive oil, and black pepper; cook over medium heat just enough to dissolve the jam. Remove from the heat, and divide mixture among 2 large bowls.

❷ Put the turkey cubes in one bowl; toss well, then cover and marinate for 30 minutes at room temperature, or longer if refrigerated. Prepare the grill. Thread the turkey cubes onto 4 skewers; reserve the marinade for basting. When the fire is ready, grill the turkey 6 to 8 minutes, turning and basting as needed.

❸ Combine romaine, arugula, and star fruit slices into the other bowl. Add the tarragon and grilled turkey, and toss lightly. Distribute salad among 4 plates, adding raspberries and mango slices to each plate.

Each serving			
Calories	321	Total Fat	5 g
Protein	28 g	Saturated Fat	0.8 g
Carbohydrates	42 g	Cholesterol	77 mg
Dietary Fiber	3 g	Sodium	69 mg

GRILLED PORK TERIYAKI AND VEGETABLE SALAD

MAKES 4 SERVINGS

This is a very flavorful salad with colorful vegetables. To vary it, add a can of drained, sliced water chestnuts for extra crunch. This is a most tasty, low-fat preparation that you will enjoy.

1/3 cup (80 ml) teriyaki sauce

1/4 cup (60 ml) seasoned rice vinegar

2 teaspoons sesame seeds

   pinch of red pepper flakes

1 (1-lb/455-g) pork tenderloin, trimmed

2 celery ribs, cut into julienne strips

2 carrots, cut into julienne strips

1 red bell pepper, cut into julienne strips

2 heads Boston lettuce, trimmed, rinsed and dried

16 snow peas, finely sliced lengthwise

❶ In a small bowl, combine teriyaki sauce, vinegar, sesame seeds, and red pepper flakes; toss well. Transfer 1/3 of the dressing to a resealable plastic bag; add the pork tenderloin, and let marinate 30 minutes at room temperature, or overnight in the refrigerator. Refrigerate remaining dressing until ready to use.

❷ Cut an 18-inch (45 3/4-cm) square of foil. Put the celery, carrot, and bell pepper strips in the center; sprinkle 1 tablespoon of the reserved dressing over the vegetables. Form a pouch (page 10). Combine lettuce and snow peas in a large bowl. Prepare the grill.

❸ When the fire is ready, lightly oil the grid. Add pork, and grill 12 minutes, covered, basting with the marinade in the plastic bag, and turning to brown all sides. Add the foil packet to the grill when you put the pork on the grill. Remove the pork and the packet from the grill at the same time, and let stand 3 or 4 minutes.

❹ Add remaining sauce to lettuce and snow peas, then add the vegetables from the packet; toss well, and distribute among 4 plates. Slice the pork thinly, then divide among each plate.

Each serving			
Calories	280	Total Fat	8.3 g
Protein	38 g	Saturated Fat	2.7 g
Carbohydrates	13 g	Cholesterol	107 mg
Dietary Fiber	3 g	Sodium	1,020 mg

GRILLED SWEET ONION SALAD WITH BABY GREENS AND GORGONZOLA

MAKES 4 SERVINGS

Baby lettuce greens are sold as mesclun mix, and are either prepackaged or sold loose by the pound. The quantity needed here is about 1/3 pound (150 g). If you don't have gorgonzola, use feta or goat cheese.

1/4 cup (60 ml) white wine vinegar

2 tablespoons fresh lemon juice

2 teaspoons grated lemon zest

1 tablespoon finely chopped fresh tarragon, or 1 teaspoon dried

1 teaspoon finely chopped fresh thyme, or 1/4 teaspoon dried

2 tablespoons olive oil

2 large sweet onions (such as Texas or Vidalia), cut into 1/4-inch (5/8-cm) slices

freshly ground black pepper to taste

4 cups baby greens, about 1/3 lb (150 g)

4 teaspoons crumbled gorgonzola

1 Combine vinegar, lemon juice, zest, tarragon, thyme, and oil in a bowl; whisk until blended.

2 Lightly brush some of the dressing mixture over the sliced onions, using about 2 tablespoons; season with black pepper.

3 Prepare the grill; spray oil on a grilling grid. When the fire is ready, place the onions on the grid, and grill about 10 minutes, turning once; avoid overly charring the onion by moving the slices to cooler spots on the grill. Remove to cool.

4 Add greens to the remaining dressing in the bowl; tossing well; distribute among 4 plates. Add some onions to the outer edge of each plate, and top with a teaspoonful of cheese.

Each serving			
Calories	116	Total Fat	8 g
Protein	2 g	Saturated Fat	1.5 g
Carbohydrates	10 g	Cholesterol	2 mg
Dietary Fiber	3 g	Sodium	45 mg

ORANGE-FENNEL DRESSING FOR GRILLED FENNEL SLICES

MAKES ABOUT 1 1/2 CUPS (360 ML)

This delicious low-fat dressing has many uses, in addition to topping grilled fennel slices on a bed of greens. It goes well with grilled chicken, turkey, and other poultry dishes, especially those that are salad-based. The dressing is especially good on a variety of vegetables, such as grilled squash. Place one or two tablespoonfuls in the center of a grilled acorn squash half, for example.

  1 teaspoon fennel seeds

  1 1/4 cup (300 ml) fresh orange juice

1/2 teaspoon arrowroot or cornstarch

  2 tablespoons water

  2 tablespoons fresh lemon juice

  1 tablespoon Dijon-style mustard

1/4 cup (14 g) finely chopped fresh fennel leaves

    freshly ground black pepper to taste

❶ Place a small skillet over medium heat. When hot, add fennel seeds. Toast them, tossing, until they take on a bit of color; add orange juice. Cook, uncovered, over medium heat until the liquid is reduced by half, 5 to 8 minutes.

❷ In a small bowl, mix the arrowroot with water; add the mixture to the skillet. Stir in lemon juice and mustard, stirring until the sauce is slightly thickened. Add a liberal amount of pepper. Serve hot.

Each tablespoon			
Calories	15	Total Fat	0.2 g
Protein	0.3 g	Saturated Fat	0 g
Carbohydrates	3 g	Cholesterol	0 mg
Dietary Fiber	0.1 g	Sodium	32 mg

GRILLED SCALLOP SALAD

MAKES 4 SERVINGS

This is an elegant salad with interesting flavors. It is very easy to prepare, and makes a perfect lunch dish. If you like this type of salad, try a variation, using two tablespoons low-sodium tamari instead of the balsamic vinegar. If you like grilled scallops, you will want to make this again.

4 plum tomatoes, peeled, seeded, and cut into small dice

2 large shallots, peeled and minced

2 tablespoons each: balsamic vinegar and fresh lemon juice
   freshly ground black pepper to taste

1 tablespoon olive oil

12 large fresh scallops

4 (1/4-inch/5/8-cm) slices red onion

4 cups (320 g) loosely packed mesclun mix, or other
   tender lettuce

❶ In a medium-size bowl, combine tomatoes, shallots, vinegar, lemon juice, and pepper. Add olive oil, whisking to combine. Combine 1/3 of the dressing with the scallops in a shallow dish; marinate 20 minutes, turning once. Prepare the grill.

❷ When the fire is ready, lightly oil the grid. Secure the onion slices in a wire basket, and grill about 3 minutes on each side, or until tender. Transfer to a dish and separate onions into rings, keeping them in 4 separate piles.

❸ In a large bowl, combine mesclun mix with remaining dressing; divide among 4 plates. Top each salad with onion rings; set aside.

❹ Spray oil on a hinged wire basket; place scallops in the basket and secure. Grill scallops 1 to 2 minutes on each side, or until they turn golden on the outer edges and are just about cooked through, basting with the marinade. Remove the scallops and arrange 3 on each plate on the outer edges of the greens.

Each serving			
Calories	141	Total Fat	5.6 g
Protein	11 g	Saturated Fat	0.8 g
Carbohydrates	13 g	Cholesterol	18 mg
Dietary Fiber	2 g	Sodium	257 mg

GRILLED PORK TENDERLOIN BATONS WITH CABBAGE AND CARROT SLAW

MAKES 4 SERVINGS

Make the slaw first, and let its flavors blend in the refrigerator before grilling the pork. The rest is easy, and this makes a very nice lunch. Add a slice or two of unadorned boiled potato, or two or three grilled asparagus stalks to the side of each plate just before serving.

1 (1-lb/455-g) pork tenderloin, trimmed

spray oil

1 tablespoon fennel seeds

2 tablespoons each: low-sodium soy sauce and Worcestershire sauce

freshly ground black pepper to taste

Cabbage and Carrot Slaw (recipe follows)

❶ Wipe the tenderloin clean with paper towels. Spray the pork with oil. Crush fennel seeds in a mortar with a pestle; rub crushed fennel into the pork. Place pork in a shallow dish; add soy and Worcestershire sauces, and marinate 2 hours or overnight.

❷ Prepare the grill. Lightly spray the grid with oil. When the fire is ready, put the tenderloin on the grill, and cook, covered, 10 to 15 minutes, turning once. Remove from grill, then let rest 5 minutes or more.

❸ Cut the pork into 1/2-inch (1 1/4-cm) slices; then slice into 1/2-inch (1 1/4-cm) strips.

❹ To serve, spoon the slaw onto each of 4 plates, then arrange the pork batons on top of the slaw. Grind black pepper over top.

Each serving			
Calories	200	Total Fat	4.7 g
Protein	34.5 g	Saturated Fat	2.6 g
Carbohydrates	3.5 g	Cholesterol	114 mg
Dietary Fiber	2 g	Sodium	28.3 mg

CABBAGE AND CARROT SLAW

MAKES 4 SERVINGS

1 cup (113 g) each shredded: green and purple cabbage

1 small red bell pepper, finely chopped

1 small carrot, grated

1/2 cup (86 g) finely chopped scallions

1/2 cup (120 ml) low-fat mayonnaise

1/4 cup (60 ml) unsweetened apple juice

1 to 2 tablespoons seasoned rice vinegar

2 tablespoons mustard seeds

freshly ground black pepper to taste

❶ In a large bowl, combine cabbage, bell pepper, carrot, and scallions; toss to blend, then set aside.

❷ In another bowl, combine mayonnaise, apple juice, and 1 tablespoon vinegar; blend well, then add mustard seeds and black pepper.

❸ Blend well, then taste and adjust seasoning with additional vinegar. Pour mayonnaise mixture over cabbage mixture, tossing well to combine.

❹ Refrigerate until ready to use. Recipe makes four side servings.

Each serving			
Calories	144	Total Fat	10.4 g
Protein	2.5 g	Saturated Fat	1.1 g
Carbohydrates	11.5 g	Cholesterol	0 mg
Dietary Fiber	3.05 g	Sodium	214.7 mg

GRILLED SCALLOPS WITH ARUGULA AND WATERCRESS

MAKES 4 SERVINGS

The combination of warm, grilled food served in a cool salad offers a pleasant contrast. This salad will make a satisfying lunch entree. You won't need much more, except for a slice of toasted or grilled grainy bread.

4 cups (320 g) loosely packed arugula

2 cups (160 g) loosely packed watercress

1 tablespoon each: Dijon-style mustard, white wine vinegar, and low-sodium soy sauce

3 tablespoons low-sodium chicken broth

2 tablespoons canola oil

1 garlic clove, minced

2 tablespoons finely chopped flat-leaf parsley

freshly ground black pepper to taste

1/2 cup (86 g) thinly sliced scallions

12 sea scallops, rinsed and patted dry

❶ Remove the tough stems from the arugula and watercress. Rinse well and spin dry, then combine in a large bowl.

❷ To make the dressing, place the mustard in a small bowl; add vinegar, soy sauce, and broth, then blend well with a wire whisk. Whisk in the oil until emulsified. Stir in the garlic, parsley, pepper, and scallions; set aside.

❸ Prepare the grill, and lightly oil the grid. Thread 3 scallops on each of 4 skewers; lightly spray oil on both sides. When the fire is ready, grill scallops about 2 minutes on each side, turning once, until the edges are lightly browned. Remove scallops from grill and skewers.

❹ Pour the dressing over the salad greens, and toss to blend. Distribute among 4 plates, and place 3 scallops on top of each. Serve immediately.

Each serving			
Calories	141	Total Fat	9 g
Protein	11 g	Saturated Fat	0.9 g
Carbohydrates	4 g	Cholesterol	18 mg
Dietary Fiber	0.8 g	Sodium	470 mg

GRILLED SEA BASS WITH SALADE NIÇOISE

MAKES 4 SERVINGS

This salad is one of my favorites because everything in it is fresh, low fat, and tasty. If you can't find sea bass, use a similar light-tasting, white fish. This has a special dressing, which you will want to use with other dishes.

1 1/4 lb (570 g) fresh sea bass fillets, rinsed and dried
spray oil

2 small heads Boston or Bibb lettuce, leaves separated, rinsed, and dried

1 small head romaine lettuce, leaves separated, rinsed, and spun dry

1 cucumber, peeled and thinly sliced

2 anchovies, rinsed well, dried, and cut into small pieces

2 pitted black olives, chopped
Italian Herb Marinade (page 20)

2 ripe tomatoes, peeled and quartered
freshly ground black pepper to taste

❶ Cut the fish fillets into bite-size pieces; thread fish onto 4 skewers. Lightly spray fish with oil.

❷ Prepare the grill and lightly spray the grid with oil. Meanwhile, prepare the salad ingredients and dressing.

❸ Tear Boston and romaine leaves into bite-size pieces. Place the lettuces, cucumbers, anchovies, and olives on a large platter. Pour the dressing over top; toss lightly. Arrange the tomatoes on the outer edge of the platter.

❹ When the fire is ready, add the sea bass skewers, and grill about 3 minutes on each side. Remove fish from the grill and skewers, place the fish pieces on top of the salad. Add freshly ground pepper over top.

Each serving (without dressing)			
Calories	188	Total Fat	4.5 g
Protein	29 g	Saturated Fat	1 g
Carbohydrates	8 g	Cholesterol	121 mg
Dietary Fiber	3 g	Sodium	208 mg

LOW-FAT FRUIT AND HERB VINAIGRETTE

MAKES ABOUT 1 CUP (240 ML)

Unlike most salad dressings in this book, this is not served at room temperature. Because of its fruit and herb flavors and nonoil base, this vinaigrette is best served chilled.

1/3 cup (80 ml) water

1/4 cup (76 g) chopped onions

  2 tablespoons frozen apple juice concentrate, thawed

  2 tablespoons cider vinegar

  2 garlic cloves, halved

  1 tablespoon honey

  1 tablespoon finely chopped fresh tarragon, or 1 teaspoon dried

  4 drops hot red pepper sauce

    freshly ground black pepper to taste

Combine all the ingredients in a blender or the bowl of a food processor; blend until smooth. Chill about 20 minutes before serving.

Each tablespoon			
Calories	11	Total Fat	0 g
Protein	0 g	Saturated Fat	0 g
Carbohydrates	3 g	Cholesterol	0 mg
Dietary Fiber	0 g	Sodium	1 mg

GRILLED SHRIMP ON LETTUCE CHIFFONADE WITH PINK CUCUMBER-YOGURT DRESSING

MAKES 8 SERVINGS

The dressing and lettuce chiffonade should be made ahead and refrigerated, but the shrimp should be grilled at the last moment. The cold, creamy seafood sauce under the hot spicy shrimp is a delight. You will enjoy this dish.

Cucumber-Yogurt Dressing (recipe follows)

4 to 6 heads limestone or Bibb lettuce (about 8 loosely packed cups of leaves)

2 lb (900 g) large shrimp (32 count), peeled and deveined

1 tablespoon chili oil

1 Prepare the dressing, and refrigerate until needed. Trim the lettuce heads; wash thoroughly and spin dry. Stack the outer leaves, then slice them as thinly as you can. Do the same with the smaller leaves, which do not need to be separated from the head. Put the lettuce chiffonade in 1 or 2 resealable plastic bags, then refrigerate until needed.

2 Prepare the grill; lightly spray the grid with oil.

3 Rinse and dry the shrimp. Put them in the dish with the reserved dressing; add the chili oil. Toss with your hands to coat the shrimp. Let marinate 30 minutes. Thread shrimp onto 8 skewers (if you use wooden skewers, be sure to soak them in water at least 30 minutes). When the fire is ready, place the skewers on the grill. Grill 3 to 4 minutes on each side, turning once.

4 To serve, mound the lettuce on 8 plates. Add about 3 tablespoons dressing over each mound, then place 1 hot shrimp skewer on top of each mound. Serve immediately.

Each serving			
Calories	54	Total Fat	2.2 g
Protein	7 g	Saturated Fat	0.4 g
Carbohydrates	3 g	Cholesterol	46.2 mg
Dietary Fiber	1.5 g	Sodium	268 mg

CUCUMBER-YOGURT DRESSING

1 cup (240 ml) low-fat or nonfat plain yogurt
1/2 cup (120 ml) ketchup
2 hard-cooked egg whites, finely chopped
1/2 red or yellow bell pepper, finely chopped
1/2 cucumber, peeled, seeded, and finely chopped
2 scallions, finely chopped
1/4 cup (28 g) finely chopped chives
3 or 4 drops hot red pepper sauce
    juice of 1/2 lemon (1 1/2 tablespoons)
    freshly ground black pepper to taste

In a large bowl, combine yogurt and ketchup, and mix well. Add remaining ingredients, blending well. Transfer 1/4 of the dressing to a shallow glass dish, large enough to hold the shrimp in a single layer. Cover the first bowl with a tight-fitting lid or plastic wrap, and refrigerate until needed; set the other container of dressing aside to marinate shrimp.

Each serving (using nonfat yogurt)			
Calories	38	Total Fat	0.11 g
Protein	2.5 g	Saturated Fat	0.02 g
Carbohydrates	7.5 g	Cholesterol	0.83 mg
Dietary Fiber	0.57 g	Sodium	222 mg

GRILLED LAYERED SHRIMP SALAD WITH CREAMY TARRAGON MUSTARD DRESSING

MAKES 4 SERVINGS

1 lb (455 g) shelled shrimp (16–20 count), deveined

spray oil

juice of 1 lemon (about 3 tablespoons)

Creamy Tarragon Mustard Dressing

1/2 (10-oz/284-g) bag prewashed fresh spinach, stems removed

2 apples, peeled, cored, and thinly sliced

1 medium red onion, very thinly sliced and separated into rings

freshly ground black pepper to taste

6 to 8 drops low-sodium soy sauce

❶ Spray the shrimp with oil, then put them in a glass dish. Add lemon juice, toss lightly, and marinate for 10 to 15 minutes at room temperature, or longer. Prepare dressing, and refrigerate until ready to use.

❷ Thread the shrimp onto 4 skewers. Spray oil on the grid, then grill the shrimp 3 to 4 minutes on each side. Remove shrimp from grill and let cool; remove shrimp from skewers, then slice into 3/4-inch (1 7/8-cm) pieces.

❸ Set aside 1 spinach leaf and 1 apple slice for garnish. Layer the spinach, apples, shrimp, onion, and black pepper in a glass 9-by-13-inch (23-by-33-cm) dish. Sprinkle soy sauce over the salad, then pour dressing over top, covering the entire salad. Garnish with reserved spinach leaf and apple slice, and sprinkle pepper over top.

CREAMY TARRAGON MUSTARD DRESSING

3/4 cup (180 ml) nonfat sour cream

1/2 cup (120 ml) nonfat plain yogurt

2 tablespoons Dijon-style mustard

2 teaspoons dried tarragon

1/4 cup (60 ml) apple juice

In a medium-size bowl, combine all ingredients except apple juice; mix well. Add apple juice, a little at a time, until the consistency is like heavy cream.

Each serving			
Calories	133	Total Fat	1.3 g
Protein	12 g	Saturated Fat	0.2 g
Carbohydrates	19 g	Cholesterol	47 mg
Dietary Fiber	2 g	Sodium	384 mg

GRILLED SHRIMP AND WATER CHESTNUT SALAD WITH CUCUMBERS, CHIVES, AND WASABI DRESSING

MAKES 4 SERVINGS

This is a lovely crunchy salad, pretty to look at and good to savor. Wasabi is a fire-hot ingredient, so be sure to follow the directions carefully when making the dressing, sampling it to reach the desired level of heat. This is a perfect luncheon dish, and needs little more than a serving of hot corn bread or a hot biscuit.

Wasabi Dressing (recipe follows)

1 lb (455 g) shelled and deveined shrimp

1 (8-oz/230-g) can whole water chestnuts, drained, rinsed, and dried

1 cucumber, peeled, seeded, and thinly sliced

2 tablespoons finely chopped chives

4 cup-shaped radicchio leaves

❶ Prepare the dressing, and store in the refrigerator until ready to use, reserving 2 tablespoons for the marinade.

❷ Combine shrimp and reserved dressing in a large bowl, and marinate for 30 minutes, tossing the shrimp 2 or 3 times. Thread the shrimp onto 4 skewers (if using wooden ones, be sure to soak them in water 30 minutes). Thread the water chestnuts onto separate wooden skewers. Prepare the grill.

❸ When the fire is ready, lightly oil the grid, and add the skewers. Grill the shrimp about 4 minutes on each side; grill water chestnuts about 3 minutes on each side. Remove shrimp and water chestnuts from the grill and skewers; combine in a mixing bowl.

❹ Add cucumber, chives, and dressing; tossing well to blend.

❺ To serve, place 1 radicchio cup on each of 4 plates; fill with the shrimp salad mixture, then serve immediately.

Each serving (shrimp with wasabi)			
Calories	125	Total Fat	1.1 g
Protein	18.5 g	Saturated Fat	.3 g
Carbohydrates	9.6 g	Cholesterol	161 mg
Dietary Fiber	2 g	Sodium	181 mg

WASABI DRESSING

MAKES 4 SERVINGS

2 tablespoons each: low-sodium soy sauce and fresh lime juice

1 tablespoon dry sherry or mirin

1 tablespoon each: sesame oil and seasoned rice vinegar

1 to 2 teaspoons wasabi paste (see note)

Combine all ingredients, except wasabi paste, in a small bowl; add wasabi paste a little at a time, tasting for desired heat. Set aside or refrigerate, covered, until ready to use.

Note: To prepare wasabi paste, follow instructions on the container of wasabi powder.

Each serving			
Calories	39	Total Fat	3.4 g
Protein	.5 g	Saturated Fat	.5 g
Carbohydrates	1.4 g	Cholesterol	0 mg
Dietary Fiber	0.03 g	Sodium	267 mg

CHAPTER 10
SWEET AND SUCCULENT GRILLED FRUIT

INTRODUCTION

Cooking fruit over the dry heat of a charcoal grill extends the taste of its natural sweetness, and adds a smoky flavor at the same time. It is surprising how good bananas, peaches, and other fruits taste when grilled. Grilled fruit is a natural extension to the idea of grilling low-fat foods for more healthful eating. Almost no fat is added when grilling fruit (perhaps a dab or two of butter, but it is not essential). Any wine or liqueur that is added is done so for flavor, as the alcohol will burn off as the fruit cooks. Little sugar is needed because of the natural sweetness of the fruit. That natural sweetness is merely enhanced on the grill, as the sugar in the fruit caramelizes. There is no question that a fresh, ripe peach is delicious in a delicate way. But there is something interesting and complex about a grilled peach that should be experienced.

All the rules that apply to grilling meat and vegetables apply to fruit, as well. Remember, one of the most important rules is to allow the coals to turn gray before adding the fruit to the fire. This usually is not a problem when you get ready to grill your fruit because most of the other grilling is already done.

I hope you will expand your grilling repertoire, and try new dishes with fruit. One good way to start would be to occasionally combine fruit in your vegetable kebabs. When you skewer potatoes or yams, why not add a big chunk of apple? Mushrooms and figs are another good combination. Or try adding grilled apple slices to a grilled chicken, turkey, or pork sandwich. If you grill a lean piece of pork or ham, add a grilled grapefruit half in place of the usual vegetable. It is more than fun; it's exciting and tasty, too.

GRILLED APPLE QUARTERS WITH CALVADOS APPLE PURÉE

MAKES 4 SERVINGS

It is best to use tart apples, such as Granny Smith, Cortland, Rhode Island Greening, and McIntosh for grilling. You can make your own applesauce or use a good store-bought brand.

   4 tart apples, partially peeled, cored, and cut into quarters

   juice of 1 whole lemon (3 tablespoons), divided

   spray oil

   1 1/2 cups (360 ml) applesauce, chilled

2 tablespoons Calvados (dry apple brandy)

   1 tablespoon brown sugar

12 dried cranberries

   pinch of cinnamon

❶ Prepare the grill. Lightly spray the grid with oil. Combine apple quarters in a bowl with half of the lemon juice; toss to coat. Thread 4 apple quarters on each of 4 long, wooden skewers (remember to soak skewers in water 30 minutes before using). When the fire is ready, grill the apples about 10 minutes, or until lightly browned and tender, turning as needed.

❷ In a small bowl, combine applesauce and Calvados; spoon some on each of 4 plates. Sprinkle with brown sugar.

❸ Top each with a skewer of apples, hot off the grill. Garnish with 3 cranberries and a dash of cinnamon per plate.

Each serving			
Calories	134	Total Fat	0.1 g
Protein	1 g	Saturated Fat	0 g
Carbohydrates	30 g	Cholesterol	0 mg
Dietary Fiber	4 g	Sodium	4 mg

GRILLED GRANNY SMITH APPLE SLICES WITH A DOLLOP OF SOFT FROZEN VANILLA YOGURT

MAKES 6 SERVINGS

Grilled apples are delicious and sweet, and make a wonderful dessert. They also may be served as a vegetable. Use apples that are firm and a bit tart. Do not peel them, as the skin helps keep their shape on the grill.

> 4 Granny Smith apples, each cored and cut crosswise into 4 (1/3-inch/7/8-cm) slices
>
> juice of 1 whole lemon (3 tablespoons)
>
> 1 to 2 tablespoons peanut or vegetable oil spray
>
> salt to taste (optional)
>
> ground cinnamon to taste
>
> 1/2 cup (120 ml) soft frozen vanilla yogurt
>
> 2 tablespoons Calvados, or 1 tablespoon maple syrup (optional)

1 Prepare the apple slices; rub lemon juice over each slice, then spray each lightly with oil. Secure apple slices in a wire basket. Grill, covered, about 6 minutes on each side, turning once. Watch the apples to avoid over-charring—if they begin to burn, move them to a cooler part of the grill. To test for doneness, run a wooden skewer through an apple slice; if the skewer goes through easily, the slices are done. Remove apple slices from the grill.

2 Season lightly with salt and cinnamon. Arrange 2 to 3 apple slices on each plate, topping with a dollop of yogurt in the center. Sprinkle Calvados over top. Serve the apple slices warm; they may be kept in a warm oven until ready to be served, or on the grill away from the coals.

Each serving (using maple syrup)			
Calories	75	Total Fat	3 g
Protein	1 g	Saturated Fat	1 g
Carbohydrates	13 g	Cholesterol	0.2 mg
Dietary Fiber	1 g	Sodium	9 mg

SMOKY APPLE BUTTER

MAKES ABOUT 1 CUP (240 ML)

To make this apple butter, which can be served in many ways, the apples first are grilled, then cooked with spices. It is excellent as an accompaniment to grilled chicken, turkey, or pork dishes. Try "buttering" your turkey burger roll with it, or serve it as a topping for lightly grilled slices of pound cake.

1 lb (455 g) Granny Smith apples, unpeeled

juice of 1 whole lemon (3 tablespoons)

1 tablespoon each: lemon and orange zest

juice of 1 orange

1 cup (240 ml) apple cider

2 tablespoons brown sugar

1/4 teaspoon ground nutmeg

❶ Slice the apples crosswise into 4 pieces. Using a melon baller, core each slice. Brush each slice lightly with some of the lemon juice. Prepare the grill.

❷ When the fire is ready, spray the grid with oil. Add the apple slices, and grill each side about 4 minutes, turning once. When lightly browned, transfer to a saucepan.

❸ Add remaining ingredients, including the lemon juice. Bring to a boil, lower the heat, and simmer, covered, for 15 minutes, stirring frequently.

❹ Remove the cover, and continue cooking and stirring until the mixture becomes quite thick; this may take about 30 minutes. Stir often to prevent scorching. Put the mixture through a food mill, then refrigerate until ready to use. This will keep refrigerated a week, and may be frozen for extended storage.

Each serving			
Calories	28	Total Fat	0.1 g
Protein	0 g	Saturated Fat	0 g
Carbohydrates	7 g	Cholesterol	0 mg
Dietary Fiber	0.6 g	Sodium	1 mg

WARMED BERRIES WITH WINE AND HONEY

MAKES 4 SERVINGS

This fruit dessert is best made when the grill has been used for other food. Warmed berries are delicious by themselves, or served with a small scoop of softened frozen vanilla yogurt. If you want to use the yogurt, put each serving in a dish, and top with the warm berries.

2 tablespoons nonfat sour cream

1 teaspoon brown sugar

1/3 cup (80 ml) unsweetened fruit juice (such as apple or pineapple)

1/4 cup (60 ml) white wine

1 tablespoon honey

2 teaspoons fruit-flavor liqueur (such as Grand Marnier, kirsch, Triple Sec, or pear brandy)

1 cup (142 g) each: raspberries, sliced strawberries, and blueberries

❶ In a small bowl, combine sour cream and brown sugar; set aside.

❷ In a foil pan, combine fruit juice, wine, honey, and liqueur. Put the container, uncovered, on the grill. Close the grill cover and heat for about 6 minutes. Lift the grill cover, add the berries, toss well, and close the grill cover again. Cook 3 to 5 minutes, just to warm the berries.

❸ To serve, spoon the berries and sauce into 4 bowls; add a dollop of the sour cream mixture to the top of each serving.

Each serving			
Calories	123	Total Fat	0.5 g
Protein	1 g	Saturated Fat	0 g
Carbohydrates	24 g	Cholesterol	0 mg
Dietary Fiber	3 g	Sodium	10 mg

BANANA, PLUM, AND PINEAPPLE KEBABS WITH RUM

MAKES 4 SERVINGS

This is a good combination of fruit to skewer and grill. I like to serve it on the skewer, set on a plate. Add some softened frozen yogurt on the side, to serve it "a la mode." The fruit should be served warm.

2 bananas, peeled and cut into 6 pieces each

8 (1 1/4-inch/3 1/4-cm) pineapple cubes

4 small black plums, pitted and cut into halves

1/4 cup (60 ml) dark rum

2 tablespoons lemon juice

1 tablespoon lemon zest

2 tablespoons butter substitute

1 tablespoon dark brown sugar

1 Combine the fruit in a shallow bowl.

2 In a small bowl, combine rum, lemon juice, zest, butter, and sugar; blend well. Pour rum mixture over the fruit, and toss carefully to coat.

3 Thread the fruit onto 4 skewers, alternating banana, plum, and pineapple pieces, beginning and ending with banana. Prepare the grill.

4 When the fire is ready, spray the grid with oil, and add the skewers. Grill 6 to 8 minutes, carefully turning the skewers and basting with the sauce frequently. Serve immediately.

Each serving			
Calories	140	Total Fat	1 g
Protein	1 g	Saturated Fat	0 g
Carbohydrates	27 g	Cholesterol	0 mg
Dietary Fiber	3 g	Sodium	2 mg

GRILLED WHOLE BANANAS WITH PEACH PRESERVES

MAKES 4 SERVINGS

You may vary the flavor of the fruit preserves in this recipe. I suggest using peach preserves here—it's wonderful with the bananas—but orange marmalade or apricot jam will be equally delicious.

4 bananas, peeled

1/3 cup (80 ml) peach preserves

2 tablespoons each: fresh lemon juice, peach or other fruit brandy, and sugar

1 cup (165 g) sliced fresh peaches or strawberries

4 mint sprigs

❶ Cut 2 (18-inch/45 3/4-cm) squares of foil, stacking them. Put the bananas in the center of the foil.

❷ In a small saucepan, combine preserves, lemon juice, and brandy. Place over medium heat, and cook until preserves are melted. Pour or brush preserves mixture over the bananas. Sprinkle the sugar over top. Make a Bundle Wrap (page 10), leaving the top open. Prepare the grill.

❸ When the fire is ready, transfer the packet to the grill. With the cover down, grill about 6 to 8 minutes.

❹ To serve, put 1 banana on each of 4 plates, dividing any remaining sauce in the packet among the servings. Divide fresh peach slices among the plates, placing the slices in the curve of each banana. Place a mint sprig in the same place, and serve immediately.

Each serving			
Calories	231	Total Fat	1 g
Protein	2 g	Saturated Fat	0 g
Carbohydrates	57 g	Cholesterol	0 mg
Dietary Fiber	3 g	Sodium	15 mg

GRILLED FIGS WITH RASPBERRIES

MAKES 4 SERVINGS

This works best with ripe figs. Although it is a seasonal dessert, it is a delicious one. Don't hesitate to serve figs this way, without the sauce, as an accompaniment to poultry, pork, and many other grilled meats.

   spray oil

1/4 cup (60 ml) each: raspberry jam, fresh lemon juice, and dark rum

  1 cup (142 g) fresh or frozen raspberries, thawed

  1 lb (455 g) ripe figs, rinsed and dried

❶ Prepare the grill. Lightly spray the grid with oil. Meanwhile, make the sauce. Combine the jam, lemon juice, and rum in a small saucepan. Bring to a boil over medium heat; cook until the jam melts and the liquid reduces by 1/3, about 6 minutes. Remove from the heat and add raspberries; toss well, then distribute among 4 plates.

❷ When the fire is ready, spray oil on the figs and put them on the grill, over indirect heat. Grill figs 15 to 20 minutes, turning once or twice, until figs are brown.

❸ Place figs on top of the sauce, and serve hot.

Each serving			
Calories	185	Total Fat	0.5 g
Protein	1 g	Saturated Fat	0.1 g
Carbohydrates	40 g	Cholesterol	0 mg
Dietary Fiber	5 g	Sodium	11 mg

GRAPEFRUIT HALVES WITH APRICOTS AND CHERRIES

MAKES 4 SERVINGS

In this recipe, the grapefruit really doesn't cook on the grill, but the heat encourages the flavors of ginger, cinnamon, honey, and other fruit to blend beautifully. This is an easy and tasty dish, and it makes a dashing presentation.

2 large grapefruit, cut into halves

4 medium-size fresh apricots, seeded and cut into 1/2-inch (1 1/4-cm) cubes

16 cherries (about 1/3 lb/150 g) cut into halves and pitted

1/4 cup (30 g) chopped pecans

2 tablespoons honey

1 tablespoon finely chopped stemmed ginger in syrup

cinnamon to taste

4 mint sprigs

❶ Remove grapefruit segments and put them in a bowl. Scrape the grapefruit shells to remove and discard the membranes.

❷ Add apricots and cherries to the bowl. Add pecans, honey, ginger, and a sprinkle of cinnamon; toss well. Fill the grapefruit shells with the fruit mixture. Prepare the grill.

❸ Prepare 4 Bundle Wraps (page 10), 1 for each filled grapefruit half; leave an opening in the top of each Bundle Wrap.

❹ When the fire is ready, place the packets on the grill. With the grill cover down, grill about 10 minutes. Remove the grapefruit from the grill and the foil; add another sprinkle of cinnamon to each, then serve garnished with a mint sprig on top.

Each serving			
Calories	161	Total Fat	6 g
Protein	2 g	Saturated Fat	0.5 g
Carbohydrates	29 g	Cholesterol	0 mg
Dietary Fiber	4 g	Sodium	1.3 mg

GRILLED PEACHES WITH ALMOND-YOGURT SAUCE

MAKES 4 SERVINGS

When using almond extract, it is best to add 1/4 teaspoon at a time to get the almond taste you wish, as this extract tends to be strong. This sauce can be used for most grilled fruit; try it on grilled bananas.

1/2 cup (120 ml) low-fat vanilla yogurt

1 tablespoon honey

1 teaspoon almond extract

8 grilled peach halves or other grilled fruit, warmed

❶ In a small bowl, combine the yogurt, honey, and almond extract; mix well.

❷ To serve, divide grilled fruit among 4 plates, glasses, or soup bowls; then top with a spoonful of sauce.

Each serving			
Calories	82	Total Fat	0.5 g
Protein	2 g	Saturated Fat	0.3 g
Carbohydrates	18 g	Cholesterol	2 mg
Dietary Fiber	2 g	Sodium	20 mg

GRILLED PEACHES WITH BRANDIED FROZEN YOGURT

MAKES 4 SERVINGS

Grilled peaches and softened brandied vanilla yogurt is a combination difficult to beat. This preparation makes a simple, wonderful dessert, but the peaches must be ripe, firm, and unblemished. I prefer freestone peaches.

4 large ripe peaches, peeled and cut into halves (see note)

1/4 cup (60 ml) orange liqueur (such as Grand Marnier, Triple Sec, or Cointreau), divided, or a mixture of 2 tablespoons lemon juice and 1 teaspoon sugar

1 pint (480 ml) frozen vanilla yogurt, softened

4 whole strawberries, sliced into fan shapes (see note)

❶ Prepare the grill. Lightly spray the grid with oil. Combine peach halves in a bowl with 2 tablespoons liqueur or the lemon juice and sugar.

❷ When the fire is ready, place the peaches on the grill, and cook about 5 minutes on each side, turning once until lightly browned.

❸ In a medium-size bowl, combine yogurt with remaining 2 tablespoons orange liqueur. (If you did not use the liqueur, add nothing.)

❹ To serve, put 2 grilled peach halves on each of 4 plates, spoon some softened yogurt over the peaches, but do not cover them. Garnish each serving with a strawberry fan.

Note: To make strawberry fans, do not remove the stem cap. Using a sharp paring knife, make five to seven thin, lengthwise cuts (depending on the size of the berry) from the tip of the berry to the stem end, without cutting through the stem. To make the strawberry fan out, gently press the berry near the stem cap.

To quickly peel peaches, place them in boiling water for about ten seconds. Remove the peaches from the boiling water and place them in a bowl of ice water; the skins should slip off easily, if the peaches are ripe.

Each serving			
Calories	193	Total Fat	2 g
Protein	6 g	Saturated Fat	1 g
Carbohydrates	37 g	Cholesterol	6 mg
Dietary Fiber	2 g	Sodium	70 mg

GRILLED KIWI WITH GINGER AND ALMONDS

MAKES 4 SERVINGS

One might not think of kiwis on the grill, but kiwis actually make a good dessert, when prepared this way. The kiwis keep their shape and pick up extra flavor from the other ingredients.

- 6 kiwis, peeled and cut crosswise into 1/4-inch (5/8-cm) slices
- 2 tablespoons each, finely chopped: candied ginger and fresh mint
- 2 tablespoons almond slivers

  juice of 1 whole lemon (3 tablespoons)
- 2 tablespoons fruit-flavored liqueur (such as Grand Marnier, Triple Sec, or kirsch)

❶ Prepare a foil packet, such as a Bundle Wrap (page 10), to fit the fruit. Place the kiwi slices, overlapping, to form a 6-inch (15 1/4-cm) square.

❷ Sprinkle ginger, mint, and almonds over the kiwi slices. Carefully spoon lemon juice and liqueur over the fruit. Fold over the corners of the foil packet, leaving the top about half open. Prepare the grill.

❸ When the fire is ready, place the packet on the grill. Close the grill cover, and grill about 15 minutes. Remove from the grill and serve by spooning the fruit and juices onto 4 dessert plates.

Serving suggestion: A dollop of softened frozen yogurt or a few raspberries or strawberries may be added to each plate.

Each serving			
Calories	150	Total Fat	2.3 g
Protein	4 g	Saturated Fat	0.1 g
Carbohydrates	28 g	Cholesterol	0 mg
Dietary Fiber	5 g	Sodium	32 mg

GRILLED PINEAPPLE SLICES WITH HONEYDEW SAUCE

MAKES 4 SERVINGS

It's often difficult to find a suitable ripe honeydew melon to purée, so check carefully because ripe melons are the only ones with any taste. I often will buy melon that is already cut and displayed in the supermarket salad bar where items are sold by the pound. I usually taste a chunk before buying it, to be sure it's ripe and sweet.

1/2 ripe honeydew melon, seeded, peeled, and cut into chunks, or
    1 lb (455 g) ready-to-eat melon pieces (see note)

2 tablespoons melon-flavored liqueur, kirsch, or Cointreau

2 tablespoons honey

    spray oil

4 1/2-inch (1 1/4-cm) slices fresh pineapple

4 mint sprigs

❶ In the bowl of a food processor or blender, combine melon, liqueur, and honey. Pulse until the melon is puréed; there should be about 1 1/2 cups (360 ml) purée. Transfer to a bowl, cover, and refrigerate to get it ice-cold.

❷ Prepare the grill. Lightly spray the grid with oil. When the fire is ready, place the pineapple rings on the grill, and cook about 6 minutes on each side, or until lightly browned.

❸ To serve, distribute the cold melon purée into 4 chilled soup bowls with rims. Place 1 slice of hot pineapple over each serving of purée, in the center of each bowl. Reserving 8 large mint leaves, finely chop remaining mint. Sprinkle chopped mint over the pineapple slices. Carefully place 2 mint leaves to the edge of each pineapple slice.

Note: Many groceries offer pre-cut fruit in the produce section for a ready-made fruit salad, or have a salad bar with fresh fruit. Buying pre-cut fruit will save time, but probably will cost more money.

Each serving			
Calories	156	Total Fat	0.5 g
Protein	1 g	Saturated Fat	0.1 g
Carbohydrates	37 g	Cholesterol	0 mg
Dietary Fiber	2 g	Sodium	18 mg

GRILLED PEACHES WITH CANTALOUPE PURÉE

MAKES 4 SERVINGS

Freestone peaches are desirable here because they are halved easily, with the stone dislodging neatly.

1/2 ripe cantaloupe, seeded, peeled, and cut into chunks
  2 tablespoons dark rum
  2 tablespoons honey
    spray oil
  4 large, ripe peaches, peeled, pitted, and cut into halves
    freshly grated nutmeg to taste
  4 fresh nasturtiums, for garnish

1 In the bowl of a food processor or blender, combine melon, rum, and honey. Pulse until the melon is puréed; there should be about 1 1/2 cups purée. Transfer to a bowl, cover, and refrigerate to get it ice-cold.

2 Prepare the grill. Lightly spray the grid with oil. When the fire is ready, place the peach halves on the grill, and cook about 5 minutes on each side, turning once, until lightly browned.

3 To serve, distribute the cold melon purée into 4 chilled soup bowls with rims. Place 2 hot peach halves on top of each serving of purée; grate nutmeg over top. Garnish each bowl with a nasturtium bloom.

Each serving			
Calories	110	Total Fat	0.3 g
Protein	1 g	Saturated Fat	0.1 g
Carbohydrates	24 g	Cholesterol	0 mg
Dietary Fiber	2 g	Sodium	7 mg

GRILLED FIGS WITH FROZEN YOGURT, MINT, AND NUTMEG

MAKES 4 SERVINGS

Grilled figs are probably the most delicious grilled fruit. Here is a wonderful way to prepare them. I put the figs on the grill just before we sit down to eat the main course. They are grilled and ready to serve by the time we are ready for dessert.

spray oil

8 fresh Black Mission figs

1 teaspoon brown sugar

1 cup (240 ml) frozen vanilla yogurt, softened

nutmeg to taste

4 mint sprigs

1 Prepare the grill and lightly spray the grid with oil. Cut 2 sheets of foil, about 6-by-10 inches (15 1/4-by-25 3/8 cm); make about 10 slits in the bottom with a sharp paring knife; curve the sides to make a tray. Spray oil on the foil, then lay the figs on top. Spray oil on both sides of each fig. When the fire is ready, put the foil tray on the grill. With the cover down, grill the figs 10 minutes. Turn them gently, then add the brown sugar. Grill 10 minutes more, with the cover down.

2 Put 2 figs on each of 4 plates; spoon some softened frozen yogurt to the side. Sprinkle each plate with nutmeg. Remove 1 mint leaf from each sprig, placing 1 leaf on each plate. Snip the remaining mint over the figs and yogurt, and serve right away.

Each serving			
Calories	135	Total Fat	2.4 g
Protein	2 g	Saturated Fat	1.3 g
Carbohydrates	29 g	Cholesterol	1 mg
Dietary Fiber	3 g	Sodium	33 mg

INDEX